The Complete Book of Corporate Forms

of

(+CD-ROM)

Second Edition

James C. Ray
Attorney at Law

SPHINX® PUBLISHING
AN IMPRINT OF SOURCEBOOKS, INC.®
NAPERVILLE, ILLINOIS
www.SphinxLegal.com

This book was formerly titled *The Most Valuable Corporate Forms You'll Ever Need*. We have updated or changed the forms, statutes, and information in addition to changing the title to ensure that it is the most current at the time of publication.

Second Edition, 2005

Published by: **Sphinx® Publishing, An Imprint of Sourcebooks, Inc.®**

Naperville Office
P.O. Box 4410
Naperville, Illinois 60567-4410
630-961-3900
Fax: 630-961-2168
http://www.sphinxlegal.com
http://www.sourcebooks.com

This publication is designed to provide accurate and authoritative information in regard to the subject matter covered. It is sold with the understanding that the publisher is not engaged in rendering legal, accounting, or other professional service. If legal advice or other expert assistance is required, the services of a competent professional person should be sought.

From a Declaration of Principles Jointly Adopted by a Committee of the
American Bar Association and a Committee of Publishers and Associations

This product is not a substitute for legal advice.

Disclaimer required by Texas statutes.

Library of Congress Cataloging-in-Publication Data
Ray, James C., 1945-
  The complete book of corporate forms: from minutes to annual reports and
everything in between / James C. Ray.-- 2nd ed.
      p. cm.
  Includes bibliographical references and index.
  ISBN 1-57248-507-8 (alk. paper)
  1. Corporation law--United States--Forms. 2. Corporation law--United
States--Popular works. I. Title.

KF1411.R388 2005
346.73'066'0269--dc22   2005014618

Printed and bound in the United States of America.
BG — 10 9 8 7 6 5 4 3 2 1

Contents

How to Use the CD-ROM

Thank you for purchasing *The Complete Book of Corporate Forms (+CD-ROM)*. In this book, we have worked hard to compile exactly what you need to get your corporation up and running, and maintain and operate it for years to come. A complete array of the necessary documents every corporation needs has been included. To make this material even more useful, we have included every document in the book on the CD-ROM that is attached to the inside back cover of the book.

You can use these forms just as you would the forms in the book. Print them out, fill them in, and use them however you need. You can also fill in the forms directly on your computer. Just identify the form you need, open it, click on the space where the information should go, and input your information. Customize each form for your particular needs. Use them over and over again.

The CD-ROM is compatible with both PC and Mac operating systems. (While it should work with either operating system, we cannot guarantee that it will work with your particular system and we cannot provide technical assistance.) To use the forms on your computer, you will need to use Microsoft Word or another word processing program that can read Word files. The CD-ROM does not contain any such program.

Insert the CD-ROM into your computer. Double-click on the icon representing the disc on your desktop or go through your hard drive to identify the drive that contains the disc and click on it.

Once opened, you will see the files contained on the CD-ROM listed as "Form #: [Form Title]." Open the file you need. You may print the form to fill it out manually at this point, or you can click on the appropriate line to fill it in using your computer.

Any time you see bracketed information [ ] on the form, you can click on it and delete the bracketed information from your final form. This information is only a reference guide to assist you in filling in the forms and should be removed from your final version. Once all your information is filled in, you can print your filled-in form.

Purchasers of this book are granted a license to use the forms contained in it for their own personal use. By purchasing this book, you have also purchased a limited license to use all forms on the accompanying CD-ROM. The license limits you to personal use only and all other copyright laws must be adhered to. No claim of copyright is made in any government form reproduced in the book or on the CD-ROM. You are free to modify the forms and tailor them to your specific situation.

The author and publisher have attempted to provide the most current and up-to-date information available. However, the courts, Congress, and your state's legislatures review, modify, and change laws on an ongoing basis, as well as create new laws from time to time. Due to the very nature of the information and the continual changes in our legal system, to be sure that you have the current and best information for your situation, you should consult a local attorney or research the current laws yourself.

• • • • •

This publication is designed to provide accurate and authoritative information in regard to the subject matter covered. It is sold with the understanding that the publisher is not engaged in rendering legal, accounting, or other professional service. If legal advice or other expert assistance is required, the services of a competent professional person should be sought.
—From a Declaration of Principles Jointly Adopted by a Committee of the American Bar Association and a Committee of Publishers and Associations

This product is not a substitute for legal advice.
—Disclaimer required by Texas statutes

Introduction

It is hoped that using this book will save you some legal fees. This book may even save you from having to hire a lawyer at some time—but that is not its purpose.

This book has three main purposes—first, to help you manage and organize your corporation so you can reduce the occasions on which you need a lawyer to few as possible; second, to help you recognize the occasions on which a lawyer's advice is essential; and third, to help you use the lawyer you hire more efficiently.

Failing to hire a lawyer when you need one is not likely to save you money. If, in reading this book, you discover that what you want to do involves more complications than you imagined, or if what you want to do involves a large sum of money, then get a lawyer. If all goes well, you can complain about paying for something you did not need after all. That is better than not hiring a lawyer and having something more serious to complain about.

Some clients believe that, having turned a matter over to the lawyers, they are released from all further responsibility. After all, you are paying a large amount of money to a lawyer to draft a contract. But this thinking makes the lawyer's job nearly impossible. You should never believe it is solely the lawyer's job to make sure the contract is right. You know your business and what is important to it. The best lawyer's ideas about that may be completely wrong, and he or she may attach importance to the unimportant (because it was important to the last client) and gloss over a critical factor. Use this book to know what to expect from your lawyer and why. And then read and understand the work your lawyer does for you. Make sure it works for you.

ORGANIZATION OF THIS BOOK

This book deals with organizing and governing a corporation—corporate decision making by shareholders and directors, and management by officers. It will help you organize decision making and record keeping, some of which you can do better than a lawyer could. (This book is not about how you operate your business in dealing with the outside world.)

The main text of this book explains the various types of resolutions and other forms typically used in governing a business. Sample forms are contained throughout the text. These are examples for an imaginary corporation to give you some idea of how your finished forms should look.

These resolutions and other documents are reproduced as fill-in-the-blank forms in Appendix C. Although the resolution forms are reproduced as Consents to Action for adoption by shareholders and directors, remember that the same resolutions can be adopted by shareholders or directors in meetings. Thus, if you find a form resolution you need reproduced as a Consent to Action but you want your shareholders or directors to adopt the resolution in a meeting, you can simply take the body of the resolution and use it in connection with the forms supplied for minutes of meetings (forms 1–3 and 5–7). For more information about Consents to Action and meetings of shareholders and directors, see Chapter 3.

Appendix A is a list of the corporation statutes for each state. This will tell you where to look for more information. You should be familiar with your state's corporation statute and keep a copy on hand. Often it provides specific rules you must follow to operate legally.

Appendix B gives web addresses for most state statutes. Another very useful address for locating statutes is

www.findlaw.com

As mentioned, Appendix C contains the blank forms you can use. Some of these forms will require you to fill in information by referring to the various resolutions in the main part of the book. Many of the forms are resolutions for adoption by the shareholders or directors, to be combined into minutes of meetings, Consents to Action, or separate resolution forms, which are explained and illustrated in Chapter 3.

The forms are intentionally simple in style. Some of them may be more simple than real life applications will allow, but the basics are here.

HOW TO USE THE FORMS

To give you a good overview of governing your corporation, read through this entire book. Then, by using the table of contents or the index, locate the section of the text that explains the form you need. This will refer you to a blank form in Appendix C. Insert the data called for in the form. In some cases this will be a few names, in others you will need to insert a lengthy resolution. You can either photocopy the blank forms and type on them, retype the entire forms, or insert your information directly onto the form using your computer and the attached CD-ROM. (see How to Use the CD-ROM on page vii.) If your board of directors or shareholders intend to adopt a particular resolution in a meeting rather than by consent to action, or if you cannot find a resolution that exactly suits your needs, look in forms 1 through 10 to find a framework that fits your situation. See Chapter 3 for more information about meetings and consents to action.

There are no references to specific statutes. This book is intended to be used by people all over the country, so no specific statute is relevant to every reader. There are a few mentions of the Revised Model Business Corporation Act of 1984 which is referred to in the text as the Model Business Corporation Act (MBCA). The purpose of such references is to help you find your way in the statutes of your state. Many states have adopted the MBCA with variations. (There is a directory of state business corporation statutes in Appendix A of this book.) If yours is one of them, the MBCA reference will look something like the citation for the corresponding provision in your state statute.

Example:

Section 1.40 of the MBCA is found in the North Carolina Business Corporation Act, found at North Carolina General Statutes, section 55-1-40. (This is abbreviated as "N.C.G.S., Sec. 55-1-40." If you look this up you will find it in books titled "The General Statutes of North Carolina," but they are commonly, and officially, referred to as "North Carolina General Statutes.")

Most state governments declare standard forms for many of the purposes described in this book. Some states have very complete sets of forms readily available for downloading on your computer. When such forms are available, it is to your advantage to use them rather than the more generic forms in this book. The states are usually quicker and more efficient when reviewing their own forms, and it may save you time. In some cases, the Secretary of State will require you to use the state's standard forms. In such cases, the forms in this book still will be of value to you as a guide to understanding the purpose of standard state forms.

Understanding Corporation and Business Basics

A corporation (literally, an *embodiment*) is an organization created to do some things human beings cannot do or cannot easily do. Corporations can combine wealth of many people and focus that wealth on large projects, such as building a large passenger airplane. At the same time, a corporation can shield its investors from liability. If a corporation becomes insolvent and declares bankruptcy, the owners may lose their investment, but no more than that.

Corporations potentially have *perpetual* existence. Corporations such as churches and universities have been around for centuries. Many incorporated businesses have long outlived their founders. Investors, employees, and customers may have to worry about a corporation's financial health, but not its old age or the danger that it will be hit by a bus.

Corporations can combine the skills and energy of all its employees. No one human being acting alone could run a complex organization such as a bank or airline. There has to be delegation. Corporations are designed to make delegation work. In fact, corporations inherently work by delegation. Since a corporation is not a real human being, it can only act through *agents* such as officers and employees. It can enlist and manage as many agents as are needed to do the job— around the clock if necessary.

REASONS TO HAVE CORPORATIONS

These are the main reasons for having corporations.

- ✪ *Continuous existence*—corporations can outlive the individuals who founded and managed them.

- ✪ *Economies of scale*—corporations can raise huge piles of money from many investors and distribute management responsibility among many agents and employees.

- ✪ *Limited liability*—corporations, not their shareholder investors, are liable for its debts and obligations.

This does not mean that a corporation's employee can avoid personal liability by being a shareholder.

Example:

Suppose Ruth is employed as a delivery truck driver by Quick Delivery, Inc. She also owns 100 shares of stock in Quick Delivery, Inc. She carelessly hits a pedestrian while making deliveries. Quick Delivery, Inc. is liable for injuries to the pedestrian because its *employee* caused the accident. The *shareholders* of Quick Delivery (including Ruth) are shielded from liability by corporate limited liability, but Ruth is personally liable, because she caused the accident.

ALTERNATIVES TO CORPORATIONS

There are many *forms* of doing business. These days, it seems that every few years lawyers and legislators invent a new one. Here is a list of the most common ones.

Sole Proprietorship

A *sole proprietorship* is a one-owner business. If you go into business by yourself, without any co-owners, you are doing business as a sole proprietorship. Essentially, you and your business are the same thing—which means that its profits are your profits, and its debts are your debts. A sole proprietor can hire employees to work for him or her, but these employees do not own any part of the business.

Sole proprietors have unlimited liability. If an employee carelessly drives a sole proprietor's delivery truck through a stoplight, the business owner is personally liable for the damages.

General Partnership

If you go into business with one or more co-owners, you have a *general partnership*. The co-owner may be your spouse, your son or daughter, or someone you met yesterday. Partners share profits and debts according to their agreement, or if there is no formal partnership agreement, then according to rules established by law.

Like sole proprietors, general partners have unlimited liability. If a partner or a partnership employee drives the company truck through a stoplight and injures a pedestrian, the partners are personally liable. Usually, the partners are *jointly and severally liable*, meaning that each partner can be sued for the whole thing, though, they may later work out a way to share the expense.

Limited Partnership

The *limited partnership* is a kind of partnership established by statutory law. The purpose is to obtain some of the benefits of corporations for people who also want some of the characteristics of partnership. It has at least one *general* partner who manages the business and who is personally liable for the partnership debts. It also has one or more *limited* partners who invest in the business and share in the profits. Limited partners do not manage the business and have *limited liability*, meaning that they are not personally liable for the debts of the limited partnership.

Limited partnerships should not be confused with *limited liability partnerships* (LLPs) (sometimes *registered limited liability partnerships*), which are general partnerships in which certain partners and professionals are not liable for malpractice committed by their partners (but are liable for malpractice they commit).

Limited Liability Company

Limited liability companies (LLCs) are becoming more and more popular. An LLC has the essential characteristics of both corporations and limited partnerships. It may have perpetual existence and limited liability for its investors (called *members*). Unlike limited partners, LLC members may participate in the management of the business.

Professionals   With regard to *professional corporations* (PCs), *professional limited partnerships* (PLPs), and *professional limited liability companies* (PLLCs), *limited liability* has some disadvantages. If your doctor, lawyer, or engineer is careless or incompetent, you do not want him or her to be shielded from personal liability for malpractice claims by virtue of the limited liability enjoyed by corporate shareholders, limited partners, and LLC members. Professionals, therefore, must operate in one of the business forms that do not allow limitation of liability on malpractice claims.

Not-for-Profit Corporations   Charitable corporations, or *not-for-profit corporations,* are usually organizations such as churches, charities, social clubs, or fraternal organizations. They are organized under special statutes that allow for certain flexibility in management and organizations. (Except in rare circumstances, a business would not be organized under such rules.)

CHOOSING TO BE A CORPORATION

Finding the right alternative for your business is complicated, and it is probably a subject you will want to discuss with your lawyer and accountant. It depends on a number of factors including the size of the business, how much capital you need, and how much money you can afford to spend on creating and maintaining the more complicated forms of doing business. It may even depend on your personality—how much patience do you have for the details of running a corporation and maintaining its *separateness* from your personal business affairs?

C Corporations   You also have to think about taxes. Most corporations are *C corporations* under the Internal Revenue Code (I.R.C.). C corporations must pay tax on income just as individuals do. When C corporations distribute income to shareholders in the form of dividends, the dividends are not tax deductions for the corporation. When the dividends are received by the shareholders, they are taxable income to the shareholders.

This is *double taxation* in that corporate profits are taxed twice—once as corporate income and once as the shareholders' income. Most people want to avoid double taxation, and there are ways to do it.

One way to avoid double taxation is for the shareholders to become employees of the corporation. Their salaries, as employees, are taxable to the shareholders/employees. But the salaries are deductible expenses for the corporation, so there is no double taxation. But this can be tricky. For example, suppose the shareholder/employee is getting a salary, but not doing any work. The tax collectors may reasonably claim that, if you are not doing any work, it is not a salary after all, but a dividend equivalent—no corporate deduction.

Another way to avoid double taxation is to choose a different form of doing business. Partners of limited and general partnerships, and members of limited liability companies are usually taxed directly on the profits of the business, while the partnerships and LLCs avoid taxes altogether.

Double taxation may not always be a bad thing. If a shareholder is in a high tax bracket, it may be beneficial in two ways: (1) he or she may not need frequent infusions of cash from the corporation and may be content to let corporate profits stay in the corporation and grow, or (2) the shareholder's personal tax rate may be higher than the corporate rate. Such a shareholder may prefer C corporation status.

S Corporations

Some corporations may elect subchapter S status under the I.R.C. and become *S corporations*. Unlike a C corporation, an S corporation is taxed in the same way as a partnership. That is, the S corporation shareholders (like general and limited partners) are taxed directly on company profits. S corporations and partnerships do not pay taxes, but S corporation shareholders and partners do. (And they have to pay the taxes, even if the S corporation does not turn the profits over to the shareholders in the form of dividends or salaries, which can be a problem.)

Unfortunately, the I.R.C. has strict rules about which corporations are allowed to elect subchapter S status. For example, S corporations are limited to a small number of shareholders and to one class of shares. Before you decide to elect subchapter S status, be sure to consult your lawyer or tax accountant.

If your corporation is currently registered as a *C corporation* and you want to change it to an *S corporation*, the **ELECTION BY A SMALL BUSINESS CORPORATION** (IRS form 2553) for making this election is included in Appendix C. (see form 110, p.356.) If you change the corporation's tax status, the directors should probably adopt a resolution for the change. Be sure to consult your tax adviser before changing the tax status.

Corporate Advantages

Here are some other possible advantages of the corporate form.

- ✪ *It may be easier to sell a corporation than another kind of business.* The reason is that, to transfer ownership of a corporation, all you have to do is sell the shares. Compare that to selling a sole proprietorship in which you have to sell the computer, the desk, the accounts receivable, the paper clips, etc.

- ✪ *It may simplify estate planning.* Suppose one of your daughters has good business sense, but the other does not. You can leave a majority control of the business to the one who is a good business manager, but still leave an ownership interest to the daughter whose talents lie elsewhere. If you leave a sole proprietorship to your kids, they will find themselves general partners in the family business with the presumption that they all have the responsibilities and liabilities that go along with a partnership.

- ✪ *A corporation may provide opportunities for saving on taxes.* For example, it may be possible to make medical insurance fully deductible.

- ✪ *Many employees would rather have a corporate employer than a partnership or sole proprietor employer.* It may seem more prestigious to the employee and it allows for better incentive plans. For example, the corporate employer can distribute some share ownership (and a share in the profits) to employees while continuing control of the business in the majority shareholders. Sharing ownership of a sole proprietorship or general partnership changes the nature of the business.

- ✪ *The corporate form of business, by its nature, separates the business from the personal affairs of its owners.* The corporation has separate bank accounts, separate property, and separate legal obligations from the owners.

Corporate Disadvantages

While there are many advantages to the corporate form, there are also disadvantages. Here are some disadvantages of the corporate form that you may want to consider.

✪   *There are a lot of details.* You have to keep separate records and separate bank accounts. There are some that you would not keep as a sole proprietor—for example, corporate minute books. Starting a corporation also involves particular procedures, such as filing articles of incorporation with the state, issuing shares, etc.

✪   *There are some extra expenses involved.* Corporations must file an annual report with the state and must pay an annual franchise tax. There is also the matter of filing federal and state income tax returns.

✪   *If your business is a corporation, you are not only an owner (shareholder), you are also an employee.* This means that you become an expense for the business, just like the other employees. Expenses such as unemployment taxes will increase. If you give yourself a perk, you have to understand that the other employees might deserve or become entitled to similar perks.

Getting Started

You have decided you want a corporation. The next step is deciding where you want it. Corporations are created, or *incorporated*, under the laws of a particular state. It does not have to be the state where you live or where the business is located, but there are factors to consider in deciding where to locate your corporation.

LOCATION OF THE CORPORATION

The law of the state where your business is incorporated controls the way your corporation is governed. It becomes the home state for many of your corporation's legal matters. Your corporation may be sued in the courts of the state where it is incorporated (as well as in the state(s) where it carries on its business).

Delaware Regardless of where the business is located, many corporations have been incorporated under the laws of Delaware. The reason is that, traditionally, Delaware laws have allowed great flexibility in designing and managing corporations. Because of this history, Delaware has a very large body of caselaw interpreting its corporate laws. Delaware courts are generally experts in matters of corporate law.

Although few states can match Delaware in the extensive body of corporate law its courts have amassed, most states have liberalized their business corporation statutes so that they are essentially comparable to Delaware's. For most people considering incorporation, Delaware's historic advantage no longer matters.

However, Delaware may still be the best choice for a corporation considering raising capital by selling shares to the public. Anyone considering such a course should consult legal counsel. (see "Buying and Selling Shares of Stock," page 75.)

Nevada   In recent years the state of Nevada has changed its business corporation laws to attract more businesses. Nevada law offers some advantages of privacy in that it does not share information with the Internal Revenue Service.

Other States   Most people considering incorporation will choose to incorporate under the laws of the state in which they live and in which the corporate business will be centered. Some advantages of doing so are as follows.

Convenience. Although incorporating in another state is not particularly difficult, it is usually easier and cheaper to deal with people closer to home.

Economy. If you incorporate in, say, Delaware but intend to carry on your business in your home state, your corporation will be a *foreign corporation* in your home state. It will have to apply for a *Certificate of Authority* to conduct business in your home state. This process is roughly comparable to the procedure for incorporation, so it multiplies the effort and expense required.

Legal jurisdiction. As mentioned, your corporation is subject to jurisdiction in the courts of the state where it is incorporated and in the states where it conducts business. If a problem occurs, it may be very inconvenient and expensive to manage a lawsuit in some state far away from your home and business.

BUSINESS CORPORATION STATUTES

Every state has its own set of statutes governing corporations. Most of them are fairly similar, but all are unique. Appendix A is a directory of state business corporation statutes. (see page 229.) A list of Web addresses where you can find the actual statutes of the states can be found in Appendix B. (see page 233.)

Close Corporation

Different states have different ideas about what a *close corporation* is. In some states, it simply means a corporation with a small number of shareholders. A typical example would be a family company in which members of the same family own all the outstanding shares of the corporation.

In other states, the term has a more formal meaning and refers to corporations that formally elect close corporation status or incorporate under special statutes. In these states, close corporations may do without boards of directors with the shareholders taking over the functions of the board.

In either case, close corporations typically place restrictions on shares to keep ownership in a small circle of people. (see "Agreements Among Shareholders," p. 90.)

Professional Corporation

Shareholders of corporations that provide professional services, such as law firms, medical practices, engineering firms, or accounting firms, (often known as *professional corporations*) do not enjoy the same limited liability as shareholders of ordinary corporations. (See "Alternatives to Corporations" in Chapter 1.)

When such businesses incorporate, they must do so under special provisions of the state law, which take into account the special nature of such businesses. In addition, such businesses may have to meet additional requirements of licensing organizations such as bar associations and medical societies.

NOTE: *Such considerations do not apply to most businesses. If your business is of a professional nature, consult with your local professional licensing body.*

CORPORATE NAMES

Businesses conducted in the corporate form are required to reveal to the public that its owners enjoy limited liability. For that reason, corporate names must contain a word or abbreviation that indicates corporate status. In most states this means that the corporate name must include one of the following words:

- ✪ Corporation or Corp.

- ✪ Incorporated or Inc.

- ✪ Company or Co.

- ✪ Limited or Ltd.

Or, if it is a professional corporation:

- ✪ Professional Corporation or P.C.

- ✪ Professional Association or P.A.

Corporations may not use a name that is the same as a name already used or reserved for use by a corporation, limited partnership, or limited liability company organized or licensed to do business in the state. The standard for determining what is permitted is very low in most states. If your company's name is *distinguishable on the record* from another, it is permitted.

– Warning –

This standard means you can choose a name that is very much like one already in use.

Example:

If *Quicky Delivery, Inc.* is already in use, you could choose *Quickly Delivery, Inc.* in most states. But even if you are allowed to incorporate under that similar name, it may infringe on the Quicky trademark, and you may be liable for such infringement, not under the business corporation statute, but under the federal or state trademark law.

Trademarks   This also means that someone else can incorporate under a name very similar to the one you have already chosen. You may be able to protect your company name by registering it under a state or federal *trademark* statute. (A trademark is a name or logo uniquely associated with a product.) For example, Coca-Cola is a trademark, and the Mercedes-Benz star logo is a trademark. (A *service mark* is a name or logo associated with services provided by a company.)

A name or logo achieves trademark or service mark status through custom and usage. The federal government and some state governments provide mechanisms for registering such marks. Any business that copies or otherwise infringes a registered trademark or service mark may be subject to injunction or to liability for damages resulting from the infringement. You may want to consider registering your company's name or logo on the appropriate registry.

To avoid infringing another company's mark, you may want to conduct a name search. (see "Name Searches" on page 14.)

It is possible to incorporate under one name and conduct your business under another *alias* or *assumed name*. This is discussed in the section "Adopting a Corporate Alias" on page 182.

Limits on Names   You may not choose a name that implies the ability to carry on a business or practice you are not permitted to engage in.

Example:

You cannot name your company *Jim's Insurance Company* unless you are licensed to sell insurance. Nor may you imply that you are a law firm, unless you are licensed as such.

Some words are *proprietary*. For example, the word "Realtor" is owned as a trademark by a professional association, and you may not use it without their permission.

Unusual Names   Trademark lawyers talk about the *strength* of a trademark or service mark. Among other things, strength means a name that is unusual. A unique name will be more easily protected from use or infringement by another business than will a less imaginative name. Usually the strongest kind of name is one you make up—a word that did not exist before you invented it and used it for your company (e.g., Xerox).

Nevertheless, other kinds of names can make very good trademarks. For example, the word "mustang" describes a kind of horse. Ford Motor Company borrowed the word and applied it to a car. Now when most people hear *Mustang*, they think of the car, not the horse. The name has acquired a *secondary meaning* in lawyer terms and is a valuable trademark.

Name Searches

When searching for a name, find out if the name you want is available. There are a number of possible checks you should make that will cost you nothing. Check business directories such as the Yellow Pages, telephone directories, and other lists of businesses to see if someone else is already using a name similar to the one you want. Enter the name you like in several Internet search engines to see if any conflicts turn up.

To ensure that you are not choosing a name that infringes the trademark of an existing business, you can conduct a more thorough and professional name search by using the services of a professional name search company. Ask your lawyer for a recommendation.

Remember, the question is not just *what is legal?* Ask yourself what makes sense. You may be able to incorporate legally under a name similar to one already in use, but it may lead to unnecessary confusion and even liability.

Reserving a Name

It is not necessary to do so, but if you have chosen a name you like, you can reserve it for your use until you get around to incorporating. If you are ready to incorporate, you can skip this step.

Reserving a name requires filing an application and paying a small fee. Most states provide fill-in-the-blank forms for this purpose. The forms are usually available online at the Secretary of State's website. Some states require that you use the standard form, and most would prefer it.

ARTICLES OF INCORPORATION

The creation of some forms of doing business is automatic. If you simply go into business for yourself, for example you repeatedly buy T-shirts and sell them for a profit, you have created a sole proprietorship. It is automatic. If you do the same thing with a co-owner, you have created a general partnership.

Corporations are different. A corporation only exists because there is a corporate statute that says corporations can be brought into existence. In order to create a corporation, you have to follow the steps set out in the statute. That is, you have to file a document called the **ARTICLES OF INCORPORATION** and pay a fee. (see form 123, p.374.)

Mandatory Information

The articles are like the corporate constitution. It can be a fairly simple document, but it has the basic information needed to establish the corporation, including:

- ❂ a corporate name meeting the proper requirements;

- ❂ the number of shares the corporation is authorized to issue;

- ❂ the street and mailing addresses of the corporation's initial *registered office* and the name of the corporation's initial *registered agent*. (This is the name and address of the person to whom official papers, such as lawsuit documents, are to be delivered. This name and address can be changed from time to time without having to amend the articles); and,

- ❂ the name and address of each *incorporator*. (Incorporators sign the **ARTICLES OF INCORPORATION**. There need be only one in most cases.)

The **ARTICLES OF INCORPORATION** may contain other optional information. It is generally best to keep the articles reasonably simple. It is not particularly easy to amend the articles (see Chapter 10), so include only what is important and more or less permanent.

NOTE: *Remember the* **ARTICLES OF INCORPORATION** *is a public document, so anyone can see it.*

Optional Information

Optional information that may be included in the articles can be found in the following list. This is not an exhaustive list, but articles may include:

✪ the names and addresses of the initial directors of the corporation (the members of the board of directors can be changed later without having to amend the articles);

✪ the purposes for which the corporation is organized;

✪ provisions regarding the management of the corporation;

✪ provisions limiting or defining the powers of the corporation, its directors, its shareholders, and its officers;

✪ a par value for shares of the corporation (see Chapter 6);

✪ a limitation on the duration of the corporation (for example, you *could* provide that the corporation will go out of existence in twenty-five years); and,

✪ in some states, a provision limiting the liability of directors resulting from negligence in carrying out his or her duties.

Most states provide fill-in-the-blank forms for this purpose, usually available online. Some states require that you use the standard form, and most would prefer it. Use the form provided by your state. An example of a typical **ARTICLES OF INCORPORATION** for Scrupulous Corporation follows.

sample of form 123: **ARTICLES OF INCORPORATION**

Articles of Incorporation
of
Scrupulous Corporation

The undersigned hereby executes these Articles of Incorporation for the purpose of incorporating under the Business Corporation Law of the State of West Carolina.

1. The name of the corporation is **Scrupulous Corporation**.

2. The number of shares the corporation shall have authority to issue is **100,000 no par value**.

3. The street address (and mailing address, if different) (including county) of the initial registered office of the corporation and the name of the registered agent of the corporation located at that address is:

**Roberta Moore, No. 4 Beach Place,
Pleasant Cove, South Coast County, West Carolina 27000**

4. (Optional) The names and addresses of the individuals who will serve as initial directors of the corporation are:

Henry Hardy **238 Prosperity Street** **New York, NY 10032**	**Roberta Moore** **No. 4 Beach Place** **Pleasant Cove,** **West Carolina 27000**	**Raymond Rodriguez** **239 Surf Street** **Pleasant Cove,** **West Carolina 27000**

5. (Optional) Additional provisions not inconsistent with law for managing the corporation, regulating the internal affairs of the corporation, and establishing the powers of the corporation and its directors and shareholders:

NONE.

6. The name and address of each incorporator of the corporation is:

Henry Hardy, 238 Prosperity Street, New York, NY

In witness whereof, these Articles of Incorporation have been subscribed by the incorporator(s) this **30th** day of **June, 2006**.

Henry Hardy
Incorporator

Filing Requirements

In most states, **ARTICLES OF INCORPORATION** are filed at the office of the Secretary of State. If you are using a standard form preferred by your state, you will probably find the address, filing instructions, and fees printed on the form.

Your corporation exists as of the time and date when the articles are filed with the Secretary. In most states, it is possible to delay the effective date by providing for a delayed effective date in the **ARTICLES OF INCORPORATION**.

ORGANIZATION

Now that your corporation exists, it needs a little organizing to fill in the shell. The company needs officers, shareholders, bylaws, and other basics. These basics are supplied in an organizational meeting, or consent to action without formal meeting.

The Organizational Meeting

The sample **ARTICLES OF INCORPORATION** on page 17 lists the individuals who will serve as the first board of directors of the corporation. (Three is a usual number, but you can have more or less. Choose an odd number, so you do not have to worry about tied votes.)

If the **ARTICLES OF INCORPORATION** names the initial board, the board members meet to organize the company. If the articles do not name the board members, the incorporators who signed the articles will name the directors and may complete the organization or turn that function over to the new directors.

The organizational meeting does not have to be a meeting at all. Any actions that may be taken in a formal directors' or shareholders' meeting may also be taken in a writing called a *Consent to Action*. This book contains numerous examples of actions taken at formal meetings and consents to action. All such minutes of meetings and *Consents to Action* should be kept permanently in the corporate minute book. (see Chapter 3, "Corporate Decision Making.")

Later you will see a consent to action by the directors of Scrupulous Corporation that organizes that corporation. Following is a list of decisions that should be considered by the directors or incorporators at the organizational meeting.

Acceptance of the articles of incorporation. The directors satisfy themselves that the company has been correctly incorporated.

Adoption of bylaws. **BYLAWS** are the rules and regulations by which the corporation governs itself. The **BYLAWS** must conform to the laws of the state in which the corporation is organized, and may not conflict with provisions in the company's **ARTICLES OF INCORPORATION**. **BYLAWS** vary a great deal from corporation to corporation.

Appendix C of this book includes typical **BYLAWS**, which will more than likely serve your purpose. (see form 125, p.378.) There are additional suggested provisions for **BYLAWS** at various places in this book dealing with a variety of subjects, such as duties of officers and indemnification of directors and officers.

Adoption of a corporate seal. The seal is a symbol of the corporation's authority. Its legal importance varies from state to state, but usually a document signed under seal is presumed by courts to be authorized by the board of directors and correct. A seal can be in any form you want. A typical seal is circular or rectangular and contains the name of the corporation, as well as its year and state of incorporation.

Adoption of a form for share certificates. Ownership of corporate shares is usually evidenced by the issuance of a certificate. The corporation should designate an official form and authorize the company's officers to issue shares on that form.

Accept offers to purchase shares. In most small corporations, the directors and officers will also be shareholders, and the shareholders will purchase their shares at the time the company is organized. (For an example of an agreement to purchase shares, see Chapter 6. See the same chapter for important information about state and federal regulation of the buying and selling of shares.)

Reimbursement. This authorizes the officers to reimburse incorporators for expenses of incorporation.

Elect officers. For more on officers, see Chapter 9.

Authorize a corporate bank account. The bank you use will have standard forms called *bank resolutions* authorizing an account at that bank. The organizational meeting should authorize the use of the bank's standard form.

Ratify the appointment of the company's registered agent and registered office. This is the same agent and office mentioned in the ARTICLES OF INCORPORATION.

Adoption of IRS Section 1244 Plan. If your corporation qualifies as a small business corporation under the I.R.C., it may be eligible for the benefits of I.R.C., Section 1244. The benefit occurs if you lose money on *Section 1244 stock*. The losses are fully deductible (up to certain limits) against ordinary income, rather than deductible as capital losses.

The Code does not require a written plan, but it is good practice to have one in the organizational records. Under current law, the amount of stock intended to qualify under a Section 1244 plan, plus the amounts received by the corporation as contributions to capital or paid in surplus, cannot exceed $1,000,000.

What follows is a sample, filled-in form 124, CONSENT TO ACTION WITHOUT FORMAL MEETING OF DIRECTORS (ORGANIZATIONAL ACTIVITY).

sample of form 124: **Consent to Action without Formal Meeting of Directors (Organizational Activity)**

Consent to Action Without Formal Meeting of Directors of

Scrupulous Corporation

Organization Activity

The undersigned, being all of the Directors of the Corporation, hereby adopt the following resolutions:

RESOLVED, that the Articles of Incorporation as filed with the Secretary of State of **this State**, and presented to the directors by the secretary of the Corporation (the secretary), are hereby accepted and approved, and that the secretary is authorized and directed to place the duplicate original of the Articles, together with the original filing receipt of the Secretary of State, in the minute book of the Corporation.

RESOLVED, that the Bylaws presented to the directors by the secretary are hereby adopted as the Bylaws of the Corporation, and that the secretary is authorized and directed to insert a copy of such Bylaws, certified as such by the secretary, in the minute book of the Corporation immediately following the Articles of Incorporation.

Seal of Scrupulous Corporation
20✳06
State of West Carolina

RESOLVED, that the corporate seal presented to the directors by the secretary is hereby adopted as the seal of the Corporation, and that an impression of such seal be made in the margin of these minutes.

RESOLVED, that the form of share certificate presented to the directors by the secretary is hereby adopted as the form of share certificate for the Corporation, and that the secretary is authorized and directed to attach a sample of such certificate to these resolutions.

RESOLVED, that stock subscription agreements for shares of the Corporation, dated **June 30, 2006**, and described below:

Name	Number of shares	Consideration
Henry Hardy	**20,000**	**$10,000**
Roberta Moore	**20,000**	**$10,000**
Raymond Rodriguez	**20,000**	**$10,000**

are hereby accepted on behalf of the corporation, and that the president and secretary, upon receipt of the consideration stated, are authorized and directed to issue certificates for such shares to the respective shareholders.

RESOLVED, that the president of the Corporation is authorized and directed to pay charges and expenses related to the organization of the Corporation and to reimburse any person who has made such payments on behalf of the Corporation.

RESOLVED, that the persons listed below are hereby appointed to the offices indicated opposite their names, and that a determination of compensation of such officers shall be delayed for consideration at a later date.

Name	Office
Raymond Rodriguez	**President**
Henry Hardy	**Vice President and Treasurer**
Roberta Moore	**Vice President and Secretary**

RESOLVED, that funds of the Corporation shall be deposited in the **Bank of Care** and that standard printed resolutions supplied by the Bank and presented by the secretary to the directors shall be adopted by the directors and incorporated and attached to these resolutions.

RESOLVED, that the registered office and registered agent of the corporation as stated in the Articles of Incorporation shall be and remain the registered office and agent of the Corporation until the same is changed by resolution of the directors in accordance with the applicable law.

RESOLVED, that the following Plan for the issuance of common stock of the Corporation and qualification of such stock as *small business corporation* stock under Section 1244 of the Internal Revenue Code of 1986, as amended, is hereby adopted:

1. The corporation shall offer and issue under this Plan, a maximum of **60,000** shares of its common stock at a maximum price of **$10.00** per share and a minimum price equal to the par value of the shares, if any.

2. This plan shall be terminated by (a) the complete issuance of all shares offered hereunder, (b) appropriate action terminating the Plan by the board of directors and the shareholders of the Corporation, or (c) the adoption of a new Plan by the shareholders for the issuance of additional stock under IRC Section 1244.

3. No increase in the basis of outstanding stock shall result from a contribution to capital under this Plan.

4. No stock offered under this Plan shall be issued on the exercise of a stock right, stock warrant, or stock option, unless such right, warrant, or option is applicable solely to unissued stock offered under this Plan and is exercised during the period of the Plan.

5. Shares of the Corporation subscribed for prior to the adoption of this Plan, including shares subscribed for prior to the date the corporation comes into existence, may be issued hereunder, provided, however, that the said stock is not in fact issued prior to the adoption of this Plan.

6. No shares of stock shall be issued under this plan for a payment which, including prior payments, exceeds the maximum amount that may be receive under the Plan.

7. Any offering or portion of an offer outstanding that is unissued at the time of the adoption of this plan is hereby withdrawn.

8. Shares issued under this Plan shall be issued in exchange for money or other property other than stock or securities. Shares issued under this Plan shall not be issued in return for services rendered or to be rendered to, or for the benefit of, the corporation. Shares may be issued under this plan in consideration for cancellation of indebtedness of the corporation, unless such indebtedness is evidenced by a security or arises out of the performance of services.

9. Any matters related to the issue of shares under this Plan shall be resolved so as to comply with applicable law and regulations so as to qualify such issue under Section 1244 of the Internal Revenue Code. Any shares issued under this Plan which are finally determined not to be so qualified, and only such shares, shall be determined not to be in the Plan, and any other Shares not so disqualified shall not be affected by such disqualification.

10. The aggregate amount offered hereunder plus the equity capital of the Corporation shall not exceed $1,000,000.

RESOLVED, that these resolutions shall be effective on **July 1, 2006.**

| *Henry Hardy* | *Roberta Moore* | *Raymond Rodriguez* |
| Henry Hardy, Director | Roberta Moore, Director | Raymond Rodriguez, Director |

ISSUING SHARE CERTIFICATES

Now that the corporation has shareholders, you will want to issue share certificates. You do not have to have a fancy form, and you can find a simple share certificate in Appendix C. (see form 35.) The issuance of shares should be recorded on a stock transfer ledger sheet. Form 109 is a **STOCK LEDGER** form that should be completed and inserted in the corporate minute book.

CORPORATE KITS

Legal stationers sell *corporate kits* which include looseleaf notebooks for use as minute books, preprinted stock certificate forms, and stock transfer registers. While convenient, it is not necessary to buy one of these kits. An ordinary looseleaf notebook may serve as your minute book, and you can buy a corporate seal from most suppliers of office equipment.

Corporate Decision Making

A corporation is the embodiment of many people working together toward a common goal. Its owners, decision makers, and managers may number in the hundreds or thousands. Such an organization must rely on a certain degree of formality to ensure that decisions are made, recorded, and communicated in an orderly and reliable way.

COLLECTIVE DECISIONS AND PROOF OF AUTHORITY

When an individual makes a decision, it is a pretty simple matter. Suppose you are thinking about a new car. You may need advice, and you may need to think about it a long time, but when the time comes to make the decision, it is a mental snap of the fingers. When you put your name on the dotted line at the dealership, that is all the evidence needed that the decision has been made.

Corporations as Persons

Under the law, corporations are *persons*, but they are only imaginary creations. They can make decisions like other persons, but how do you know when an imaginary person has made a decision, and how do you prove it?

Corporations, like puppets, only act and move when their shareholders, officers, and directors say. Since a corporation is a collective body made up of the separate individuals who are its shareholders, officers, and directors, a corporation can only make a collective decision. Collective decisions are made in meetings of one kind or another.

Since a corporation is separate from the collection of individuals who own and manage it, there must be some form of communication between it and its masters. This separation is extremely important because without it, the corporation may, for some purposes, cease to exist.

Piercing the Corporate Veil

If a corporation's owner runs the corporation's business in a way that makes it inseparable from his or her existence as an individual, then it is under the legal doctrine known as *piercing the corporate veil*, and a court may ignore the corporation altogether. The result may be that a plaintiff or creditor can satisfy a judgment out of the owner's personal assets rather than the corporation's.

Proof of this critical separation is shown by:

- ✪ keeping the formal lines of communication open between owners and directors;

- ✪ the way you call and conduct shareholders' and directors' meetings; and, particularly,

- ✪ the way you record the decisions made in the meetings.

Of course there are other important steps to take in avoiding piercing the corporate veil. For example, make sure you keep the corporation's bank account and other assets separate from your personal business.

Proof of Authority

When you went into the car dealer's office and put your signature on the contract to buy a car, the salesperson did not need to ask, *how do I know you really intend to be bound by this contract?* You were there in person, and the dealer could see that you yourself signed it. A corporation cannot do that. Not being an individual, a corporation cannot sign its own name. It must act through an agent. If you sent your next door neighbor to buy the car for you, and your neighbor signed your name on the line, the salesperson certainly would ask that question, and your neighbor would have to show some kind of *proof of authority*.

A corporation has the same problem. How would you go about proving that the corporation really wants a new car and that its agent, usually an officer, really has the power to sign the company's name on the contract? The proof can only be found in the written record of the decision-making process. A corporation *decides* when its shareholders or directors meet to make collective decisions, and, because the corporation cannot speak for itself, the outside world learns about the decision by having a look at the record.

FORMAL MINUTES

One of the primary records is the *minutes* of corporate meetings. Minutes are basically a written summary of what occurs at meetings of the board of directors and meetings of the shareholders. Boards of directors usually have regularly scheduled meetings weekly or monthly. Shareholders do not meet as often as the board. Typically, they only meet once a year. However, as important matters sometimes cannot wait for the next regular meeting, sometimes there is a need for special meetings both of the board of directors and of the shareholders.

In corporations with a large number of directors, smaller *committees* are sometimes formed as a more efficient way of conducting business. Form 1 or 2 can be adapted for committee meetings by simply designating the name of the committee after the name of the corporation.

Appendix C includes forms for use for the various types of meetings. Space is provided on these forms to fill in the name of your corporation, other basic information, and whatever minutes apply to the particular meeting. Form 1 is to record **MINUTES OF REGULAR MEETING OF THE BOARD OF DIRECTORS**. Form 2 is for **MINUTES OF SPECIAL MEETING OF THE BOARD OF DIRECTORS**. Form 5 is for the **MINUTES OF ANNUAL MEETING OF THE SHAREHOLDERS**; and, Form 6 is for **MINUTES OF SPECIAL MEETING OF THE SHAREHOLDERS**.

On the following pages are examples of what the written record of three corporate decisions might look like. The first is from a special meeting of the shareholders (form 6). The second is from a special meeting of the board of directors (form 2). The third is from a special meeting of the Executive Committee of the board of directors (also using form 2).

sample of form 6: **MINUTES OF A SPECIAL MEETING OF THE SHAREHOLDERS**

Minutes of Special Meeting of
the Shareholders of
Scrupulous Corporation

A special meeting of the Shareholders of the Corporation was held on the date and at the time and place set forth in the written notice of meeting, or waiver of notice signed by shareholders, and attached to the minutes of this meeting.

The following shareholders were present:

Shareholder	No. of Shares
Henry Hardy	**20,000**
Raymond Rodriguez	**15,000**
Della Driskell	**15,000**
Calvin Collier	**15,000**
Hugh Hardy	**20,000**
Roberta Moore	**15,000**

The meeting was called to order and it was moved, seconded, and carried that **Raymond Rodriguez** act as Chairman and that **Roberta Moore** act as Secretary.

A roll call was taken and the Chairman noted that all of the outstanding shares of the Corporation were represented in person or by proxy. Any proxies are attached to these minutes.

Minutes of the preceding meeting of the Shareholders, held on **January 5, 2006**, were read and approved.

Upon motion duly made, seconded, and carried, the following resolution(s) was/were adopted:

The Chairman informed the shareholders that Mr. Henry Hardy, citing his advanced age, had resigned from the board of directors, effective July 9, 2006, and recommended that the shareholders act promptly to fill the vacancy created by his resignation. He then asked the shareholders for nominations for the position of director.

Mr. Calvin Collier nominated Ms. Della Driskell, a shareholder who was present at the meeting. There were no additional nominations, and Ms. Driskell was elected by the unanimous vote of the shareholders to serve as director of the corporation to complete Mr. Hardy's term and until her successor is elected and qualified.

There being no further business, the meeting adjourned on the **19th** day of **July, 2006**, at **1** o'clock **p**.m.

Roberta Moore
Secretary

sample of form 2: **MINUTES OF A SPECIAL MEETING OF THE BOARD OF DIRECTORS**

Minutes of Special Meeting of the Board of Directors of Scrupulous Corporation

A special meeting of the Board of Directors of the Corporation was held on the date and at the time and place set forth in the written notice of meeting, or waiver of notice signed by directors, and attached to the minutes of this meeting.

The following directors were present: **Della Driskell, Roberta Moore, Raymond Rodriguez, and Calvin Collier**.

The meeting was called to order and it was moved, seconded, and carried that **Raymond Rodriguez** act as Chairman and that **Roberta Moore** act as Secretary.

Minutes of the preceding meeting of the Board, held on **January 9, 2006**, were read and approved.

Upon motion duly made, seconded, and carried, the following resolution(s) was/were adopted:

The Chairman called the meeting to order at 10:45 a.m. He then asked the President to present a report.

The President reported on the need of a delivery vehicle for the company's use.

Mr. Hardy moved the adoption of the following resolution which, after discussion, was duly adopted by the unanimous vote of the Directors:

RESOLVED, that the Corporation shall purchase an automobile at a cost of not more that $28,000 which, in the opinion of the President of the corporation, shall be suitable for making deliveries to customers.

FURTHER RESOLVED, that the President or his designees are authorized and directed to negotiate such purchase for the corporation and to execute such contracts or other documents as may be necessary or desirable to complete the purchase.

There being no further business, the meeting adjourned on the **19th** day of **July, 2006**, at **1** o'clock **p**.m.

Roberta Moore
_____
Secretary

Approved:

Raymond Rodriguez
_____

sample of form 2: **Minutes of a Special Committee Meeting**

Minutes of Special Meeting of
the Board of Directors of
Scrupulous Corporation (Executive Committee)

A special meeting of the Board of Directors of the Corporation was held on the date and at the time and place set forth in the written notice of meeting, or waiver of notice signed by directors, and attached to the minutes of this meeting.

The following directors were present: **Della Driskell, Roberta Moore, Raymond Rodriguez, and Calvin Collier.**

The meeting was called to order and it was moved, seconded, and carried that **Raymond Rodriguez** act as Chairman and that **Roberta Moore** act as Secretary.

Minutes of the preceding meeting of the Board, held on **January 9, 2006**, were read and approved.

Upon motion duly made, seconded, and carried, the following resolution(s) was/were adopted:

The President reported on progress in negotiating the purchase of a new delivery vehicle as authorized by the Directors on June 06, 2006. He informed the Committee that, in his opinion, rather than purchasing a car as had been discussed in such meeting, it would be to the company's advantage to purchase a small van that would carry a larger load and allow more efficient deliveries. Such a van, he said, could be purchased for $28,000, the amount authorized in the Directors' original resolution. Since the directors' authorization had specified the purchase of an automobile, the President thought it necessary to seek the Committee's advice on whether it would be appropriate to purchase the van instead.

Ms. Driskell moved the adoption of the following resolution which, after brief discussion, was adopted by the unanimous vote of the members of the committee.

RESOLVED, that the purchase of a delivery van, shall be deemed to be consistent with the Directors' intent in adopting its resolution on June 06, 2006, and the President is therefore authorized to proceed with the purchase of a van at a cost of not more than $28,000.

There being no further business, the meeting adjourned on the **19th** day of **July, 2006**, at **1** o'clock **p**.m.

Roberta Moore
_____
Secretary

Approved:

Raymond Rodriguez
_____

Running a business requires hundreds of decisions. Not all of them are important enough to command the attention of the directors or shareholders. The business corporation statutes of the various states usually allow another method of making corporate decisions, which can greatly reduce the expense and inconvenience of frequent meetings.

A **CONSENT TO ACTION WITHOUT FORMAL MEETING OF DIRECTORS** may be very useful when a needed decision can be reached without a face-to-face discussion among the directors. (see form 4, p.246.) It is particularly helpful when the decision makers are scattered and cannot meet without expensive and time-consuming travel.

NOTE: *Throughout this text, examples of decision making by directors and shareholders appear in the form of* **Consents to Action**. *This is because, for most small corporations, written consents are more convenient than calling a formal meeting. You should remember, though, that anything that can be decided in a consent to action can be decided in a meeting and vice versa. There are some decisions that are so important that they should probably be made in a face-to-face meeting. Some of these occasions are noted in the text.*

Most states require that in order to be effective, consents to action or *written consents* must be in writing and signed (consented to) by all the shareholders or directors entitled to vote. That requirement means that a company with a large number of shareholders will not reasonably be able to use this method. You would never be able to collect the large number of signatures needed. However, for most boards of directors and directors' committees, and for the shareholders of some small corporations, it is a very useful device indeed.

Many states (notably Delaware) now allow written consents to be effective when signed by only the number of directors that would be needed to take the action in a meeting, usually a majority of the directors in office. However, copies of such majority consents must be sent to *all* the directors.

Also, for those small corporations with only one director or shareholder, written consents avoid the awkward feeling of one person having a meeting alone. While form 4 is for the directors' consent,

CONSENT TO ACTION WITHOUT FORMAL MEETING OF SHAREHOLDERS is for the shareholders' consent. (see form 8, p.250.) Spaces are provided to fill in the name of your corporation and the details of what action is being approved. Following, you will find two examples.

sample of form 4: **CONSENT TO ACTION WITHOUT A MEETING BY DIRECTORS**

Consent to Action Without Formal Meeting of Directors of

Scrupulous Corporation

The undersigned, being all of the Directors of the Corporation, hereby adopt the following resolutions:

WHEREAS, the President of the corporation has reported on the need of the corporation for an automobile for use in making deliveries to the company's customers and the directors have concluded that it is in the interest of the corporation to purchase an automobile for the purposes described in the President's report, it is therefore

RESOLVED, that the Corporation shall purchase an automobile at a cost of not more that $28,000 which, in the opinion of the President of the corporation, shall be suitable for making deliveries.

FURTHER RESOLVED, that the President or his designees are authorized and directed to negotiate such purchase for the corporation and to execute such contracts or other documents as may be necessary or desirable to complete the purchase.

RESOLVED, that these resolutions shall be effective at **11:00 a**.m., on **June 06, 2006**.

Raymond Rodriguez
Director

Della Driskell
Director

Calvin Collier
Director

Roberta Moore
Director

sample of form 8: **Consent to Action**
without Formal Meeting of Shareholders—

Consent to Action Without Formal Meeting of Shareholders
of
Scrupulous Corporation

The undersigned, being all of the shareholders of the Corporation, hereby adopt the following resolutions:

WHEREAS, Mr. Henry Hardy, citing his advanced age, has resigned from the board of directors of the corporation, effective July 9, 2006, thereby creating a vacancy on the board of directors, and WHEREAS, it is the wish of the shareholders to fill the vacancy promptly, it is therefore

RESOLVED, that Ms. Della Driskell is hereby elected to serve as director of the corporation to complete the remainder of Mr. Hardy's term and until her successor is elected and qualified, and

RESOLVED, that these resolutions shall be effective at **11:00 a**.m., on **June 06**, 2006.

Henry Hardy
Henry Hardy, Shareholder

Raymond Rodriguez
Raymond Rodriguez,
Shareholder

Della Driskell
Della Driskell, Shareholder

Calvin Collier
Calvin Collier, Shareholder

Hugh Hardy
Hugh Hardy, Shareholder

Roberta Moore
Roberta Moore, Shareholder

MINUTE BOOKS—THE CORPORATE MEMORY

The corporate *minute books* are the log books, or the diary, of a corporation. A corporation has no useful memory. If it relies on the various memories of its shareholders, officers, and directors, it will have as many conflicting memories as it does shareholders, officers, and directors. Such memories are notorious for fading or, worse yet, evolving to suit the purposes of the individuals trying to remember.

Purpose

The minute books, then, are the official memory of the corporation. The persons who participate in management and decision making are responsible for agreeing on the official version of events and recording them. Once approved, the official record is legally presumed to be the correct version of events, and anyone who denies their accuracy (in a court of law, for example) has to prove them inaccurate.

The minutes should not be taken lightly; although, unfortunately, many times they are. Often meetings open with a statement from the chair to the effect that *unless there is objection, the chair will omit the reading of the minutes of the last meeting* or someone will *move that the minutes of the last meeting be approved without reading.* There is seldom any objection. But the formal *reading* is supposed to be for the purpose of approving the accuracy of the minutes of the previous meeting. A director who fails to review the old minutes and make objection to any inaccuracy he or she finds before the formal approval may regret it.

Distribution

Do not imagine that the minutes of a directors or shareholders meeting will be kept secret. There are many times that good business will require the distribution of official *certified* copies of the minutes to outsiders (see forms 11 and 12), and times that a court or administrative agency (e.g., the IRS) will *subpoena* minutes. Some closely regulated businesses must turn over the minutes to a regulatory agency as a matter of course. In many cases, the shareholders of a corporation may have a statutory right to look at the minutes of the directors meetings as well as the shareholder minutes. So when you put something down in the minute book, imagine it being read by the person you would least like to have read it. It could easily happen.

Compilation and Writing

Some say that the more detail you have in the minutes, the better. If the purpose of the minutes is to show that the directors are doing a conscientious job and carefully giving lengthy consideration to each important issue to come before them, then detail is important. Following this line of reasoning, you would want the minutes to reflect the pros and cons and describe the vigorous give-and-take of the meeting.

Example:

Suppose the board of directors decides to lead the corporation into a new line of business by acquiring a new subsidiary. It is a big investment, and a year later it proves to be a questionable one. An unhappy shareholder sues the directors for their careless management. The directors will want to defend themselves by showing that, although their decision may not have worked out well, they were far from careless and had made a well-informed, reasonable business judgment.

The directors will want to introduce into evidence the minutes of the meeting at which they made the decision to show the care with which they deliberated. If the minutes are complete and show a reasonable basis for the decision, it may make the difference in mounting a successful defense.

Others say too much detail in the minutes can be a dangerous practice.

Example:

Suppose there is a heated debate about some issue, and one of the directors tells the rest that if they make a certain decision, "there will be hell to pay, and the corporation will be belly-up in a year." The majority disregards the warning and makes the decision. The secretary dutifully records the decision along with the dissenting director's warning. The decision quickly proves to be a bad one, and when the year is up, the company is in trouble.

A disgruntled shareholder sues the directors for their incompetent management and introduces the minutes into evidence at trial. The directors will look pretty bad since the minutes will show that they had fair warning from the wise dissenter that their decision was a foolish one.

So detail in the minute books can be a double-edged sword.

There are legitimate reasons for taking a concise approach, stating the decisions made, and noting dissenting views when the dissenting directors request it. There are also reasons for taking the detailed approach, demonstrating that the directors take their duties seriously, and investigating all sides of each issue. There is no reason, however, to include details that can only prove to be embarrassing. For example, if one director expresses the opinion that the other directors are "insufferable twits," it is hard to imagine any future occasion on which it will be advantageous to have that remark on the record.

It can also be a mistake to be anything other than consistent in the approach taken. If the secretary fills page after page of the minute book with detailed reports of meetings, and then reports one meeting in uncharacteristic lack of detail, the comparison will invite the question, *what happened at this meeting that they are trying to hide?* Or, if the secretary usually writes minutes in a concise style, but for one meeting goes to unusual lengths in reporting detail, someone may want to know why and decide it warrants special investigation.

Forms 1 and 2 are to record **MINUTES** of your directors' meetings, and forms 5 and 6 are to record **MINUTES** for your shareholders' meetings. Space is provided to fill in the name of your corporation, various standard provisions, and the minutes of the particular meeting. Use additional pages (form 3 for directors and form 7 for shareholders), and attach them to the form, if necessary.

Following are two reports of the same events showing two different styles of reporting minutes.

Sample of **DIRECTOR'S MEETING MINUTES REPORTING DISCUSSION AND VOTE ON THE PURCHASE OF REAL PROPERTY (DETAILED FORM)**

Mr. Hugh Hardy, the chairman of the meeting then asked the President, Mr. Rodriguez, to present a report on the company's needs for additional office space.

Mr. Rodriguez noted that the offices presently occupied by the company had been purchased in 2004 when its employees had numbered fewer than fifty. Since that time, the staff had increased to more than one hundred, necessitating the crowding of two or more employees into spaces originally intended for only one. In addition, the company had been forced to rent temporary office space for the accounting division in another building which, although it was only a few miles away, nevertheless required frequent trips back and forth and complicated computer links and resulted in a waste of time and extra expenses.

The company's present building, although in need of renovation, is in sound structural condition, Mr. Rodriguez reported, but not able to be expanded on the land presently owned by the company. However, it had recently been reported to management that the vacant land adjacent to the company building is available for purchase, and Mr. Rodriguez had approached its owners about purchasing the land with a view toward expanding the company headquarters.

Mr. Rodriguez reported that the asking price for the vacant lot is $150,000, but he thought he could negotiate the price down to as low as $135,000. He next presented to the meeting charts showing the comparative costs of (a) continuing operations as is, with the expectation that additional off-premises space would need to be rented within the next 24 months, (b) selling the present building and building or renting space elsewhere capable of serving the entire operation, or (c) acquiring the adjacent lot and expanding the current facilities. The third option indicated savings of 20% and 15% over the cost of the first two respectively over a five-year period. (The report presented by Mr. Rodriguez is filed in management storage file No. 04-56.)

Mr. Hugh Hardy commented that the most economical decision is not always the wisest, and wondered whether the erection of a new building might be desirable considering the public relations advantages of such a move. Mr. Rodriguez agreed that the public relations would be valuable, but believed that restoring and renovating the current headquarters would result in equally beneficial public notice and result in substantial savings as well.

Ms. Driskell questioned several specific assumptions underlying Mr. Rodriguez's report, and then announced her satisfaction with their reasonableness. She then moved the adoption of the following resolutions:

RESOLVED, that the President is authorized and directed to negotiate a contract for the purchase of the lot adjacent to the company's headquarters as described in his report (management storage file No. 04-56) for a cash purchase price of not more than $145,000.

FURTHER RESOLVED, that the officers of the corporation are authorized to execute such contract together with such other documents as may be necessary or desirable to complete the described purchase within 120 days of the date of this resolution.

Ms. Moore seconded the motion, and the Chairman asked whether there was any further discussion.

Ms. Moore asked Mr. Rodriguez whether 120 days would be sufficient to complete the purchase. Mr. Rodriguez replied that he believed the time was sufficient, but would anticipate that the board would grant an extension of the time if proved necessary. The consensus of the board was that reasonable extensions would be granted.

Mr. Henry Hardy objected to the purchase of the property for cash, believing it to place an unneeded burden on the company's cash position. He recommended that the acquisition be financed through a bank loan secured by a mortgage on the property. Mr. Rodriguez said that he expected to finance the building expansion with such a mortgage, as indicated in his comparison figures, but thought the transaction would be more expeditiously completed if the land were purchased for cash, and that a rapid completion of the purchase would be a strong negotiating point with the seller.

There being no further discussion, the chairman asked for a vote on the resolutions. The resolutions were adopted with four votes in favor. Mr. Henry Hardy voted against the resolutions and asked that his vote and his objection to the cash purchase arrangement be noted in these minutes.

Sample of **DIRECTOR'S MEETING MINUTES REPORTING DISCUSSION AND VOTE ON THE PURCHASE OF REAL PROPERTY (CONCISE FORM)**

Mr. Rodriguez next reported on the company's need for additional office space, explaining that the number of employees has expanded greatly since its present location was first occupied. A copy of the President's report is filed in management storage file No. 04-56. The directors noted that figures presented by Mr. Rodriguez in his report predicted that the company would gain substantial savings over a five-year period by purchasing and expanding onto the vacant lot adjacent to the company's present location compared to the renting of additional needed space or relocation of the company's operation elsewhere.

The following resolutions, moved for adoption by Ms. Driskell, seconded by Ms. Moore, were adopted after discussion of the President's report.

RESOLVED, that the President is authorized and directed to negotiate a contract for the purchase of the lot adjacent to the company's headquarters as described in his report (management storage file No. 04-56) for a cash purchase price of not more than $145,000.

FURTHER RESOLVED, that the officers of the corporation are authorized to execute such contract together with such other documents as may be necessary or desirable to complete the described purchase within 120 days of the date of this resolution.

There were four votes in favor of adoption. Mr. Henry Hardy objected to the purchase of the property for cash rather than financing the purchase with a bank loan. He voted against adoption of the resolution, asking that his opposition be noted in these minutes.

An alternative to writing all of the resolutions in the **MINUTES** is to have a separate sheet for each resolution. Form 9, **RESOLUTION OF THE BOARD OF DIRECTORS**, and form 10, **RESOLUTION OF THE SHAREHOLDERS**, can be used for this purpose. These resolutions can then be attached to the **MINUTES**.

The benefit is that it will later be easier for the secretary to simply copy the appropriate resolution and attach it to a certification statement (form 11 for directors or form 12 for shareholders) if necessary (instead of having to search through the minutes to find the resolution, then rewriting it to certify).

A decision may be correctly recorded and preserved in the minute book, but most corporations are not happy for just anyone to look through the records, anymore than you would want just anyone to look through your diary. When necessary, however, it is possible to take a bit of the minute book out and certify the excerpt as being accurate and a genuine record of the corporation's decision. The need for this will affect the way minutes of meetings and, particularly, resolutions are written. The person usually responsible for excerpting and certifying the records is the corporate secretary who is also responsible for seeing that the minutes of meetings are in good order.

A certified copy follows of the resolutions adopted in the example of a directors' consent without formal meeting on page 41. Notice that the secretary has drafted the resolution so that, when they are excerpted, it makes sense. That is, you can read just the resolution out of the context of the rest of the minutes and tell what decision is being made and what authority is being granted to whom.

Suppose the seller of the vacant lot next door to the company office wants to make sure that the company president really has authority to negotiate the purchase of the property. By looking at the following certificate, the seller, without being shown the full record of the board's deliberations on the matter, will be able to see that the president does have the necessary authority.

Notice that the secretary has indicated that she is indeed the secretary. She will place the corporation's official seal next to her signature.

The presence of the seal is important. It means that anyone reading the document is able to rely on the truth of it without double-checking to make sure that the person signing really is the secretary and is representing the corporation in this matter.

The **CERTIFIED COPY OF RESOLUTIONS ADOPTED BY THE BOARD OF DIRECTORS** is for your corporate secretary to use to certify resolutions of the directors. (see form 13, p.255.) To certify resolutions of shareholders use the **CERTIFIED COPY OF RESOLUTIONS ADOPTED BY THE SHAREHOLDERS**. (see form 14, p.256.) Following is an example of a certification in which the resolution has been copied from the **MINUTES** of the meeting.

If a separate resolution sheet (form 9 or form 10) had been used, a copy of the resolution sheet could simply be attached.

sample of form 13: **CERTIFIED COPY OF RESOLUTIONS ADOPTED BY THE BOARD OF DIRECTORS**

Certified Copy of Resolutions Adopted by the Board of Directors of

Scrupulous Corporation

I HEREBY CERTIFY that I am the Corporate Secretary of **Scrupulous Corporation**, that the following is an accurate copy of resolution(s) adopted by the Board of Directors of **Scrupulous Corporation**, effective July 10, 2006, and that such resolutions continue in effect as of the date of this certification:

RESOLVED, that the President is authorized and directed to negotiate a contract for the purchase of the lot adjacent to the company's headquarters as described in his report (management storage file No. 04-56) for a cash purchase price of not more than $145,000.

FURTHER RESOLVED, that the officers of the corporation are authorized to execute such contract together with such other documents as may be necessary or desirable to complete the described purchase within 120 days of the date of this resolution.

Signed and the seal of the Corporation affixed, **July 21, 2006.**

Seal of Scrupulous Corporation
20✳06
State of West Carolina

Roberta Moore
Roberta Moore,
Secretary

Board of Directors

The board of directors are the overseers and strategic decision makers of the corporation. Directors are selected by the shareholders and their duty is to see that the corporation is operated in the best interests of the shareholders.

THE PLACE OF THE DIRECTORS WITHIN THE CORPORATION

The Model Business Corporation Act (MBCA) says "all corporate powers shall be exercised by or under the authority of, and the business and affairs of the corporation managed under the direction of, its board of directors..." (MBCA, Sec. 8.01).

It is important to know what directors are not. A director ordinarily does not represent the corporation. Just because you are a director does not mean you have any power to act as agent for the corporation by negotiating deals, by signing contracts, or for any other purpose. A single director has no power and cannot act alone (unless, of course, he or she is the *sole* director). Only the *board of directors* (or a committee of the board) can make a decision, and that must be done in a meeting or by written consent as described in Chapter 3.

THE SIZE OF THE BOARD OF DIRECTORS

There is no one, right size for a board of directors. What works for one corporation may not work for another. What works at one stage of a corporation's development may not work at another.

It also depends a lot on the personalities of the people involved. Do you work well with a group? Are there people (usually shareholders) who will feel left out or be disgruntled if they are not made directors? Maybe someone genuinely deserves a voice on the board. Maybe such people will be less trouble on the board than off.

Example:

A group of shareholders constantly complained that the board of directors was not declaring dividends frequently enough or big enough. After years of complaining, they finally gained representation on the board, and, faced with the true responsibility of running the company, immediately voted to cut the dividends further.

The **ARTICLES OF INCORPORATION** creating your corporation probably refers to an initial board of directors, specifying the number of members. It may or may not list the names of its members. (see form 123, p.374.) The initial board, if it is named in the articles, will constitute the board until a change is made.

NOTE: *It is possible for the articles to indicate that the permanent board will have a specified number of members. If such is the case, only an amendment to the* **ARTICLES OF INCORPORATION** *can change the number.*

Usually the **BYLAWS** will specify the size of the board. In that case, the number may be changed by amendment to the bylaws. Or, the **BYLAWS** will specify a range within which the number may be set by simple resolution of the directors or shareholders.

Changing the Size of the Board by Resolution

Your **BYLAWS** may say something like:

The number of directors constituting the board of directors shall be not fewer than three nor more than nine as may be fixed from time to time, within such range, by the shareholders or by the board of directors.

If the **BYLAWS** specify a range for the size of the board, a resolution adopted by the board of directors or the shareholders (check your **BYLAWS** to see if it is one or the other or either) will set the board at the size you want.

If you have a choice, it may be better to have this resolution adopted by the board rather than the shareholders. Once the shareholders adopt a resolution, there may be some doubt as to whether the board can then adopt a subsequent resolution changing what the shareholders have done. Thus, once the shareholders have acted, the board may then be limited.

Resolutions may be adopted either at a meeting (and incorporated into the minutes of the meeting using form 1, 2, 5, or 6) or by written consent (by incorporating it into form 4 or 8). Following is an example of a written consent to change the size of the board of directors.

sample of form 15: **DIRECTORS' CONSENT TO ACTION**
ESTABLISHING THE SIZE OF THE BOARD OF DIRECTORS

Consent to Action without Formal Meeting by the Directors of Scrupulous Corporation

The undersigned directors of the corporation hereby adopt the following resolution:

RESOLVED, that pursuant to **Article 3, Section 2** of the bylaws of the corporation, the number of directors constituting the board of directors shall be **three**, and that such shall be the number of members of the board of directors until changed in a manner authorized by the articles of incorporation and the bylaws of the corporation.

This resolution shall be effective at **10 a**.m. on the **8th** of **August, 2006**.

Henry Hardy	*Roberta Moore*	*Raymond Rodriguez*
Henry Hardy, Director	Roberta Moore, Director	Raymond Rodriguez, Director

---

Changing the Size of the Board by Amendment to the Bylaws

Your **BYLAWS** may say something like *the number of directors constituting the board of directors shall be three*, making no reference to a range of numbers. If so, you may change the number by amending the **BYLAWS**. Check the section of your **BYLAWS** that tells how the **BYLAWS** may be amended. It will likely say that the amendment may be accomplished by a vote of the directors, but it may require a vote of the shareholders for some purposes.

The following is an example of a resolution to change the **BYLAWS**, which would be adopted by the directors or shareholders, depending upon your corporation's rules for how **BYLAWS** must be changed.

sample of form 16: **DIRECTORS' CONSENT TO ACTION ESTABLISHING THE SIZE OF THE BOARD OF DIRECTORS BY AMENDMENT TO THE BYLAWS**

Consent to Action without Formal Meeting by the Directors of

Scrupulous Corporation

The undersigned directors of the corporation hereby adopt the following resolution:

RESOLVED, that **Article 3, Section 2** of the bylaws of the corporation is amended to read as follows:

"The number of directors constituting the board of directors shall be **three**."

This resolution shall be effective at **10 a**.m. on the **8th** of **August, 2006**.

Henry Hardy
Henry Hardy, Director

Roberta Moore
Roberta Moore, Director

Raymond Rodriguez
Raymond Rodriguez, Director

ELECTING DIRECTORS

Directors are elected by the shareholders. Ordinarily, the election takes place at the annual shareholders meeting. (See Chapter 7 for discussion of the relevant forms.) In most corporations, the vote required is a majority of those present and voting at the meeting. On some occasions directors may be elected at a special meeting or without there being a meeting at all.

Remember that anything that can be done in a shareholders' meeting may be done by written consent if it is signed by all (in some states a majority) of the shareholders. Following is a **SHAREHOLDERS' CONSENT TO ACTION ELECTING DIRECTORS**.

sample of form 17: **SHAREHOLDERS' CONSENT TO ACTION ELECTING DIRECTORS**

**Consent to Action without Formal Meeting
by the Shareholders of
Scrupulous Corporation**

The undersigned shareholders of the corporation hereby adopt the following resolution:

RESOLVED, that the following individuals are elected directors of the corporation to serve until their successors are qualified and elected:

**Roberta Moore
Henry Hardy
Raymond Rodriguez**

This resolution shall be effective at **9 a.**m. on the **28th** of **July, 2006**.

Roberta Moore	*Henry Hardy*
Roberta Moore, Shareholder	Henry Hardy, Shareholder
Della Driskell	*Hugh Hardy*
Della Driskell, Shareholder	Hugh Hardy, Shareholder
Raymond Rodriguez	*Calvin Collier*
Raymond Rodriguez, Shareholder	Calvin Collier, Shareholder

You cannot require a person to serve as director without his or her consent. In most cases, a chosen director's written consent is not necessary, but it does not hurt. There are a few situations, for example, if the corporation is subject to Securities and Exchange Commission proxy rules (see Chapter 7), in which written consent is required.

Written consent, like **DIRECTOR'S CONSENT TO SERVE**, does not prevent the director from resigning at any time. (see form 18, p.260.) The following statement, alone or incorporated into a letter from the nominee director to the corporation, will suffice.

sample of form 18: DIRECTOR'S CONSENT TO SERVE

Date: **July 10, 2006**
To: The Board of Directors, **Scrupulous Corporation**

I hereby consent to serve as director of **Scrupulous Corporation** if elected.

Henry Hardy
Henry Hardy

Ordinarily, directors who are not also officers of the corporation (and therefore paid an officer's salary for the services they provide) receive some type of remuneration. The payments can be calculated in any number of ways, but most often consist of a daily allowance (or per diem) plus some form of reimbursement for travel, lodging, and the like. Usually, the directors themselves set the remuneration, sometimes at the recommendation of management.

A simple resolution preserved in the minutes of the directors' meetings will suffice; although, the **BYLAWS** could also be drafted to provide for compensation. The following is an example of a directors' resolution that provides different levels of compensation for directors who must travel substantial distances and those who live close to the site of the meeting.

sample of form 19: **Directors' Consent to Action Establishing Directors' Fees**

Consent to Action without Formal Meeting by the Directors of

Scrupulous Corporation

The undersigned directors of the corporation hereby adopt the following resolution:

WHEREAS, management of the corporation has recommended to the board of directors a system for the remuneration of directors for their services, and

WHEREAS, the board of directors, after consideration, has concluded that the recommendations of management are in the best interests of the corporation in maintaining a board of directors the members of which are able and willing to serve diligently, it is therefore,

RESOLVED, that each director of the corporation shall be paid the following fees:

1. For attendance at each meeting or series of meetings lasting fewer than three hours, **$500.00**.

2. For attendance at each meeting or series of meetings lasting three hours or more in one day, **$750.00**.

3. For each overnight stay away from the director's usual residence required by attendance at a meeting or series of meetings, in addition to the fees provided above, **$250.00** plus reimbursement for lodgings up to **$150.00** per night.

4. For travel involving distances more than **100** miles to or from a meeting, directors shall be reimbursed for the actual cost of such travel. Travel by private automobile shall be reimbursed at the rate and in the manner provided for reimbursement of employees of the company from time to time.

This resolution shall be effective at **11 a**.m. on the **6th** of **June, 2006**.

Henry Hardy	*Roberta Moore*	*Raymond Rodriguez*
Henry Hardy, Director	Roberta Moore, Director	Raymond Rodriguez, Director

RESIGNATION, REMOVAL, AND REPLACEMENT OF DIRECTORS

Directors are usually elected for terms of one year each. It sometimes happens, however, that vacancies may occur on the board of directors at other times. Directors may resign, become ill, or even be removed by the shareholders for one reason or another.

Removal of a Director by the Shareholders

Most states allow the shareholders of a corporation to vote for the removal of a director from office before his or her term is over. It may be done either in a meeting or by written consent. In some corporations, the **ARTICLES OF INCORPORATION** allow for removal of a director only *for cause*.

In some corporations, directors are elected by groups of voters. For example, the holders of preferred shares may elect one director, and the holders of common shares may elect two. If this is the case, only the group of shareholders who elected the director may remove him or her.

Another complication may arise if the shareholders elected the directors *cumulatively*. (see Chapter 7.) In that case, a director may not be removed if the number of votes against the removal would be enough to elect the director by cumulative voting.

In any case, a careful review of your state's law and your **ARTICLES OF INCORPORATION** is in order. Professional legal advice is always desirable.

If the removal takes place at a meeting, as opposed to written consent, the notice of the meeting (form 31 or form 32) should inform the shareholders that one of the purposes of the meeting is to remove a director and to fill the vacancy created.

On the following page is an example of a resolution adopted by the shareholders by written consent. The resolution removes a director *for cause*, in which the cause is a consistent failure to attend meetings.

If it is not required to state a cause, it is usually best not to state one in the formal resolution. In that case, the first two paragraphs of the following example should be omitted. Of course, in the shareholders meeting, there may be discussion of the reasons for asking the shareholders to remove the director. (Be careful to avoid defamatory statements.) That discussion may be recorded in the minutes of the meeting without being part of the resolution.

sample of form 20: **Shareholders' Consent to Action Removing a Director for Cause**

Consent to Action without Formal Meeting by the Directors of Scrupulous Corporation

The undersigned directors of the corporation hereby adopt the following resolution:

WHEREAS, it has been reported by the secretary of the corporation that **Absentia Morgan**, a director of the corporation, has **failed to attend five consecutive meetings of the board of directors**, and

WHEREAS, it has been recommended to the shareholders that, for the reason stated above, **Ms. Morgan** should be removed from the board of directors, it is therefore

RESOLVED, that, at the effective date and time of this resolution, **Absentia Morgan** shall be removed from the board of directors of the corporation, and that there shall be a vacancy on the board of directors.

This resolution shall be effective at **1 p.**m. on the **3rd** of **August, 2006**.

Henry Hardy
Henry Hardy, Director

Roberta Moore
Roberta Moore, Director

Raymond Rodriguez
Raymond Rodriguez, Director

Resignation of a Director

When a director resigns, it is usually done by a written notice directed to the corporation—its president or its board of directors. It can be done without a written notice, but there is less chance of confusion if there is a signed piece of paper somewhere that definitely states the director's intent and the effective date of the resignation.

There is no need to give a reason for the resignation, but often a resigning director will. If the corporation is publicly held, the SEC has special rules about making public the reasons for a director's resignation. (see Chapter 7.)

sample of form 21: **RESIGNATION OF A DIRECTOR**

Date: **January 15, 2006**

To: The Board of Directors of **Scrupulous Corporation**

I hereby resign as director of **Scrupulous Corporation** effective **January 16, 2006** at **5 p**.m.

Sincerely,

Calvin Collier
Calvin Collier

Once a vacancy has occurred on the board of directors, it may be filled either by the shareholders or by the remaining directors. An example of a resolution for the replacement of a director by the shareholders following the director's voluntary retirement is found after the heading "Consent to action without formal meeting by the shareholders" on the sample form below.

The following are two examples of a resolution to replace a director— one by the shareholders and the other by the remaining directors. This type of resolution would be included in form 1, 2, 4, 5, 6, or 8, depending upon whether it is adopted in a meeting or by written consent.

sample of form 22: **SHAREHOLDERS' CONSENT TO ACTION**
REPLACING A DIRECTOR

Consent to Action without Formal Meeting by the
Shareholders of
Scrupulous Corporation

The undersigned shareholders of the corporation hereby adopt the following resolution:

WHEREAS, the **resignation** of **Calvin Collier as director** of the corporation has created a vacancy on the board of directors, and

WHEREAS, the shareholders wish to fill the vacancy, it is therefore

RESOLVED, that **Raymond Rodriguez** is elected to serve as director of the corporation for the remainder of the term for which **Calvin Collier** was elected and until **his** successor is qualified and elected.

This resolution shall be effective at **10 a.**m. on the **30th** of **January, 2006**.

Roberta Moore	*Henry Hardy*
Roberta Moore, Shareholder	Henry Hardy, Shareholder
Della Driskell	*Hugh Hardy*
Della Driskell, Shareholder	Hugh Hardy, Shareholder
Raymond Rodriguez	*Calvin Collier*
Raymond Rodriguez, Shareholder	Calvin Collier, Shareholder

It frequently happens that the secretary of the corporation will be asked to assure someone dealing with the corporation that certain individuals are in fact the directors of the corporation. Form 24 will serve the purpose, and the following is an example.

sample of form 24: **SECRETARY'S CERTIFICATION OF BOARD MEMBERSHIP**

Certification of Secretary of Board of Directors Membership of

Scrupulous Corporation

I HEREBY CERTIFY that I am the Corporate Secretary of **Scrupulous Corporation**, that the individuals listed below are the duly elected directors of the Corporation, and that they continue to hold the office of director on the date of this certification:

Raymond Rodriguez	**Henry Hardy**
Della Driskell	**Calvin Collier**

Signed and the seal of the Corporation affixed, **July 15, 2006**.

Seal of Scrupulous Corporation

20✳06

State of West Carolina

Roberta Moore

Roberta Moore,
Secretary

COMMITTEES OF THE BOARD OF DIRECTORS

Committees of the board of directors can be highly useful for some corporations. For one thing, they streamline decision making by reducing the number of decision makers. It is easier to reach consensus among three committee members than, say, twelve board members.

Also, it allows quicker reaction time. If your directors are scattered across the country, all with busy schedules, it is no easy task to get them together for a meeting. But create a committee of directors who live close at hand and you may be able to call a meeting on a few hours' notice.

Finally, you can use a committee to concentrate on the various areas of expertise of your board members on the matters most suited to their talents. For example, creating an audit committee made up of board members with financial and accounting experience may be most helpful in dealing with state taxes.

Committees may act within the powers granted to them by the **BYLAWS** or by the board. State laws do put some limitations on committee powers. Among other powers denied to committees, the MCBA includes the power to declare dividends, the power to adopt, amend, or repeal bylaws, and the power to fill vacancies on the board or its committees. (MBCA, Sec. 8.25.)

Creating a Committee of the Board

Committees may be created by the **BYLAWS**. Frequently, the **BYLAWS** will already provide for the existence of particular committees, and for these committees the board need only adopt a resolution appointing its members. (You must select the members from among the properly elected directors.) In most cases, the **BYLAWS** will provide a mechanism for creating committees and appointing their members (usually by vote of a majority of the directors in office when the action is taken).

Following are examples of two resolutions. The first creates a three-member executive committee and appoints its members. The second increases the size of the committee and fills the vacancies created.

sample of form 25: **DIRECTORS' CONSENT TO ACTION CREATING A COMMITTEE OF THE BOARD AND NAMING THE MEMBERS**

Consent to Action without Formal Meeting by the Directors of Scrupulous Corporation

The undersigned directors of the corporation hereby adopt the following resolution:

RESOLVED, that there is created an executive committee of the board of directors consisting of **three** members, and further

RESOLVED, that to the extent permitted by law and the bylaws of the corporation, the executive committee shall have the full powers and act with the full authority of the board of directors when the board of directors is not in session, and further

RESOLVED, that the following individuals are appointed to serve as members of the executive committee of the board of directors until their successors are appointed and qualified:

Roberta Moore
Henry Hardy
Raymond Rodriguez

This resolution shall be effective at **2 p**.m. on the **7th** of **February, 2006**.

Henry Hardy	*Roberta Moore*	*Raymond Rodriguez*
Henry Hardy, Director	Roberta Moore, Director	Raymond Rodriguez, Director

---

sample of form 26: **DIRECTORS' CONSENT TO ACTION CHANGING THE SIZE AND MEMBERSHIP OF A COMMITTEE–**

Consent to Action without Formal Meeting by the Directors of Scrupulous Corporation

The undersigned directors of the corporation hereby adopt the following resolution:

RESOLVED, that the number of members of the **executive** committee of the board of directors is increased from **two** to **three**, and further

RESOLVED, that the following individual is appointed to fill the vacancy created by the increase in the sized of the committee to serve as a member of such committee until their successors are elected and qualified:

Roberta Moore

This resolution shall be effective at **2 p**.m. on the **7th** of **Februrary, 2006**.

Henry Hardy	*Roberta Moore*	*Raymond Rodriguez*
Henry Hardy, Director	Roberta Moore, Director	Raymond Rodriguez, Director

Kinds of Committees

There can be many kinds of committees. A corporation is free to pick and choose among them or to create new committees for any purpose that seems useful, so long as it is consistent with limitations imposed by law. There can be *standing committees* with regularly scheduled meetings, and there can be special *ad hoc committees* created to fill temporary needs.

The latter are particularly useful when some issue raises a conflict of interest with one or more members of the board. An ad hoc committee may be created, which excludes the conflicted directors and allows the remaining impartial directors to form a quorum and dispose of the issue without their participation.

Following are four examples of resolutions amending the **Bylaws** to create committees. These are four different kinds of committees that are frequently found useful. As usual, such resolutions can be adopted by either consents to action or in meetings.

sample of form 27: **Directors' Consent to Action Amending the Bylaws to Establish an Executive Committee**

Consent to Action without Formal Meeting by the Directors of

Scrupulous Corporation

The undersigned directors of the corporation hereby adopt the following resolution:

RESOLVED, that the bylaws of the corporation are amended by the addition of a new **Article 3, Section 9** reading in its entirety as follows:

"Section 8. Executive Committee. There shall be an Executive Committee of the board of directors which shall, to the extent permitted by law, and subject to such limitations as may be imposed from time to time by the board of directors, exercise the powers of the board of directors when the board is not in session. The number of members of the Executive Committee shall be established, and may be changed from time to time, by resolution of the Board of Directors. The members of the Executive Committee shall be appointed by a majority of the number of directors in office when the appointment is made and shall serve at the pleasure of a majority of the board in office."

Further RESOLVED, that the initial number of members of the Executive Committee shall be two, and the initial members of the Executive Committee shall be:

Henry Hardy
Raymond Rodriguez

This resolution shall be effective at **4 p.**m. on the **2nd** of **March, 2006**.

Henry Hardy
Henry Hardy, Director

Roberta Moore
Roberta Moore, Director

Raymond Rodriguez
Raymond Rodriguez, Director

sample of form 28: DIRECTORS' CONSENT TO ACTION AMENDING THE BYLAWS TO ESTABLISH AN AUDIT COMMITTEE

Consent to Action without Formal Meeting by the Directors of Scrupulous Corporation

The undersigned directors of the corporation hereby adopt the following resolution:

RESOLVED, that the bylaws of the corporation are amended by the addition of a new **Article 3, Section 10** reading in its entirety as follows:

"Section 10. Audit Committee. There shall be an Audit Committee of the board of directors, which shall supervise the auditing and examination of the books of account of the corporation by employees and independent auditors of the corporation. The Audit Committee shall meet with the independent auditors not fewer than [number] times during each fiscal year and shall have such other powers and duties as may from time to time be authorized by the board of directors. The number of members of the Audit Committee shall be established, and may be changed from time to time, by resolution of the Board of Directors. The members of the Audit Committee shall be appointed by a majority of the number of directors in office when the appointment is made and shall serve at the pleasure of a majority of the board in office."

Further RESOLVED, that the initial number of members of the Audit Committee shall be **two**, and the initial members of the Audit Committee shall be:

Roberta Moore

Henry Hardy

This resolution shall be effective at **4 p.**m. on the **2nd** of **March, 2006**.

Henry Hardy
Henry Hardy, Director

Roberta Moore
Roberta Moore, Director

Raymond Rodriguez
Raymond Rodriguez, Director

sample of form 29: **DIRECTORS' CONSENT TO ACTION AMENDING THE BYLAWS TO ESTABLISH AN PERSONNEL COMMITTEE**

Consent to Action without Formal Meeting by the Directors of

Scrupulous Corporation

The undersigned directors of the corporation hereby adopt the following resolution:

RESOLVED, that the bylaws of the corporation are amended by the addition of a new **Article 3, Section 11** reading in its entirety as follows:

"Section 11. Personnel Committee. There shall be a Personnel Committee of the board of directors which shall consider and make recommendations to the board of directors regarding recruiting and compensating officers and senior employees of the corporation, the compensation of directors, compliance with applicable laws regarding employment practices, and other matters regarding personnel management, and the Committee shall have such other powers and duties as may from time to time be authorized by the board of directors. The number of members of the Personnel Committee shall be established, and may be changed from time to time, by resolution of the Board of

Directors. The members of the Personnel Committee shall be appointed by a majority of the number of directors in office when the appointment is made and shall serve at the pleasure of a majority of the board in office."

Further RESOLVED, that the initial number of members of the Personnel Committee shall be **two**, and the initial members of the Personnel Committee shall be:

Roberta Moore
Raymond Rodriguez

This resolution shall be effective at **10 a.**m. on the **1st** of **March, 2006**.

Henry Hardy
Henry Hardy, Director

Roberta Moore
Roberta Moore, Director

Raymond Rodriguez
Raymond Rodriguez, Director

sample of form 30: **Directors' Consent to Action Amending the Bylaws to Establish a Nominating Committee**

Consent to Action without Formal Meeting by the Directors of Scrupulous Corporation

The undersigned directors of the corporation hereby adopt the following resolution:

RESOLVED, that the bylaws of the corporation are amended by the addition of a new **Article 3, Section 12** reading in its entirety as follows:

"Section 12. Nominating Committee. There shall be a Nominating Committee of the board of directors which shall consider available candidates for director of the corporation and shall make recommendations to the board of directors regarding the filling of vacancies which may occur from time to time in the membership of the board of directors. The number of members of the Nominating Committee shall be established, and may be changed from time to time, by resolution of the Board of Directors. The members of the Nominating Committee shall be appointed by a majority of the number of directors in office when the appointment is made and shall serve at the pleasure of a majority of the board in office."

Further RESOLVED, that the initial number of members of the Nominating Committee shall be **two**, and the initial members of the Nominating Committee shall be:

Henry Hardy
Roberta Moore

This resolution shall be effective at **10 a.**m. on the **1st** of **March, 2006**.

Henry Hardy
Henry Hardy, Director

Roberta Moore
Roberta Moore, Director

Raymond Rodriguez
Raymond Rodriguez, Director

Directors' Meetings

Members of the board of directors have no power to act alone. The board acts as a group, and usually makes its decisions in a meeting.

NOTE: *Do not forget that any action that can be taken by the directors in a meeting can be taken without a meeting by written consent. (see Chapter 3.)*

MEETING FREQUENCY

The **BYLAWS** of most corporations require only one *regular meeting*, which usually follows the annual meeting of the shareholders. Many corporations have other regularly scheduled meetings. There is no rule on this. You have directors' meetings as often as they are needed.

Many corporations find it useful to have regularly scheduled meetings, usually at least quarterly, timed to coincide with the availability of quarterly financial results. Some companies have them monthly or even weekly. It may depend on the condition of the company. A company going through difficult times may decide to have weekly meetings for a time until conditions improve.

One of the advantages of regularly scheduled meetings is that they are dependable. Your directors can plan schedules around regular meetings. Even if you cancel some of them due to a lack of anything to talk about, regular meetings save time and telephone calls, because you do not have to continually find dates when no one on the board has a scheduling conflict.

Some corporations—especially small ones whose directors may also be day-to-day managers—do not have regularly scheduled meetings (other than the one following the annual shareholders meeting). These companies call *special meetings* whenever they are useful. Of course, even the corporations with frequent regular meetings may find it useful from time to time to call a special meeting.

If you have directors who are not involved in the company's affairs on a daily basis, you may owe it to them and to the corporation to have directors meetings frequently. If you do not, you may be not allowing the directors a fair chance to fulfill their duties to be informed and to make decisions in the best interests of the company and its shareholders.

WHO ATTENDS MEETINGS

There is no rule on who should attend a directors' meeting. Of course the directors must have notice of the meetings, and the board cannot conduct business without the necessary quorum. Common sense says that some representative of management should be present so that the directors will know what needs to be discussed and will be able to inquire about the company's condition. Also, there should be someone to record the minutes, usually the corporate secretary.

Beyond that, it is up to the directors. They need the people who can give them the information they need to make the decisions they have to make. It may include various officers and a wide variety of outside advisors such as lawyers, accountants, personnel experts, etc.

WHO MAY ATTEND MEETINGS

Is there anyone who has a right to attend directors' meetings other than the directors? Generally speaking, no. Some courts have said that a director has a right to insist on the presence of his or her own legal counsel for the purpose of giving advice about the director's duties or liabilities. Shareholders do not have a right to be informed about or to attend directors' meetings without an invitation from the board. Neither do officers of the company who are not also members of the board.

NOTICE OF DIRECTORS' MEETINGS

It is an important point of corporate law that you cannot have a meeting of the directors where business is conducted (i.e., where resolutions are adopted) unless *notice* goes to all the directors. Each director must have a fair chance to come to the meeting and to deliberate and vote. In the case of regularly scheduled meetings, notice is not necessary in most corporations because regularity is notice enough. However, some companies' **BYLAWS** or **ARTICLES OF INCORPORATION** require notice even for regular meetings.

Even if there is no requirement, it may be good practice to give the directors a reminder, especially if the regular meetings are infrequent. The form **NOTICE OF REGULAR MEETING OF BOARD OF DIRECTORS** is useful for that purpose. (see form 31, p.273.)

For special meetings of the directors, notice is always necessary, and timing is important. The **BYLAWS** will say how far in advance of the meeting you have to give notice. Use **NOTICE OF SPECIAL MEETING OF THE BOARD OF DIRECTORS** for this. (see form 32, p.274.)

Format   There is no special format required for such notices, as long as the necessary information is included. For most companies, there is no requirement that notice be in writing. However, as is very frequently the case, writing is best because the writing will be around to provide proof that notice was given. A notice can also be a simple letter on the corporate letterhead, as in the first of the two examples that follow.

Most **BYLAWS** do not require the notice to contain information about the matters to be discussed or decided at the meeting; although, many corporate managers make it a practice to enclose a proposed agenda, such as the **AGENDA OF MEETING OF BOARD OF DIRECTORS**. (see form 34, p.276.) Directors usually appreciate the information and it may allow the directors to be better prepared. Sooner or later, conscientious directors will insist on seeing reports and other information on which they are expected to rely *before* the meeting.

sample of form 31: **NOTICE OF REGULAR MEETING OF BOARD OF DIRECTORS—**

Scrupulous Corporation
No. 4 Beach Place
Pleasant Cove, West Carolina 27000

October 3, 2006

Calvin Collier
123 Megabucks Avenue
New York, NY 10031

RE: Notice of Meeting of Board of Directors

Dear Calvin,

This letter will remind you that the regular meeting of the **Scrupulous Corporation** board of directors will be held on **November 6, 2006** at **7:00 p**.m., at **the corporation conference room**.

We hope you will be able to attend and that you will join us for dinner in the company dining room following the meeting.

For your information, I have enclosed a tentative agenda together with several reports we will be discussing at the meeting.

Roberta Moore
Roberta Moore
Corporate Secretary

---

sample of form 32: **NOTICE OF SPECIAL MEETING OF BOARD OF DIRECTORS**

Notice of Special Meeting of the Board of Directors of

Scrupulous Corporation

Date: **October 3, 2006**

TO: All Directors

There will be a special meeting of the board of directors on on **November 6**, **2006** at **7:00 p**.m., at **the corporation conference room**.

The primary purpose of this meeting is: **Purchase of new truck**.

Roberta Moore
_____

Roberta Moore,
Corporate Secretary

Inevitably an occasion will arise when the required notice of a meeting does not get out at all, or does not get out in time. Fortunately the directors can waive notice *either before or after the meeting takes place and even if the director fails to show up for the meeting*. The waiver must be in writing. Of course you cannot require the director to waive notice, but if he or she will agree to do so voluntarily, the **WAIVER OF NOTICE OF MEETING OF BOARD OF DIRECTORS** will serve the purpose. (see form 33, p.275.) An example of such a waiver is on page 66.

Some corporations ask directors to sign such a form at each meeting just to take care of the possibility that, unknown to the corporate secretary, there has been a mistake in giving notice to which someone may later object. The Model Business Corporation Act says notice is automatically waived if the director shows up and participates in the meeting anyway. (MBCA, Sec. 8.23.)

sample of form 33: **WAIVER OF NOTICE OF MEETING OF BOARD OF DIRECTORS**

Waiver of Notice of Meeting of Board of Directors of

Scrupulous Corporation

The undersigned director(s) or the Corporation hereby waive any and all notice required by law by the articles of incorporation or bylaws of the Corporation, and consent to the holding of a ☒ Regular ☐ Special meeting of the Board of Directors of the Corporation on **November 6, 2006** at **7:00 p**.m., at **the corporation conference room**.

Name: *Henry Hardy*   Date: *11/6/06*

Name: *Roberta Moore*   Date: *11/6/06*

Name: *Hugh Hardy*   Date: *11/6/06*

Name: *Raymond Rodriguez*   Date: *11/6/06*

Name: *Calvin Collier*   Date: *11/6/06*

Name: *Della Driskell*   Date: *11/6/06*

Agenda   What goes on at directors' meetings varies from company to company and from meeting to meeting. Some are very formal and some informal. It depends on the personalities of the people involved, the number of participants, and even the nature or number of issues to be discussed. There is no requirement that you have a formal **AGENDA OF MEETING OF THE BOARD OF DIRECTORS**, but it is usually worth the effort to make sure everything is covered. (see form 34, p.276.) Plus, directors like it. The following is an example of an agenda.

sample of form 34: **AGENDA OF MEETING OF BOARD OF DIRECTORS**

Agenda of Meeting of the Board of Directors of

Scrupulous Corporation

Date of Meeting: **November 6, 2006**

1. Introductory remarks by the Chairman.   5. Other business.
2. Approval of the minutes of last meeting.   6. Adjournment.
3. Report of the Chief Financial Officer.
4. Salary report of V.P.-Personnel.

(Lunch to be served approximately 12:15 p.m. in the company dining room.)

KEEPING RECORDS

It is the duty of the corporate secretary to see that accurate minutes are kept of all formal directors', shareholders', or committee meetings. This does not mean the secretary must be the one with a pencil and pad of paper at the meeting taking notes. Minutes may be recorded by anyone the secretary designates. It may be one of the company stenographers or lawyers. When the board is in *executive session* (meaning that only directors and specifically designated persons are present), the minutes may be kept by one of the directors.

Most people find it difficult to keep accurate minutes and participate in the meeting, so it is usually better to pick someone who is not expected to contribute to the discussion and can, therefore, concentrate on taking good notes.

For a discussion of the importance of the corporate minute book and keeping good records, refer to Chapter 3.

The following are examples of minutes of a directors' meeting, showing how various matters would be filled in for the description of events.

Sample **MINUTES OF DIRECTORS' MEETING DESCRIBING
A REPORT BY AN OFFICER**

The chairman of the meeting next asked Mr. Simpson, Vice President - Operations, to present a report on efforts to upgrade the company's data processing equipment.

Mr. Simpson referred to a written report that had been distributed to the directors in the information package accompanying the written notice of the meeting (a copy of which may be found in management storage file No. 04-58). He described in general terms the specifications of the system he expects to recommend to the directors, and summarized the savings that may be expected from personnel efficiencies to be gained through use of the proposed system. He reported that he is continuing discussions with several potential suppliers of equipment and expects to have firm bids from at least three suppliers available for consideration by the Board at its next regular meeting.

After brief questioning by several members of the Board, the Chairman thanked Mr. Simpson for his thorough report and excused him from the meeting.

Sample MINUTES OF DIRECTORS' MEETING DESCRIBING A REPORT BY AN INDEPENDENT AUDITOR

Mr. Tex A. Voydence, representing Bean-Counter Associates, the Company's independent auditors, and Mr. Calvin Collier, Treasurer, then joined the meeting. Mr. Voydence presented the completed audited financial statements of the Corporation for the fiscal year ended June 30, 2006, and a written report on the auditors' findings with regard to the Company's accounting and internal auditing procedures. A copy of the financial statements and audit report are located in management confidential file no. 05-739.

Mr. Voydence summarized the report. **[Describe highlights of report as presented by auditor]**. Mr. Voydence then asked whether there were any questions regarding the financial statements or the report.

Mr. Ray Rodriguez asked Mr. Collier whether management had any comments or questions regarding the information that had been presented. **[Describe comments of CFO and any additional questions.]**

The Chair of the meeting then suggested that the meeting go into executive session so that the directors could ask any additional questions they might have. Those present for the executive session were the directors and Mr. Voydence.

Ms. Della Driskell then asked Mr. Voydence to comment on the degree of cooperation the auditors had received from management and employees during the audit process. Mr. Voydence assured the directors that the Company had been highly cooperative and mentioned that Mr. Collier had been particularly helpful during the process.

Mr. Hugh Hardy asked whether there was any information that management had been reluctant to reveal to the auditors or had requested the auditors not to reveal to the directors. Mr. Voydence assured the board that there had not.

Ms. Driskell asked whether there had been any disagreements between management and the auditors about accounting methods or decisions or the presentation of the financial statements. Again, Mr. Voydence said that there had not.

Mr. Rodriguez asked whether there was any additional information that the auditors thought should be disclosed to the board or concerns that should be discussed. Mr. Voydence replied that there was not.

The Chair expressed the board's gratitude to Bean-Counter Associates for their good work, and the executive session was ended.

Sample **DIRECTORS' RESOLUTION ACCEPTING THE REPORT OF A COMMITTEE OF THE BOARD—**

The Chairman next requested Ms. Driskell, Chair of the Personnel Committee, to present the report of the Committee.

Ms. Driskell informed the meeting that the Personnel Committee had met earlier in the day to consider compensation packages for senior officers of the company for the coming year. She distributed a report entitled "Compensation Scheme—2005" a copy of which is stored in Confidential Management File no. 05-13. It was the recommendation of the Personnel Committee that the salaries detailed on such report should be established by the Board as salaries for the coming year for the President, Senior Vice Presidents, Vice Presidents, and Corporate Secretary, and that the health plan and other employee benefits in effect for the current year be carried over for the coming year.

After brief discussion by the Directors, Mr. Rodriguez moved the adoption of the following resolution. The motion was seconded by Mr. Hardy and adopted by the unanimous vote of the Directors.

RESOLVED, that the report and recommendations of the Personnel Committee presented to the Board are hereby adopted, that the salaries of the President, Senior Vice Presidents, Vice Presidents, and Corporate Secretary for the fiscal year beginning January 1, 2006, shall be established at the rates shown on the report entitled "Compensation Scheme—2006" (Confidential Management File no. 06-13), and that the employee health plan and other benefits as described in the "Scrupulous Corp. Employee Benefits Handbook, 2005" shall be continued during such fiscal year.

The Chairman thanked Ms. Driskell and the other members of the Personnel Committee for its excellent work.

Frequently, the corporate secretary will be asked to certify the authenticity of various actions by the board of directors. Use a **CERTIFIED COPY OF MINUTES OF MEETING OF THE BOARD OF DIRECTORS**. (see form 11, p.253.) Following are two examples of such a certification. One is for when the secretary is asked to certify the minutes of an entire meeting. (see form 11, p.253.) One is for a **CERTIFIED COPY OF RESOLUTIONS ADOPTED BY THE BOARD OF DIRECTORS**. (see form 13, p.255.)

sample of form 11: **CERTIFIED COPY OF MINUTES OF MEETING OF THE BOARD OF DIRECTORS**

**Certified Copy of Minutes of Meeting
of the Board of Directors of
Scrupulous Corporation**

I HEREBY CERTIFY that I am the Corporate Secretary of **Scrupulous Corporation**, and that the following is an accurate copy of minutes of the meeting of the Board of Directors of the corporation, held on **May 17, 2006**:

See attached copy of minutes.

Signed and the seal of the Corporation affixed, **September 22, 2006**.

Seal of Scrupulous Corporation	*Roberta Moore*
20✳06	Roberta Moore,
State of West Carolina	Secretary

---

sample of form 13: **CERTIFIED COPY OF RESOLUTIONS ADOPTED BY THE BOARD OF DIRECTORS**

**Certified Copy of Resolutions Adopted by
the Board of Directors of
Scrupulous Corporation**

I HEREBY CERTIFY that I am the Corporate Secretary of **Scrupulous Corporation**, that the following is an accurate copy of resolution(s) adopted by the Board of Directors of the corporation, effective **May 17, 2006**, and that such resolutions continue in effect as of the date of this certification:

See attached copy of resolution.

Signed and the seal of the Corporation affixed, **September 22, 2006**.

Seal of Scrupulous Corporation	*Roberta Moore*
20✳06	Roberta Moore,
State of West Carolina	Secretary

Shareholders

Ownership of a corporation is divided into shares. As owners of corporation, the shareholders have the power to make the kinds of decisions an owner makes—should I sell my property or buy more? how should my property be managed? Corporate shareholders usually make such decisions in shareholders' meetings.

THE PLACE OF THE SHAREHOLDER WITHIN THE CORPORATION

Shareholders are not the corporation, and they do not represent the corporation. Like an individual director, an individual shareholder has no power to bind the corporation or to make a decision for the corporation (unless there is only one shareholder). The shareholders own the corporation, but they do not own the assets of the corporation and have no rights as such to use or exercise control over any asset of the corporation.

Shareholders do have the power, acting as a body, to act as the ultimate decision makers for the corporation, deciding certain fundamental issues directly and the rest indirectly through the election of directors.

This and the next chapter are mostly about how shareholders make those decisions.

CREATING SHAREHOLDERS

A corporation sells its shares to raise money (capital) with which to carry on its business. This *stock* of capital turns into buildings, equipment, and all the other assets of the corporations. The shareholders who buy the *shares of stock* are therefore owners of the corporation.

Owning Shares

Shareholders have two important rights: first, the right to vote in shareholders meetings, thereby exercising control over the corporation; and second, the right to share in distributions of the corporation's profits and, in case the corporation dissolves, its assets.

Par Value

In the nineteenth century, when corporation law was relatively primitive, *par value* had a useful purpose in that it represented a sort of core value, the amount of capital the company needed to begin and maintain its business. That amount of capital (the *authorized capital* the corporation was allowed to raise by its **ARTICLES OF INCORPORATION**) divided by the number of shares that could be issued by the company equaled the par value of each share. If a corporation sold shares for less than par value, a prohibited practice, the shares were said to be *watered*.

There was no standard for determining what the authorized capital of any particular corporation should be, so incorporators would choose a convenient figure that yielded a par value comfortably less than the expected selling price of the shares. In many cases it was one dollar. Sometimes the authorized capital would be determined merely by the tax rates imposed by statute on new corporations.

Example:

A statute might charge a minimum tax of $40.00 on new corporation filings that would permit the creation of a company with up to $100,000 in authorized capital. As a result, most start-up companies in that state would have $100,000 in authorized capital and be permitted to sell 100,000 shares of stock, par value $1.00 per share. This said nothing about how much capital the company could raise, since

$1.00 par value shares could be sold for any amount above that price. So, if the corporation sold 50,000 shares for $200 each, it would collect $10 million in capital.

You can see that par value provides no useful information about the value of a company, and for that reason, modern corporation laws make par value optional. That is, they permit *no par* stock. Some states eliminate the concept entirely. Most corporations, however, do still have par value shares (if for no other reason than blindly following tradition).

Stock Certificates
A *stock certificate* is not a share of stock. It certifies that the person named on the certificate is the owner or *holder* of the number of shares stated on the certificate. As long as certain basic information is included on the certificate, any format will do, so long as it is adopted by the directors as the company's official certificate form. It can be a plain sheet of paper with the information typed on, or it can be an elaborately engraved form with nice pictures. There is a simple **COMMON STOCK CERTIFICATE** in Appendix C. (see form 35, p.277.)

The front side of form 35 indicates ownership of shares. Usually, certificates are numbered sequentially from the first certificate issued. The term "fully paid and nonassessable" means at least the par value of the shares (for example, $1.00 par value shares multiplied by 150 shares owned equals $150) has been collected by the corporation in payment for the shares. This further means that the shareholder is not subject to further assessment related to the shares, no matter how much money the corporation may lose or need.

"Transferable only on the books of the corporation" means that a purchaser of the shares from the holder named on the certificate will not be recognized as the new owner until the change of ownership is recorded in the stock records of the company. That will be done only if the named holder or the holder's authorized agent (it does not have to be a lawyer) appears in person to direct that the change in ownership be recorded.

This transfer procedure may be accomplished by using the form that usually appears on the back of a stock certificate, which is actually a *power of attorney*. Frequently, the name of the attorney-in-fact is left blank and later filled in with the name of the secretary or treasurer of the corporation who actually records the transfer on the company books. There is a blank space for the shareholder's Social Security number or Taxpayer Identification Number. It is there to help the company with its IRS reporting obligations.

Stock certificates are usually signed by two officers of the company. Which two varies from company to company. Check your **BYLAWS** to see what is appropriate. The paragraph beginning "Upon request..." is used only when the corporation is authorized to issue more than one class or series of shares (which will be discussed later). Following is an example of a simple stock certificate.

sample of form 35: **COMMON STOCK CERTIFICATE**

Front side:

Certificate No.: 000004   No. of Shares: 20,000

Scrupulous Corporation

Incorporated under the laws of the State of **West Carolina**

Authorized Capital Stock: **20,000** shares.

Par Value: ❏ $_____ per Share   ☒ No Par Value

THIS CERTIFIES THAT **Henry Hardy** is the owner of **20,000** fully paid and nonassessable shares of the capital stock of **Scrupulous Corporation** transferable only on the books of the corporation by the holder of this certificate in person or by the holder's duly authorized attorney upon surrender of this certificate properly endorsed.

Upon request, and without charge, the corporation will provide written information as to the designations, preferences, limitations, and relative rights of all classes and series of shares and the authority of the board of directors to determine the same for future classes and series.

IN WITNESS WHEREOF, **Scrupulous Corporation** has caused this certificate to be signed by its duly authorized officers and its corporate seal to be affixed on **January 8, 2006**.

Seal of Scrupulous Corporation	*Raymond Rodriguez* ,
20✳06	President
State of West Carolina	*Roberta Moore* ,
	Secretary

Back side:

FOR VALUE RECEIVED, the undersigned hereby sells, assigns, and transfers to _____, _____ of the shares represented by the certificate on the reverse side, and irrevocably appoints _____ attorney, with full power of substitution, to transfer such shares on the books of **Scrupulous Corporation**.

DATED: _____, _____.

_____

Witness: _____

Social Security number or other Taxpayer Identification Number of the assignee: _____

BUYING AND SELLING SHARES OF STOCK

Since the 1930s, the *buying and selling of corporate securities* (a term that includes stocks and bonds), has been carefully regulated by both Federal and state governments. The *Securities and Exchange Commission* (SEC) is the Federal agency with responsibility to administer U.S. laws on the subject, chiefly the *Securities Act of 1933* and the *Exchange Act of 1934*. State statutes on the subject, called *blue sky laws*, are usually administered by the Secretary of State, the same official that oversees incorporations and other corporate matters.

Registration and Exemptions

The details of securities regulation are beyond the scope of this book. But you should know that the regulatory scheme says that *every* sale of a corporate security (whether the seller is the corporation or an individual investor) is regulated and can only take place if "registered" in the manner required by law, unless a specific exemption from the requirement is available.

Registration of securities is a costly (usually more than $1,000,000 in expenses) and difficult process, so it is fortunate that exemptions are plentiful. However, there must be an exemption or there must be a registration. Even an inadvertent violation of these requirements can be even more costly.

How do you know if there is an exemption available to you? The sale of a small number of shares to very few shareholders who will be closely involved in the operation of the company will almost certainly be exempt from registration. But the only certain answer to the question depends on the facts in each case. If there is any doubt, competent legal advice is essential.

Original Issue Shares

Original issue shares are those sold by the issuing corporation to the shareholders, as opposed to shares which, once issued, may be sold by the shareholder to another person. The sale of original issue shares is done pursuant to a contract between the company and the investor called a **STOCK SUBSCRIPTION AGREEMENT**. (see form 36, p.279.) The following is an example.

sample of form 36: **STOCK SUBSCRIPTION AGREEMENT**

Stock Subscription Agreement
Scrupulous Corporation

In consideration of the mutual promises contained in this agreement and other lawful and sufficient consideration, the receipt of which is hereby acknowledged, **Scrupulous Corporation** (the "Corporation"), a **West Carolina** corporation, agrees to issue, and the undersigned purchaser agrees to subscribe to and purchase 20,000 shares of the common stock of the Corporation for cash at the price of $10,000.00. The purchase price for the shares shall be payable in full upon issuance of the shares by the Corporation.

Purchaser: **Henry Hardy, 238 Prosperity Street, New York, NY 10032   Soc. Sec. No. 999-99-9999**

[Name, address, and Social Security number or Taxpayer Identification Number of purchaser]

Date: **January 2, 2006**

Henry Hardy
[Signature of Purchaser]

Scrupulous Corporation

By: *Roberta Moore*

Stock Options   A *stock option* is the right to buy shares of stock in the future at a predetermined price. Such arrangements are often used as employee incentives under the assumption that an employee who has the right to buy shares five years from today at today's prices will work extra hard to make sure that, in five years, the company's shares will be worth more than today. An investor who believes the value of the company will increase over time will see the purchase of an option as a valuable asset.

The sale or other transfer of an option to buy shares is also subject to the SEC and blue sky regulations. In addition to the possibly complex issues resulting from that regulation, the tax consequences of stock options and employee incentive plans need to be considered (these are beyond the scope of this book).

An option contract must, like any other contract, be supported by some bargained-for consideration. If there is no consideration, then the promise of the corporation to sell its stock for the stated price is not enforceable by the courts. The option may be given as employee compensation or the consideration could be any number of things, such as money or a promise to work for the company or to assume new duties.

Following is an example of a resolution to grant an option as employee compensation. There is a **STOCK OPTION AGREEMENT** form in Appendix C. (see form 37, p.280.) Following the resolution is an example of such an agreement.

sample form 37: **DIRECTORS' CONSENT TO ACTION GRANTING A STOCK OPTION TO AN OFFICER**

Consent to Action without Formal Meeting by the Directors of

Scrupulous Corporation

The undersigned directors of the corporation hereby adopt the following resolution:

RESOLVED, that for value received, there is granted to **Raymond Rodriguez** (the "Grantee") an option to purchase **1,000** shares of the **common stock** of the corporation. The purchase price of the shares will be **$15.00** per share, payable in cash upon his exercise of the option. The option shall be evidenced by and subject to the terms and conditions of a written Stock Option Agreement in the form presented by management to and now approved by the directors,

Further RESOLVED, that management of the corporation is hereby authorized and directed to take such action and execute such documents as may be necessary or desirable to give effect to the above resolution.

This resolution shall be effective at **2 p**.m. on the **22nd** of **August, 2006**.

Henry Hardy	*Roberta Moore*	*Raymond Rodriguez*
Henry Hardy,	Roberta Moore,	Raymond Rodriguez,
Director	Director	Director

---

sample of form 38: **STOCK OPTION AGREEMENT**

Stock Option Agreement
Scrupulous Corporation

In consideration of the mutual promises contained in this agreement and other lawful consideration, the receipt and sufficiency of which is hereby acknowledged, **Scrupulous Corporation** (the "Corporation), a **West Carolina** corporation, hereby grants to **Della Driskell** (the "Grantee") an option to purchase shares of the Corporation upon the following terms and conditions:

1. Consideration of the Grantee. The grant of an option in this agreement is made in consideration of **providing market services to the corporation**.

2. Number of shares and price. The option granted in this agreement (the "Option") is an option of the Grantee to purchase **2,000** shares of the **common** shares of the Corporation. The purchase price of the shares will be **$2.00** per share, payable in cash upon the exercise of the option.

3. Time and method of exercise. The Option may be exercised in whole or in part by the Grantee at any time and from time to time before **December 31, 2008** by delivery to the Corporation at its principal office written notice of the Grantee's intent to exercise the option stating the number of shares being purchased and accompanied by the purchase price of the shares being purchased. The option may be exercised as to whole numbers of shares only.

4. Adjustments of the number of shares subject to the Option. In the event of any share dividend, share split, or other recapitalization effecting the shares of the Company, or a merger of the Corporation in which it is the surviving corporation, the number of shares subject to the Option will be automatically adjusted to equitably reflect such change or merger. In the event of the dissolution of the Corporation, or a merger or other fundamental change following which no shares of the corporation may be issued, the Option will terminate, but the Grantee will have a reasonable opportunity to exercise the Option immediately before such event. Except as provided in this paragraph, the Grantee shall have no rights as a shareholder of the Corporation with respect to the shares subject to the Option until such shares are issued upon exercise of the Option.

5. No transfer. The Option may not be transferred by the Grantee other than by will or the laws of inheritance.

The Corporation and the Grantee have executed this Stock Option Agreement under seal on **August 22, 2006**.

Grantee:

Della Driskell

Della Driskell

| Seal of Scrupulous Corporation |
| 20✳06 |
| State of West Carolina |

Scrupulous Corporation:

By: *Raymond Rodriguez*

Raymond Rodriguez, President

Attest:

Roberta Moore

Roberta Moore, Secretary

Once it has been agreed that original issue shares will be sold pursuant to a **Stock Subscription Agreement**, **Stock Option Agreement**, or other circumstances, it may be appropriate for the directors to authorize the actual issuance of shares to the purchasers. They may do so in a resolution such as the example that follows. This resolution would be included with form 1, 2, or 4.

When the corporation was created, it may have adopted a *Section 1244 Plan* under federal tax laws. Shares issued under such a plan receive favorable tax treatment if they are later sold for a loss or become worthless. If such a plan is in effect (you can tell by looking in the corporate minutes), the resolution issuing the shares should mention it.

sample of form 39: **Directors' Consent to Action Issuing Stock being Purchased**

Consent to Action without Formal Meeting by the Directors of

Scrupulous Corporation

The undersigned directors of the corporation hereby adopt the following resolution:

WHEREAS, pursuant to a Section 1244 Plan adopted by the corporation on **January 6, 2006**, the person(s) named below have agreed to purchase the number of shares stated opposite his or her name, for the consideration indicated, pursuant to a subscription agreement dated **January 6**, **2006**, it is therefore

RESOLVED, that the **treasurer** of the corporation, or his or her designee, is authorized and directed, upon receipt by the corporation of the stated consideration, to issue certificates representing the number of **common** shares of the corporation indicated to the persons named below:

Name of purchaser(s):	No. of shares:	Consideration received:
Roberta Moore	1,000	$10,000.00
Calvin Collier	1,000	$10,000.00

This resolution shall be effective at **10 a**.m. on the **22nd** of **August**, **2006**.

Henry Hardy   *Roberta Moore*   *Raymond Rodriguez*
Henry Hardy, Director   Roberta Moore, Director   Raymond Rodriguez, Director

---

sample of form 40: **Directors' Consent to Action Issuing Stock Following the Exercise of an Option**

Consent to Action without Formal Meeting by the Directors of

Scrupulous Corporation

The undersigned directors of the corporation hereby adopt the following resolution:

WHEREAS, the person(s) named below have exercised options for the number of shares stated opposite his or her name, for the consideration indicated, pursuant to an option agreement dated **September 1**, **2006**, it is therefore

RESOLVED, that the **treasurer** of the corporation, or his or her designee, is authorized and directed, upon receipt by the corporation of the stated consideration, to issue certificates representing the number of **common** shares of the corporation indicated to the persons named below:

Name of purchaser(s):	No. of shares:	Consideration received:
Raymond Rodriguez	**1,000**	**$15,000.00**

This resolution shall be effective at **10 a**.m. on the **3rd** of **November, 2006**.

Henry Hardy

Henry Hardy, Director

Roberta Moore

Roberta Moore, Director

Raymond Rodriguez

Raymond Rodriguez, Director

Buying and Selling Shares Already Issued

A share of stock, like any other piece of property, may be sold or given away by its owner. Usually the owner can transfer shares without any advance permission from the corporation or other shareholders. In smaller corporations, there is sometimes a **Shareholders' Agreement** that places limits on the rights of an owner to dispose of his or her shares. (see form 45, p.288.) It is even possible for the ownership of shares to change without the corporation knowing about it, but few shareholders would want this to happen.

If the company does not know you are a shareholder, it will not know to send you the dividend check. Obviously, it is important for the corporation to know who its owners are, or at least to be able to communicate with them—so there must be a list of shareholders and some way of amending the list. See the **Stock Ledger** in Appendix C. (see form 109, p.355.)

Often the shares of large corporations are held in *street name* by *nominees* and the corporation does not know the identity of many of its shareholders. This is to facilitate the transfer of shares through brokerage accounts. There is a system by which such corporations can communicate with their real shareholders through the nominees.

Endorsement. The back side of the **Common Stock Certificate** (form 35) serves two purposes. It is written evidence that the owner has transferred his or her shares to a new owner, and it authorizes the responsible officer of the company to amend the list of shareholders to include the new owner.

After the endorsement form is completed and signed, the stock certificate should be turned over to the new owner who will then present it to the appropriate officer—usually the treasurer or secretary. The officer will change the shareholder list and issue a new certificate to the new owner. The officer will write "CANCELED" on the face of the old certificate and keep it with the list of shareholders.

Notice that form 35 allows some, or all, of the shares represented by a certificate to be transferred to the new owner.

Example:

Suppose Mr. Brown's certificate represents 1,000 shares of Scrupulous Corporation and he only wants to sell 250 of them to the new owner, Mr. N. Vestor II. The certificate would be completed and turned over to the treasurer as usual, but the treasurer would issue two new certificates. One would represent 750 shares issued to Brown and another representing 250 shares to Vestor. The witness may be any adult who has no interest in the transaction.

The example that follows is the completed back side of the stock certificate form.

sample of form 35: ENDORSEMENT OF A STOCK CERTIFICATE
(BACK OF FORM ONLY)

FOR VALUE RECEIVED, the undersigned hereby sells, assigns, and transfers to **Bertram Buyer**, **two-hundred fifty (250)** of the shares represented by the certificate on the reverse side, and irrevocably appoints **Roberta Moore** attorney, with full power of substitution, to transfer such shares on the books of **Scrupulous Corporation**.

DATED: **August 10, 2006**.

Raymond Rodriguez
Raymond Rodriguez

Witness: *C.M. Sine*
C.M. Sine

Social Security number or other Taxpayer Identification Number of the assignee: **000-00-0000**

Occasionally it is inconvenient to use the endorsement printed on the stock certificate. For example, it may be desirable to complete the transaction by mail, and therefore safer to send the unendorsed certificate in one package and the document authorizing the transfer in another. A **STOCK POWERS SEPARATE FROM CERTIFICATE** is used for this purpose instead of the endorsement form printed on the back side of the certificate. (see form 41, p.284.)

Following is an example of form 41. Again, the witness may be any adult who has no interest in the transaction.

sample of form 41: **STOCK POWERS SEPARATE FROM CERTIFICATE**

Stock Powers Separate from Certificate

In exchange for valuable consideration, the receipt and sufficiency of which is hereby acknowledged, the undersigned hereby sells, assigns, and transfers to **Huge Hardy**, **5,000** shares of the stock of **Scrupulous Corporation** registered on the books of the Corporation in the name of the undersigned and represented by Certificate(s) number **000010**

The undersigned hereby irrevocably appoints **Roberta Moore**, **Corporate Secretary**, attorney, with full power of substitution, to transfer such shares on the books of the Corporation.

Executed on **March 31, 2006**.

Henry Hardy
_____
Henry Hardy

Witness: *Calvin Collier*
_____
Calvin Collier

Social Security number or other Taxpayer Identification Number of the assignee: **000-00-0000**

Buying Shares Back from Shareholders

There are many reasons a corporation may want to buy its shares from shareholders, such as if:

✪   the corporation is small and there is probably no market for the shares outside the corporation;

✪   a shareholder who is dissatisfied with the way the corporation is being run, but is not in a position to force a change in direction, may have no way to disassociate from the corporation other than to sell the shares back to the company; or,

✪   the corporation may merely wish to reduce the number of its shareholders.

Some shares and other corporate securities are said to be *redeemable*. This means that the corporation has the power to force the shareholder to sell the shares to the corporation under certain conditions. There can also be a class of shares that allow the shareholder to force the corporation to buy his or her shares.

These subjects are beyond the scope of this book; however, the resolution on page 87 is useful for the more common situation in which the corporation and the shareholder agree, for whatever reason, that it would be useful for the corporation to acquire the shareholder's interest in the company.

There are some limits on the power of the directors to authorize such a purchase. It is, after all, a distribution of the company's money (or other assets) to a shareholder and is subject to the same limitations as the dividend. (see Chapter 8.) Moreover, it is an unequal distribution. That is, the shareholder who sells shares to the company is getting a distribution of assets the other shareholders are not getting.

The directors may have personal liability if the purchase of the shareholder's interest is unfair to the other shareholders, is unfairly advantageous to one of the directors voting in favor of it, or is otherwise harmful to the company.

The **ARTICLES OF INCORPORATION** of some corporations forbid the company to resell shares that have been purchased from shareholders. In such a case, the number of shares authorized by the articles must be reduced by the number of shares repurchased.

Example:

Suppose the **ARTICLES OF INCORPORATION** authorize a company to issue 1000 shares, and 250 of them have been issued to Shareholder A. The corporation would then have left 750 *authorized but unissued shares*, which it could sell to other people.

Suppose the corporation later repurchases the 250 shares from Shareholder A. According to the Model Business Corporation Act (MBCA, Sec. 6.31), the repurchased shares again become authorized but unissued and the corporation would have 1000 of them to sell.

If the articles forbid the resale of shares purchased from shareholders, then the number of authorized but unissued shares must somehow be reduced back to 750. (Notice that it does not matter that you do not intend to resell the shares. The number authorized must be reduced regardless.) It must be done by an amendment to the **ARTICLES OF INCORPORATION**. (see Chapter 12.)

Unlike most such amendments, the MBCA allows this one to be done by the directors with no shareholder vote. The company must file the amendment with the Secretary of State (or other appropriate agency in your state) where the company is incorporated.

Following is a resolution of the board of directors authorizing the repurchase of a shareholder's shares. It presumes that the corporation's **ARTICLES OF INCORPORATION** forbids it to resell such shares and that the articles must therefore be amended to reduce the number of authorized shares. If (as is more likely) the articles do not forbid such resales, the third paragraph in the following resolution may be deleted as in the next example.

sample of form 42: **DIRECTORS' CONSENT TO ACTION AUTHORIZING PURCHASE OF A SHAREHOLDER'S STOCK AND REDUCING THE NUMBER OF AUTHORIZED SHARES**

Consent to Action without Formal Meeting by the Directors of

Scrupulous Corporation

The undersigned directors of the corporation hereby adopt the following resolution:

WHEREAS, **Della Driskell** has offered to sell to the corporation, and the corporation wishes to purchase **100** shares of the **common** stock of the corporation previously issued to such shareholder, it is therefore

RESOLVED, that the corporation shall purchase **100** shares of the **common** stock of the corporation from **Della Driskell** for **$10.00** per share, such transaction to take place on of before **December 19**, 2006, and further

RESOLVED, that the articles of incorporation of the corporation shall be amended to reduce the number of authorized shares by the number of shares so purchased, such amendment to be effective on the date such transaction is completed or within a reasonable time thereafter, and further

RESOLVED, that the officers of the corporation are authorized and directed to file articles of amendment with the Secretary of State of West Carolina giving effect to such amendment in a timely manner, and further

RESOLVED, that the officers of the corporation are authorized and directed to take such actions as may be necessary or desirable to give effect to the above resolutions.

This resolution shall be effective at **10 a.**m. on the **31st** of **October,** 2006.

Henry Hardy
Henry Hardy,
Director

Roberta Moore
Roberta Moore,
Director

Raymond Rodriguez
Raymond Rodriguez,
Director

sample of form 43: **DIRECTORS' CONSENT TO ACTION AUTHORIZING PURCHASE OF A SHAREHOLDER'S STOCK (NO REDUCTION IN AUTHORIZED SHARES)**

Consent to Action without Formal Meeting by the Directors of

Scrupulous Corporation

The undersigned directors of the corporation hereby adopt the following resolution:

WHEREAS, **Della Driskell** has offered to sell to the corporation, and the corporation wishes to purchase **100** shares of the **common** stock of the corporation previously issued to **her**, it is therefore

RESOLVED, that the corporation shall purchase **100** shares of the **common** stock of the corporation for **$15.00** per share, the transaction to take place on or before **December 19, 2006**, and further

RESOLVED, that the **treasurer** of the corporation or his or her designee is authorized and directed to take such acts as may be necessary or desirable to give effect to the above resolution.

This resolution shall be effective at **10 a.**m. on the **31st** of **October, 2006**.

Henry Hardy
Henry Hardy, Director

Roberta Moore
Roberta Moore, Director

Raymond Rodriguez
Raymond Rodriguez, Director

Sometimes it is desirable to increase or decrease the total number of authorized shares. Typically, an increase may be needed to create sufficient shares to pay a share dividend (see Chapter 8) and decreases have previously been discussed. If such a change is to be made, in most states, it can be accomplished with no more than a directors' resolution to amend the **ARTICLES OF INCORPORATION**. (For example, see MBCA Sec. 10.05.) In other situations, the articles will need to be amended by shareholder action. (see Chapter 12.) Next is a directors' consent to action increasing the number of authorized shares.

sample of form 120: **ARTICLES OF AMENDMENT REDUCING THE NUMBER OF AUTHORIZED SHARES**

Articles of Amendment of

Scrupulous Corporation

The Articles of Incorporation of **Scrupulous Corporation** are hereby amended as follows:

1. **The name of the corporation is Scrupulous Corporation.**

2. **The number of authorized common shares of the corporation is hereby reduced by 10,000.**

3. **After such reduction, the number of common shares authorized shall be 90,000.**

4. **This amendment was adopted on October 26, 2006, by the board of directors without shareholder action as permitted by statute.**

The date of these Articles of Amendment is **November 1, 2006**.

Scrupulous Corporation

By: *Raymond Rodriguez*

Raymond Rodriguez, President

STOCK TRANSFER LEDGER

It is critically important for a corporation to keep a record of the names and addresses of its shareholders, because shareholders are the persons who have the power to select directors and the persons entitled to a share of the company's profits. Such lists take many forms. In larger corporations, shareholder lists are kept by professional *transfer agents*.

The **STOCK LEDGER** in Appendix C is a simple form for keeping lists of shareholders. (see form 109, p.355.) A sample of a **STOCK LEDGER**, completed to show the issuance of shares to a new shareholder, follows.

sample of form 109: **STOCK LEDGER**

Cert. No.	No. of Shares	Date Acquired	Shareholder Name and Address	From Whom Transferred	Amount Paid	Date of Transfer	To Whom Transferred	Cert. No Surrendered	No. of Shares Transferred	Cert. No.
1	1000	5/10 /06	Robert Brown 23 Investor Cr. Raleigh, NC 27605	Original Issue	$10/ share	8/3/06	N. Vestor II 10001 First Ave Turner, GA 31714	1	250	2, 3
2	250	8/3 /06	N. Vestor II 10001 First Ave Turner, GA 31714	R. Brown	unknown					
3	750	5/10 /06	Robert Brown 23 Investor Cr. Raleigh, NC 27605							

AGREEMENTS AMONG SHAREHOLDERS

With few exceptions, shareholders have no duty to look out for each other. Each shareholder is free to vote his or her shares for his or her own interests even though it may not be in the best interests of the other shareholders or the corporation (there are some limits on the damage a controlling shareholder is allowed to do). Each shareholder is allowed to sell his or her shares for the best price available from any willing buyer.

This system works well for the shareholders of a corporate giant, but may not be the best way to run a small corporation. If there are only a few shareholders, most or all of whom are closely involved in the business, the identity of the other shareholders and their plans for the corporation may be critically important.

For this reason, shareholders enter into a variety of **SHAREHOLDERS' AGREEMENTS** among themselves about the way the corporation is to be managed. (see form 45, p.288.) They may agree on who the officers and directors will be, whether the corporation will be allowed to consider merger with another, or even what kind of business the corporation will be allowed to transact. Form 45 is an agreement among the shareholders of a corporation that each of the shareholders will be assured representation on the board of directors and a job as an officer.

Form 45 provides that each officer will have the same salary. Of course any number of possible arrangements could be made.

NOTE: *If the salaries are in the same proportion as share ownership, the IRS may argue that they are not salaries at all, but dividends and therefore not deductible to the corporation.*

NOTE: *The only shareholders bound by the agreement are the ones who sign it. Any new shareholders with new shares issued by the corporation may not be subject to the agreement.*

sample of form 45: **SHAREHOLDERS' AGREEMENT REGARDING DIRECTORS AND OFFICERS**

Shareholders' Agreement

This agreement is made by and among **Scrupulous Corporation** (the "Corporation") and the undersigned shareholders of the corporation (the "Shareholders" collectively, or "Shareholder" individually) on **August 9, 2006**.

In consideration of the premises and of the mutual promises and conditions contained in this agreement, the Corporation and the Shareholders agree for themselves, their successors, and assigns, as follows:

1.   The number of directors of the corporation shall be **4**. So long as he or she shall own shares in the Corporation, each Shareholder shall have the right to serve as a director of the Corporation or to designate a person to serve as director. Any such person named must be reasonably capable of performing the duties of a director.

2.   So long as he or she shall own shares in the Corporation, each shareholder shall have the right, but shall not be required, to serve as an officer of the Corporation. The compensation paid to each Shareholder during each calendar year for his or her services as an officer of the Corporation shall be equal to the compensation paid to each other Shareholder of the corporation for services as an officer. The titles and duties of each Shareholder so employed by the Corporation shall be as determined by the Board of Directors from time to time.

3.   The Shareholders shall vote their shares in such a way as to give effect to the provisions of this agreement.

4.   Every certificate representing shares owned by the parties to this agreement shall prominently bear the following legend: "The shares represented by this certificate are subject to the provisions of a Shareholders' Agreement dated **August 9, 2006**, a copy of which is on file in, and may be examined at, the principal office of the Corporation."

IN WITNESS WHEREOF, the parties have executed this Agreement under seal on the date indicated above.

```
┌─────────────────────────────────┐
│   Seal of Scrupulous Corporation │
│                                  │
│            20✱06                 │
│                                  │
│     State of West Carolina       │
└─────────────────────────────────┘
```

Scrupulous Corporation

By: *Raymond Rodriguez*
Raymond Rodriguez, President

Attest: *Roberta Moore*
Roberta Moore, Secretary
(Seal)   (Seal)

Henry Hardy   *Hugh Hardy*
Henry Hardy, Shareholder   Hugh Hardy, Shareholder
(Seal)   (Seal)

Calvin Collier   *Della Driskell*
Calvin Collier, Shareholder   Della Driskell, Shareholder

The most common type of **SHAREHOLDERS' AGREEMENT** is one that places restrictions on the transfer of shares. The owners of a small business usually think of themselves as partners, more or less, even if the business is a corporation. The success of the business may depend on the personalities involved and how well they get along. If one *partner* sells his or her interest, or leaves it in his or her will to someone the others detest, catastrophe may result.

A **SHAREHOLDERS' AGREEMENT** can prevent that by keeping each shareholder from transferring shares to an outsider without first offering it to the other shareholders for the same price or a price determined by formula. The existing shareholders get a chance to look the potential new shareholder over, and if they do not like what they see, they can buy the shares themselves.

You may ask why the contract does not simply say no shareholder can sell his or her shares without the permission of the others. The reason is that the courts will not enforce such an agreement. It is a *restraint on alienation,* which is frowned on everywhere in the law.

Courts carefully interpret agreements, which makes it difficult for shareholders to sell their shares. The methods for determining the price at which the shares can be purchased are often complex and should be carefully tailored to each company. Thus, **SHAREHOLDERS' AGREEMENTS** of this type are too long and complex to fit comfortably in this book.

CREATING A NEW CLASS OF SHARES

Most corporations begin with authority to issue one class of shares. However, it may be useful to create one or more additional classes or to divide a class of shares into subgroups called *series*.

Classes and Series of Shares

A class or series of shares is a group of shares that have the same rights as the others in the same class or series. Usually, the rights in question are the right to vote (in which case the group is called a *voting group*), the right to receive dividends, and the right to divide the assets of the corporation in the event it is dissolved. It may also refer to the right of the corporation to redeem the shares, as previously discussed.

Traditionally, there have been two broad classes of shares—*common* and *preferred*. Sometimes these classes have been subdivided into various series designated by letters or numbers. Modern corporation statutes allow almost unlimited flexibility in the design of various classes and series. Somewhere, however, among all the shares taken as a whole, the shareholders must have all the power to vote on the issues on which shareholders are permitted to vote. Also, shareholders must have the right to receive all the remaining assets of the corporation upon dissolution.

Most corporations get along nicely without having more than one class of shares, and that class will be called the common shares. Common shares traditionally have one vote per share on all matters that may be voted on by shareholders *and* a right to receive dividends only if the directors decide to declare one.

By default, modern corporate statutes give preferred shareholders the same voting rights as common shareholders. In practice, however, preferred shareholders have only limited voting rights. They usually enjoy predetermined dividends that the directors must declare and pay before they may pay a dividend on the common shares. Preferred shareholders may also enjoy a *preference* in dividing the corporate assets upon dissolution.

Preferred shares allow the corporation to sell shares for additional capital without unduly reducing the control powers enjoyed by the common shareholders. The preferred investors are willing to trade away the right to vote on mundane corporate matters such as the election of directors for the relative certainty of the preferred dividend.

Convertible Shares

Convertible shares are those that, under certain circumstances, may be converted from one class or series into another, or even into another type of security such as from stocks to bonds.

Creating a Separate Class of Shares in the Articles of Incorporation

The **ARTICLES OF INCORPORATION** describe the capital structure of the company. If there is only one class of shares, the description may be very simple, such as:

The number of shares the corporation is authorized to issue is 100,000.

The shares then issued will be referred to as the common shares of the corporation.

Additional classes of shares may be created when the **ARTICLES OF INCORPORATION** are first filed, in which case the relevant provision will look more like the following form example.

The articles may also be amended later to establish a new class of shares and fully describing attributes of the new shares such as voting rights, dividend preferences, and liquidation preferences (see Chapter 12). The amendment, which would have to be approved by shareholders, would resemble the examples given below.

Power of Directors to Establish Preferences

The provision of the **ARTICLES OF INCORPORATION** could state in detail the preferences, limitations, and relative rights of each class. If you know what they are at the time the articles are drafted, there is no reason not to do so. However, the MBCA allows later consideration of such details when the time comes to issue the first preferred shares. The directors may then decide on the preferences and file an amendment to the articles with the state, as shown in the two examples on pages 95 and 96.

If the **ARTICLES OF INCORPORATION** are set up to authorize preferred shares, then the directors may, at any time they choose, decide to establish the preferences of the shares, amend the articles accordingly, and proceed to issue the preferred shares.

Unlike most other amendments to the **ARTICLES OF INCORPORATION**, this is one that may be adopted by the directors without a vote of the shareholders. The next two examples show a typical arrangement for preferred shares, but do not by any means exhaust the possibilities. Different classes of shares can be designed in ways limited only by imagination and can serve a wide variety of corporate and financial purposes.

sample of form 46: **DIRECTORS' CONSENT TO ACTION**
ESTABLISHING PREFERRED STOCK

Consent to Action without Formal Meeting
by the Directors of
Scrupulous Corporation

The undersigned directors of the corporation hereby adopt the following resolution:

RESOLVED, that pursuant to Article 2 of the articles of incorporation of the corporation, there is created a class of preferred shares, series A, with the preferences, limitations, and relative rights stated in the following amendment to the articles of incorporation, and further

RESOLVED, that Article 2 of the articles of incorporation is amended to read as follows:

2. The number of shares the corporation shall have authority to issue is 100,000 divided into two classes as follows:

Class	Series	Par Value	Number of shares authorized
Common	**n/a**	**No par**	**50,000**
Preferred	**A**	**No par**	**50,000**

When, and if legally declared by the board of directors, the record holder of each share of Preferred stock, Series A, shall be entitled to receive cash dividends at the annual rate of $**1.00** per share payable in equal quarterly installments beginning on **July 1, 2006**. Cash dividends on Preferred shares shall be cumulative from the first dividend payment following the issuance of the share, and shall be declared and paid, or set apart for payment, before any cash dividends shall be paid on the Common stock.

Further RESOLVED, that the President of the corporation and his/her designees are authorized and directed to take such actions, including filing Article of Amendment, as may be necessary or desirable to give effect to this resolution.

This resolution shall be effective at **10 a.**m. on the **2nd** of **October, 2006**.

Henry Hardy
Henry Hardy, Director

Roberta Moore
Roberta Moore, Director

Raymond Rodriguez
Raymond Rodriguez, Director

sample of form 120: **AMENDMENT TO ARTICLES OF INCORPORATION ESTABLISHING PREFERRED STOCK**

Articles of Amendment of

Scrupulous Corporation

The Articles of Incorporation of **Scrupulous Corporation** are hereby amended as follows:

1.   The name of the corporation is **Scrupulous Corporation**.

2.   The following amendment to Article **2** of the articles of incorporation of the corporation was adopted by the board of directors on [date]:

> Article **2**. The number of shares the corporation is authorized to issue is **100,000**, which shall be divided into two classes as follows:

Class	Series	Par Value	Number of shares authorized
Common	**n/a**	**No par**	**50,000**
Preferred	**A**	**No par**	**50,000**

When and if legally declared by the board of directors, the record holder of each share of Preferred stock, Series **A**, shall be entitled to receive cash dividends at the annual rate of **$1.00** per share payable in equal quarterly installments beginning on **July 1**, 2006. Cash dividends on Preferred shares shall be cumulative from the first dividend payment following the issuance of the share and shall be declared and paid, or set apart for payment, before any cash dividends shall be paid on the Common stock.

The date of these Articles of Amendment is **July 19, 2006**.

Each class and series of stock should have its own form of certificate that can be clearly distinguished from the others so that purchasers will know what they are buying.

Preferred Stock Certificates

A **PREFERRED STOCK CERTIFICATE** is in Appendix C. (see form 47, p.290.) The following is an example of such a certificate for 100 shares of preferred stock, series A, for Scrupulous Corp. Compare it to form 35 (**COMMON STOCK CERTIFICATE**). The back side of the certificate is similar to form 35.

sample of form 47: **Preferred Stock Certificate (Front Side)**

Certificate No.: **000001-PA**
No. of Preferred Shares, Series **A**: **10,000**

Scrupulous Corporation
PREFERRED STOCK, SERIES **A**

Incorporated under the laws of the State of **West Carolina**

Authorized Preferred Stock, Series **A**: **10,000** shares, No Par Value.

THIS CERTIFIES THAT **Della Driskell** is the owner of **10,000 shares** fully paid and nonassessable shares of the capital stock of **Scrupulous Corporation** transferable only on the books of the corporation by the holder of this certificate in person or by the holder's duly authorized attorney upon surrender of this certificate properly endorsed.

Upon request, and without charge, the corporation will provide written information as to the designations, preferences, limitations, and relative rights of all classes and series of shares and the authority of the board of directors to determine the same for future classes and series.

IN WITNESS WHEREOF, **Scrupulous Corporation** has caused this certificate to be signed by its duly authorized officers and its corporate seal to be affixed on **April 10, 2006**.

Raymond Rodriguez   ,
Raymond Rodriguez, President

Roberta Moore   ,
Roberta Moore, Secretary

CERTIFICATION OF SHARES BY SECRETARY

On occasion it may become necessary to verify the total number of shares to some third party (such as a government agency, lender, or investor). A **Certification of Secretary (of Outstanding Shares)** can be used for this purpose. An example of form 121 follows.

sample of form 121: **CERTIFICATION OF SECRETARY OF OUTSTANDING SHARES**

Certification of Secretary of

Scrupulous Corporation

I HEREBY CERTIFY that I am the Corporate Secretary of **Scrupulous Corporation** that I am the custodian of the stock records of said corporation, and that the total number of shares of the capital stock of the corporation issued and outstanding on **May 31, 2006**, is **100,000 no par value common** shares.

Signed and the seal of the Corporation affixed, **May 31, 2006**.

```
Seal of Scrupulous Corporation

        20✳06

   State of West Carolina
```

Roberta Moore
_____
Roberta Moore, Secretary

LOST OR DESTROYED STOCK CERTIFICATES

A stock certificate is not a share of stock. It is only the physical representation of a share. When a certificate gets lost or destroyed, it does not affect the ownership of the share represented. But losing a certificate can be a headache for the corporation and, therefore, for the shareholder.

Example:

Suppose a lost certificate representing 1,000 shares falls into the hands of a dishonest person who then sells the shares to an innocent buyer. If the corporation issues a new certificate for 1,000 shares to the original owner who lost the certificate, and the buyer later shows up with the original certificate asking to be recognized as a legitimate shareholder, suddenly the corporation may have more shares outstanding than it thought.

To prevent or at least minimize the damage caused by such an embarrassment, corporations have procedures for dealing with lost or destroyed certificates. They are usually found in the **BYLAWS** and are derived from the Uniform Commercial Code, not the business corporation statute.

Normally the **BYLAWS** will require the owner of a lost, stolen, or destroyed certificate to make certain representations to the corporation. A form like the **LOST OR DESTROYED STOCK CERTIFICATE INDEMNITY AGREEMENT AND AFFIDAVIT** may be used for these representations. (see form 48, p.292) In it, the shareholder agrees to indemnify the corporation if the replacement of the certificate results in any loss to the corporation (e.g., if the corporation later has to buy its own shares on the open market to issue to the good faith purchaser that later shows up in the way described in the previous example).

Sometimes corporations require the shareholder to purchase a security bond to protect the corporation against such losses. On the following page is an example of form 48 completed.

sample of form 48: Lost or Destroyed Stock Certificate
Indemnity Agreement and Affidavit

Lost or Destroyed Stock Certificate Indemnity Agreement and Affidavit

The undersigned, being duly sworn, hereby affirms the following:

1. The undersigned is record holder of **500** shares (the "Shares") of the stock of **Scrupulous Corporation** (the "Corporation"). The Shares were represented by stock certificate number **000009** issued on **May 1, 2006** (the "Certificate").

2. The undersigned is the sole owner of the Shares, having never endorsed, delivered, transferred, assigned, or otherwise disposed of them or the Certificate in such a way as to give any other person any interest in the Shares.

3. The undersigned has duly searched for the Certificate, has been unable to find it, and believes the Certificate to be lost, destroyed, or stolen.

4. In order to induce the Corporation to issue a new stock certificate to replace the Certificate, the undersigned agrees to indemnify, defend, and hold harmless the Corporation, its shareholders, directors, and officers from any and all claims, losses, or damages whatsoever arising out of or related in any manner to the Certificate or arising out of the issuance of a replacement certificate.

Dated: **September 5, 2006**   _Hugh Hardy_
                                                 Hugh Hardy

STATE OF   **New York**

COUNTY OF   **Westchester**

On **September 5**, **2006**, there personally appeared before me, **Hugh Hardy**, who ❑ is personally known to me ☒ produced **New York driver's license** as identification, and being duly sworn on oath stated that the facts stated in the above Affidavit are true.

John Galt
John Galt
Notary Public

My Commission Expires: **June 30, 2008**

chapter 7

Shareholders' Relationships and Meetings

As co-owners of a business, shareholders must try to cooperate on some level with each other and with the directors they have chosen to oversee the business. The relationship varies with the size and type of the business and with the personalities involved.

LIVING WITH SHAREHOLDERS

The relationships among the officers, directors, and shareholders of corporations vary from outright hostility to absolute unity of purpose. Remarkably, the law accommodates all these varied relationships, allowing cooperation when it is possible and remedies when they are necessary. The dynamics of the relationships vary with the number of shareholders.

Shareholders and Close Corporations

Close corporations are small in the sense that they have few shareholders. What makes them close is that the shareholders, being few in number, are able to take a close interest in the business. Usually the shareholders are also directors, officers, or both. Often they are all members of the same family.

Disputes among the shareholders, officers, and directors of close corporations are frequent enough, but usually they take the form of warring camps within a family—literally or figuratively. There is little opportunity for the officers or directors as groups to ally themselves against the shareholders because the relationships are too intertwined.

Most state laws allow for special treatment of close corporations. Some corporate statutes regulate them as a separate category. Others govern all corporations by the same set of rules, but allow smaller corporations to adopt rules recognizing their special circumstances. The MBCA, for example, allows corporations with fifty or fewer shareholders to dispense with the board of directors (MBCA, Sec. 8.01(c)) and give its function to the shareholders directly.

Shareholders and Medium Corporations

Between close corporations and the corporate giants of the world are a great many medium-sized corporations. Shareholder relationships often seem most difficult in these companies. They are too large to allow the shareholders to feel that they are in direct control, and yet not so large that the shareholders feel unable to have any influence.

They are difficult from a regulatory standpoint, too. Medium-sized corporations are often on the edge between the loose regulation applied to privately owned companies, and the much more stringent regulation burdening publicly owned companies. Too frequently the regulatory burden falls heavily on medium-sized companies, which often feel too strapped for cash to hire expensive lawyers.

A lot of the regulatory burden has to do with shareholder relationships—raising capital and keeping shareholders adequately informed. If shareholder relations are hostile, the danger of expensive litigation is high.

Shareholders and Very Large Corporations

A corporation with a large number of shareholders is likely under the effective control of its officers and directors. There may be a few influential shareholders, but the great majority of shareholders never attend a shareholders meeting or even meet the people in control. The Securities and Exchange Commission will regulate shareholder relations in such a corporation, but the corporation will have the legal staff and funds to deal with the regulators with minimum inconvenience. This chapter is directed to close corporations and those on the smaller side of the medium-sized group.

SHAREHOLDERS' MEETINGS

The law requires one shareholders' meeting a year and calls it the *annual meeting*. Although the meeting is required, failure to hold it on the date specified in the **BYLAWS** is not a serious problem for smaller corporations. You can hold it on a different date and call it the substitute annual meeting. If a year passes without such a meeting, the shareholders are entitled to complain and force a meeting by going to court.

Often **BYLAWS** will set a specific date every year on which the annual meeting is to be held. Frequently the date is inconvenient and must be changed. If it is, the meeting, whenever held, is properly called a substitute annual meeting. A more convenient arrangement is for the **BYLAWS** to allow the directors some flexibility in choosing the date of the annual meeting. The date should be a sufficient amount of time after the close of the fiscal year to allow the financial reports for the year to be completed and distributed to the shareholders before the meeting. Thus, most annual meetings are held in the spring, after the close of the fiscal year on the preceding December 31st.

The date for the annual meeting as set in the **BYLAWS** may be changed by amending the **BYLAWS**. On the following page is a resolution amending the bylaws to allow for a flexible meeting date. Next is a directors' resolution setting a specific date, time, and place for the annual meeting within the period allowed by the amended **BYLAWS**. Most **BYLAWS** already allow flexibility as to the time and location of the meeting; although, a few require the meeting to be held at the company's principle offices.

The second example may also be modified to set the time and place for a substitute annual meeting by inserting the word "substitute" as appropriate. (Form 51 already does this for you.)

sample of form 49: DIRECTORS' CONSENT TO ACTION AMENDING BYLAWS
CHANGING THE DATE FOR THE ANNUAL MEETING

Consent to Action without Formal Meeting by the Directors of Scrupulous Corporation

The undersigned directors of the corporation hereby adopt the following resolution:

RESOLVED, that **Article 2, Section 1** of the bylaws of the corporation is amended to read in its entirety as follows:

"Section 1. Annual meeting. The annual meeting of the shareholders shall be held on any day of the month of **May** of each year as may be determined by the board of directors."

This resolution shall be effective at **4 p**.m. on the **4th** of **January**, **2006**.

Henry Hardy
Henry Hardy,
Director

Roberta Moore
Roberta Moore,
Director

Raymond Rodriguez
Raymond Rodriguez,
Director

---

sample of form 50: DIRECTORS' CONSENT TO ACTION SETTING THE TIME AND PLACE
OF THE ANNUAL MEETING

Consent to Action without Formal Meeting by the Directors of Scrupulous Corporation

The undersigned directors of the corporation hereby adopt the following resolution:

RESOLVED, that, pursuant to Article 2, Section 1 of the bylaws of the corporation, the annual meeting of shareholders shall take place at 10:00 a.m. on the 5th day of May, 2006 at the ballroom of the Airport Hotel, Pleasant Cove, West Carolina, and further

RESOLVED, that officers of the corporation are authorized and directed to give such notice of the meeting to shareholders of record on April 20, 2006 as may be required by law and the bylaws of the corporation.

This resolution shall be effective at **10 a**.m. on the **3rd** of **April**, **2006**.

Henry Hardy
Henry Hardy,
Director

Roberta Moore
Roberta Moore,
Director

Raymond Rodriguez
Raymond Rodriguez,
Director

sample of form 52: **Directors' Consent to Action Calling for a Special Shareholders' Meeting**

Consent to Action without Formal Meeting by the Directors of Scrupulous Corporation

The undersigned directors of the corporation hereby adopt the following resolution:

RESOLVED, that, pursuant to Article **2**, Section **2** of the bylaws of the corporation, a special meeting of shareholders shall take place at **10:00 a**.m. on the **15th** day of **November** at **the ballroom of the Airport Hotel, Pleasant Cove, West Carolina**, and further

RESOLVED, that the meeting is called for the following purpose(s):

To consider a proposal by the directors to relocate the company's business to New City, West Carolina.

and further

RESOLVED, that the appropriate officers of the corporation are authorized and directed to give such notice of the meeting to shareholders of record on **November 1, 2006** as may be required by law and bylaws of the corporation.

This resolution shall be effective at **10 a**.m. on the **2nd** of **October, 2006**.

Henry Hardy   *Roberta Moore*   *Raymond Rodriguez*

Henry Hardy,   Roberta Moore,   Raymond Rodriguez,
Director   Director   Director

Special Meetings

The company may also call a shareholders' meeting at any time and for whatever purpose may be useful. Officers and directors usually do not enjoy the process of planning and conducting shareholders meetings, so extra ones are rare. If an item of business can wait for the next annual meeting, it probably will, but sometimes it cannot wait. For example, if the company is merging with another company, the board of directors is likely to call a special meeting.

The statutes, and probably the **Bylaws,** will allow a variety of people to call such meetings. If only the board of directors could do it, other than the annual meeting, there would be no way for the shareholders to meet and discuss the bad job being done by the board of directors.

The following examples are calls for meetings made by the directors, the president, and a group of shareholders representing more than 10% of the outstanding shares of the corporation. A **President's Call for Special Meeting of the Shareholders** is in Appendix C. (see form 53, p.297.) There is also a **Shareholder's Call for Special Meeting of the Shareholders**. (see form 54, p.298.)

sample of form 53: **PRESIDENT'S CALL FOR SPECIAL MEETING OF THE SHAREHOLDERS**

President's Call for Special Meeting of the Shareholders

To the Secretary of **Scrupulous Corporation**

Pursuant to Article **2**, Section **2** of the bylaws of the Corporation, there is hereby called a special meeting of the shareholders of the Corporation to be held on **March 22, 2006**, at **10:00 a**.m., at **the corporation's conference room**, for the following purpose(s):

discussion and vote on whether new warehouse should be purchased

You are hereby authorized and directed to give such notice of the meeting to shareholders of record on **March 1, 2001** as may be required by law and the bylaws of the Corporation.

Dated: **February 23, 2006**

Raymond Rodriguez
Raymond Rodriguez, President

---

sample of form 54: **SHAREHOLDERS' CALL FOR SPECIAL MEETING OF THE SHAREHOLDERS—**

Shareholders' Call for Special Meeting of the Shareholders

To the Secretary of **Scrupulous Corporation**

Pursuant to Article **2**, Section **2** of the bylaws of the Corporation, the undersigned shareholders of **Scrupulous Corporation**, representing not less than one-tenth of the shares entitled to vote on the issues described below, hereby request that the President call a special meeting of the shareholders of the Corporation to be held on **March 1, 2006**, at **10:00 a**.m., at **the corporation's conference room**, for the following purpose(s):

discussion and vote on whether new warehouse should be purchased

You are hereby authorized and directed to give such notice of the meeting to shareholders of record on **March 1, 2001** as may be required by law and the bylaws of the Corporation.

Dated: **February 23, 2006**

Henry Hardy
Henry Hardy; 10,000 shares
Calvin Collier
Calvin Collier; 2,500 shares

NOTE: *Do not forget that any action that can be taken by the shareholders in a meeting can be taken without a meeting by written consent. (see Chapter 3.)*

Notice of Meetings

Unless the right is waived (using form 58, which will be discussed later), shareholders must have written notice of any meeting held. The corporate secretary usually is responsible for making sure the notice is sent. If the secretary fails or refuses to do so (which sometimes happens when the meeting is called by the president or a group of disgruntled shareholders), the person or group responsible for calling the meeting may send out the notice.

Record Date

The ownership of many large corporations changes constantly. The ownership of a close corporation may never change. When change is constant, there must be some way of deciding which of the shareholders will get notice. For that reason, a convenient date is chosen and shareholders of record on that *record date* are given notice.

Of course, it may be that someone who is a shareholder on that date may not be a shareholder when the meeting comes around. If that is the case, the owner on the record date may simply give a proxy to the new shareholder so that he or she can vote the recently transferred shares.

NOTE: *Corporations used to "close the books" on the record date and not record any transfers between that date and the date of the meeting, but that is now a rare practice.*

The **BYLAWS** may provide rules for selecting the record date. If not, the MBCA allows the directors to choose a date within limits. (MBCA, Sec. 7.07.) The statute and **BYLAWS** probably have a default record date if the directors fail to select one.

The default date in the MBCA is the close of business the day before the first notice is given to shareholders. (MBCA, Sec. 7.05(d).) For close corporations in which shares are seldom if ever transferred, this default date is usually sufficient.

Usually, the notice of an annual meeting need not state the particular matters to be discussed; although, many corporations do so nevertheless.

Notice of Annual Meeting

There are some exceptions, however. Some matters (mergers and the like) are of such fundamental importance to the corporation that the shareholders are entitled to notice whenever such issues are up for a decision. If any matter other than the ordinary election of directors is to be discussed and voted on at an annual meeting, it would be wise to see your lawyer to make sure notice is adequate.

– Warning –

If the corporation is regulated by the Securities and Exchange Commission, the regulations require that substantial information be sent along with the notice. (Companies regulated by the Securities and Exchange Commission are beyond the scope of this book.)

Your **BYLAWS** will have a provision setting a window of time within which notice must be sent. The MBCA requires you to give notice not less than ten nor more than sixty days before the meeting. (MBCA, Sec. 7.05(a).)

Use the **NOTICE OF AN ANNUAL MEETING OF SHAREHOLDERS** to meet the notice requirements. (see form 55, p.299.) The same form may be used for a substitute annual meeting by inserting the word "substitute" as appropriate (i.e. before the word "Annual" in the title and so on). An example of such a notice follows.

sample of form 55: **NOTICE OF ANNUAL SHAREHOLDERS' MEETING**

Notice of Annual Meeting of the Shareholders of
Scrupulous Corporation

Date: **April 3, 2006**
TO: All Shareholders

The annual meeting of the shareholders of the Corporation will be a special meeting of the board of directors on **April 24, 2006**, at **11:00 a.**m., at **Dewey, Cheatham & Howe, 420 East 59th Street, Suite 2416 New York, NY**.

The purposes of the meeting are:
1.   **To elect directors.**
2.   **To transact such business as may properly come before the meeting and any adjournment or adjournments thereof.**

By order of the board of directors:

Roberta Moore
Roberta Moore,
Corporate Secretary

Notice of Special Meetings

The significant difference between the notice required for special meetings and that required for annual meetings is that, for special meetings, the purpose of the meeting must be described in the notice. The warning about companies regulated by the Securities and Exchange Commission on page 108 applies here as well. A **NOTICE OF A SPECIAL MEETING OF THE SHAREHOLDERS** is in Appendix C. (see form 56, p.300.) An example follows.

sample of form 56: **NOTICE OF SPECIAL MEETING OR THE SHAREHOLDERS**

Notice of Special Meeting of the Shareholders of Scrupulous Corporation

Date: **April 3, 2006**

TO: All Shareholders

The annual meeting of the shareholders of the Corporation will be a special meeting of the board of directors on **April 24, 2006**, at **11:00 a.**m., at **420 East 59th Street, Suite 2416 New York, NY**.

The purposes of the meeting are:

Discuss and vote on merger with Honor Corporation. (Lunch at The Pizza Palace will follow meeting.)

By order of the board of directors:

Roberta Moore
Roberta Moore,
Corporate Secretary

Secretary's Affidavit

The law requires that notice be sent; not that the secretary sign an affidavit to that effect. However, sometimes disputes about the validity of a corporate action may arise months or years after it is taken. A written record that the proper notice was given can be a life saver. An **AFFIDAVIT OF MAILING** provides such a record. (see form 57, p.301.) It should be kept in the corporate minute book along with the minutes of the meeting. The odd phrase, "caused...to be deposited," covers the likelihood that the secretary did not actually mail the notice, but ordered it done. An example follows.

sample of form 57: **AFFIDAVIT OF MAILING (CORPORATE SECRETARY)**

Affidavit of Mailing

The undersigned, being duly sworn, hereby affirms the following:

1.   I am the Corporate Secretary of **Scrupulous Corporation** (the "Corporation").

2.   On **May 18, 2006**, I caused notice of the **annual** meeting of the shareholders of the Corporation to be deposited in the United States Post Office at **New York, NY**, in sealed envelopes, postage prepaid, addressed to each shareholder of the Corporation of record on **May 15, 2006** at his or her last known address as it appeared on the books of the Corporation.

3.   A copy of such notice is attached to and incorporated by reference into this affidavit.

Date: **May 19, 2006**

Roberta Moore
Roberta Moore,
Secretary

STATE OF   **New York**

COUNTY OF   **Jamaica**

On **May 19, 2006**, there personally appeared before me, **Roberta Moore**, who, being duly sworn, deposed and said that he/she is the Secretary of **Scrupulous Corporation**, and that the facts stated in the above Affidavit are true.

John Galt
John Galt
Notary Public
My Commission Expires: **June 30, 2008**

Waiver of Notice

Like notice of a directors' meeting (see Chapter 5), the notice of a shareholders' meeting may be waived. Waivers should be kept with the minutes of the meeting. If notice is not required, of course it need not be waived. So mention of an annual meeting in the **SHAREHOLDER'S WAIVER OF NOTICE** is only for those annual meetings that include matters for which notice is required by statute. (see form 58, p.302.) If you are doing any such thing in which notice would be required by statute, you should be in contact with your lawyer. An example of a waiver follows.

sample of form 58: **SHAREHOLDER'S WAIVER OF NOTICE**

Shareholder's Waiver of Notice

The undersigned Shareholder(s) of **Scrupulous Corporation** hereby waive any and all notice required by law or by the articles of incorporation or bylaws of the Corporation and consent to the holding of ❑ the annual ☒ a special meeting of the shareholders of the corporation on **June 18, 2006** at **7:00 p**. m., at **the corporation's headquarters conference room** for the following purposes:

Election of directors and any other matters.

Raymond Rodriguez   Date: *6/18/06*
Shareholder

Henry Hardy   Date: *6/18/06*
Shareholder

Calvin Collier   Date: *June 18, 2006*
Shareholder

Della Driskell   Date: *6/18/06*
Shareholder

PLANNING AND CONDUCTING MEETINGS

Getting ready for a shareholders' meeting is not a welcome task, but it is an important one. In the corporate giants of the world, there are people whose job descriptions include planning the annual meeting. In smaller companies, the job falls to people who already have a desk full of things to do and are therefore tempted to cut corners. Shareholder relations are often more sensitive in the smaller companies than the larger, so avoid the temptation if you can. It may be the only chance you have to meet your shareholders. The bad news is that a lot of shareholders do not go to annual meetings unless they are already unhappy.

Never forget that the company (or at least the group of people who run the company) is on display. Your good attitude and careful preparation may soothe a concerned shareholder. An attitude that gives the shareholders the impression that the meeting is only a necessary inconvenience may give the shareholders the idea that that is what you think of them, too.

Lawyers   Unless you know for sure that the meeting will be uneventful and the shareholders docile, it may be a good idea to have your lawyer there. If you know there will be angry shareholders present or that there is a possibility of cumulative voting (see "Voting" starting on page 117), you definitely want your lawyer available at the meeting. Always remember that the shareholders are taking what you say seriously.

Example:

One CEO was carefully warned by his lawyer that even informal predictions or representations made at a meeting might be held against the CEO later, if some shareholder bought or sold shares relying on that information. At the meeting, the CEO, understandably excited about the company's prospects, found it hard not to predict the future. In front of the assembled shareholders, he turned to the lawyer and asked, "Can I speak off the record?" The lawyer said "No."

You are responsible for what you say. By forgetting that and asking the lawyer's permission to ignore his advice, the CEO had inadvertently given the shareholders the impression that maybe what he was saying was in some way not reliable.

Place for Meeting

Most **Bylaws** allow the meeting to be held at any place the directors choose. Officers and directors are likely to choose the place most convenient for them. That may be, but is not necessarily, the best choice. If there is room for the meeting at the company offices and you are enthusiastic or at least content to allow the shareholders to have a close look at the operation, then it is a good location. If you cannot make a good impression, or if the shareholders would be uncomfortable there, think about a meeting room off the premises.

Agenda

An *agenda* for any meeting is a good idea. It does not have to be distributed to the shareholders, but may be. An **Agenda of Meeting of the Shareholders** is included in Appendix C. (see form 59, p.303.)

Script

A *script* is what each person will say at the meeting, word-for-word. A script looks unnecessarily elaborate, but can be very important, especially if the person presiding is uncomfortable being in charge of formal meetings. It can make the meeting appear more "professional" to the shareholders attending the meeting. It should be distributed to anyone with a part to play.

An example of an **Agenda** can be found below, and an example of a script for a meeting begins on page 114. Your **Bylaws** may designate a person, usually the president or the chairperson of the board, to preside at shareholders' meetings. Usually the **Bylaws** allow that person to designate an alternate.

sample of form 59: **Agenda of Meeting of the Shareholders**

Agenda of Meeting of the Shareholders of Scrupulous Corporation

Date of Meeting: **June 18, 2006**

1. Call to order and welcome of shareholders and guests by the President.
2. Announcement regarding call of meeting, notice, and presence of a quorum by the Secretary.
3. Report on business developments since the last share holders' meeting and discussion of financial statements.
4. Election of directors.
5. Ratification of independent accountants.
6. [Other matters specified in the notice.]
7. Other matters.
8. Adjournment.

Sample **SCRIPT OF A SHAREHOLDERS' MEETING**

Script
Annual Meeting of Shareholders
Scrupulous Corporation
Date of Meeting: [date]

PRESIDENT: The annual meeting of the shareholders of Scrupulous Corporation is called to order. My name is [name] and I am President of the Company. I would very much like to welcome all of our shareholders. It is a pleasure to have you here at the company's offices, and I hope your visit is enjoyable.

We have some other distinguished guests here today that I would like to recognize. I will ask each to stand and be recognized, but for the sake of time, I ask you to hold any applause until the last introduction is complete.

First is a representative of our independent accountants, [Mr./Ms. Name]. of the firm of [Firm name], who will be available throughout the meeting to answer any questions you may have about the financial statements you have received.

Next is [Mr./Ms. Name] of the law firm [Firm name], our company attorney.

Next I am pleased to introduce the members of the board of directors who are present and who have contributed in a very significant way to the company's success during the last year: [Names of board members.]

Seated next to me are the Chief Financial Officer of the Company, [Mr./Ms. Name] and the Secretary of the Company, [Mr./Ms. Name] who will be speaking to you in a moment.

Finally, we are pleased to have as a special guest here [Mr./Ms. Name] who was the company's top salesperson for the past year. I hope you will have an opportunity to meet and offer your personal thanks to [First Name] for the outstanding job [he/she] and the other company employees have done this past year.

I now ask the Secretary to report on the call of the meeting.

SECRETARY: Thank you, [Mr./Ms.] President. Pursuant to the bylaws of the corporation, the board of directors, by resolution adopted [Date] called this annual meeting of the shareholders of [Name of corporation] and established [Record date] as the record date for the determination of shareholders entitled to notice of and to vote at this meeting.

Notice of the meeting was mailed to the shareholders of record on [Date]. My affidavit regarding the mailing is on file with the company.

An alphabetical list of the shareholders and their addresses and number of shares held by each as of the record date is available at this meeting for reference and has been available for inspection for the period required by the bylaws of the Company.

Of the [Number of outstanding shares] shares of common stock of the company outstanding on the record date, shareholders holding [Number of shares represented at the meeting] are present at this meeting in person or by proxy. This number represents [Percentage of outstanding shares represented at the meeting] which number constitutes a quorum for the transaction of business.

PRESIDENT: Thank you, [Name]. A quorum being present, I declare this meeting duly constituted for the transaction of all business. Before we begin the matters to be voted on by shareholders, I would like to ask [Mr./Ms. Name], our Chief Financial Officer, to briefly report on developments of the past year.

CFO: [CFO's report. Questions from the shareholders regarding report.]

PRESIDENT: Thank you, [Name]. [Additional comments by the President on the CFO's report or the Company generally.]

Next we go to the items to be voted on by shareholders. The nominating committee of your board of directors has nominated all of the current board members to stand for reelection. All of the members have served in that capacity for some time, and I believe you are familiar with their qualifications and their excellent service.

Voting for the directors today will be by ballot. I believe you were given a ballot when you arrived at the meeting, but if any more are needed, please let me know now. [Pause to distribute additional ballots if necessary.] I now ask if there are any other nominations for the board of directors from the shareholders present at the meeting.

PRESELECTED SHAREHOLDER #1: I move that the nominations for directors be closed.

PRESELECTED SHAREHOLDER #2: I second the motion.

PRESIDENT: Will those in favor of closing the nominations please so indicate. [Pause] Will those opposed please so indicate. [Pause] The motion is carried, and nominations for directors of the corporation are closed.

I now ask that you mark your ballots in the spaces provided. When you are finished they will be collected and counted. [Pause for voting]

While the votes are being counted, I suggest that we proceed to the next matter to be decided, the ratification of [Firm name] as the company's independent auditors. I offer the following resolution:

"RESOLVED, that the appointment by the board of directors of [Firm name], Certified Public Accountants, as independent auditors for the company in connection with the fiscal year ended [Ending date of the current fiscal year] is hereby approved, ratified, and confirmed."

SHAREHOLDER #1: I move that the resolution presented regarding the appointment of independent auditors be adopted.

SHAREHOLDER #2: I second the motion.

PRESIDENT: Voting on the resolution presented will be by voice vote. All those in favor of adopting the resolution presented please so indicate. [Pause] All those opposed please so indicate. [Pause] Hearing no votes in opposition to the motion, I declare the motion duly adopted.

[Disposition of other matters specified in the meeting notice.]

I now ask the Secretary to report on the results of the election of directors.

SECRETARY: [Mr./Ms.] President, each of the nominees for director has received at least [Number in excess of majority] votes which is in excess of the number required for election.

PRESIDENT: Thank you. Each having received a number of votes exceeding that required for election, I declare the nominees for director duly elected to serve as directors.

If there is no further business to come before the meeting, I would entertain a motion that the meeting be adjourned.

SHAREHOLDER #1: I move that the meeting be adjourned.

SHAREHOLDER #2: I second the motion.

PRESIDENT: All those in favor please so indicate. [Pause] All those opposed please so indicate. [Pause] Thanks to all of you for your presence and cooperation. I declare this meeting to be adjourned.

VOTING

Unlike directors, shareholders do not have to cast their votes in person. A director is an elected servant of the corporation and accordingly owes the corporation his or her best personal judgment on the issues up for vote. A shareholder owns shares for his or her own interest and may chose whether to vote and how. More practically, if the thousands of shareholders of a corporate giant had to personally attend meetings in order to vote, there would never be a *quorum,* and no decisions could be made.

Voting by Proxy

A shareholder's *absentee ballot* is called a *proxy* form. It is, of course, not really an absentee ballot. It is a kind of power of attorney in which the shareholder appoints an agent to attend the meeting and cast the shareholder's vote. The shareholder may allow the proxy unlimited discretion to decide how the vote should be cast or may tell the proxy exactly how the vote must be cast.

Like the buying and selling of stock, all voting by proxy is regulated to some degree by the U.S. Securities and Exchange Commission and by state regulators. Anyone who *solicits a proxy* (that is, talks a shareholder into giving his or her proxy to the person asking for it) using false or misleading information is guilty of a kind of fraud and is subject to severe penalties. Anyone who solicits more than a very few proxies to vote the shares of a corporation, and the management of companies with large numbers of shareholders, may be subject to very elaborate reporting and notification requirements, which are beyond the scope of this book.

For that reason, the proxy forms in this book are not intended to be used when a person seeks to gather multiple proxies in the hope of influencing the outcome of an election. However, they are appropriate when a shareholder, for the sake of convenience or necessity, wishes another person to cast the shareholder's vote under various circumstances.

The **APPOINTMENT OF PROXY** form gives the proxy general voting powers for a period of time. (see form 60, p.304.) It is usable at any shareholders' meeting that occurs while it is in effect. Proxy forms are valid for eleven months unless another expiration date is given on the form. (MBCA, Sec. 7.22(c).) Another **APPOINTMENT OF PROXY** form appoints a proxy for just one meeting. (see form 61, p.305.) Still another **APPOINTMENT OF PROXY** form limits the vote to one meeting with specific instructions on how to vote. (see form 62, p.306.)

Usually, the shareholder can revoke a proxy appointment at any time up to the moment a vote is cast. The exception is when it is *coupled with an interest*, meaning that the proxy has some ownership interest (e.g., a security lien) or other contractual right specified by statute. (MBCA Sec. 7.22(d).)

Examples of different proxy statements follow. The phrase "with full power of substitution" means the proxy may appoint a substitute proxy. The examples below do not deal with the possibility of cumulative voting. (see discussion on page 120.) If cumulative voting is reasonably likely to occur, specific instructions should be added to the proxy form as appropriate.

sample of form 60: **APPOINTMENT OF PROXY (GENERAL)**

Appointment of Proxy

The undersigned Shareholder (the "Shareholder") of **Scrupulous Corporation** (the "Corporation") hereby appoints **Hugh Hardy** as proxy, with full power of substitution, for and in the name of the Shareholder to attend all shareholders meetings of the Corporation and to act, vote, and execute consents with respect to any or all shares of the Corporation belonging to the Shareholder as fully and to the same extent and effect as the Shareholder. This appointment may be revoked by the Shareholder at any time; but, if not revoked, shall continue in effect until **March 31, 2007**.

The date of this proxy is **October 3, 2006**.

Hugh Hardy
_____
Shareholder

---

sample of form 61: **APPOINTMENT OF PROXY (FOR PARTICULAR MEETING)**

Appointment of Proxy

The undersigned Shareholder (the "Shareholder") of **Scrupulous Corporation** (the "Corporation") hereby appoints **Hugh Hardy** as proxy, with full power of substitution, for and in the name of the Shareholder to attend the ❑ annual ☒ special shareholders' meeting of the Corporation to be held on **October 12, 2006**, at **7:00 p**.m., at **the corporation's headquarters conference room**, and to act and vote at such meeting and any adjournment thereof with respect to any or all shares of the Corporation belonging to the Shareholder as fully and to the same extent and effect as the Shareholder. Any appointment of proxy previously made by the Shareholder for such meeting is hereby revoked.

The date of this proxy is **October 3, 2006**.

Hugh Hardy
Shareholder

---

sample of form 62: **APPOINTMENT OF PROXY (FOR A SPECIFIC ACTION)**

Appointment of Proxy

The undersigned Shareholder (the "Shareholder") of **Scrupulous Corporation** (the "Corporation") hereby appoints **Hugh Hardy** as proxy, with full power of substitution, for and in the name of the Shareholder to attend the ❑ annual ☒ special shareholders' meeting of the Corporation to be held on **October 12, 2006**, at **7:00 p**.m., at **the corporation's headquarters conference room**, and to act and vote at such meeting and any adjournment thereof with respect to any or all shares of the Corporation belonging to the Shareholder as directed below and in his or her discretion as to any other business that may properly come before the meeting or any adjournment:

To vote on filling the current vacancy on the board of directors, and to vote for the purchase of a building for new corporate offices.

Any appointment of proxy previously made by the Shareholder for such meeting is hereby revoked.

The date of this proxy is **October 3, 2006**.

Calvin Collier
Shareholder

Cumulative Voting

Shareholder elections are a fairly harsh version of democracy. The majority rules, and there is not much in the way of a *Bill of Rights* for the minority. Usually, if you control 51% of the outstanding shares, you get to choose all the directors. However, there are some curbs on this majority tyranny. One of them is *cumulative* voting.

Under this system, each shareholder multiplies the number of shares he or she controls times the number of directors up for election. The result is the number of votes each shareholder may cast, and he or she may spread them around in any way—all for one nominee, equally among all nominees, etc. If you own enough shares, and the math works out, you may be able to elect at least one director by yourself even though you own less than a majority of all the shares.

Not every corporation allows its shareholders this right. It depends on state law and the **ARTICLES OF INCORPORATION**. If your corporation allows cumulative voting and you think some shareholder may invoke that right at an upcoming meeting, it would be doubly wise to invite your lawyer to the meeting. The vote counting can be a nightmare, and it frequently comes up when the shareholder invoking the right is already angry at the current board of directors. Voting by ballot in a cumulative voting election is practically essential.

Ballot Voting

Some states require that shareholder votes be cast by ballot rather than by voice vote or some other means. Elsewhere it is optional. For corporations with more than a handful of shareholders, in matters in which there is any substantial disagreement, ballot voting is a practical necessity for two reasons—it provides a written record of how votes were cast and it makes counting votes much easier.

Regarding the latter, think of the situation in which you have three shareholders sitting in a row. One owns ten shares, one owns fifty, and the third, one-hundred. Two shareholders vote "yes" and one votes "no." Has the issue passed? Unless you can look at each shareholder and tell how many shares he or she owns, you do not know.

A **SHAREHOLDER BALLOT** that might be used in an election of directors is in Appendix C. (see form 63, p.307.) An example follows.

sample of form 63: **SHAREHOLDER BALLOT**

Shareholder Ballot

Annual Shareholders Meeting of

Scrupulous Corporation

Held on: **April 7, 2006**

The undersigned shareholder and/or proxy holder votes the shares described below as follows:

FOR ELECTION OF DIRECTORS:

Name of director	Shares voted for	Shares voted against
1. **Henry Hardy**	150	0
2. **Raymond Rodriguez**	150	0
3. **Della Driskell**	150	0
4. **Calvin Collier**	100	50
5. **Hugh Hardy**	150	0
6. **Roberta Moore**	150	0

Number of shares voted by the undersigned in person: **850**
Number of shares voted by the undersigned as proxy: **50**
Total shares voted by this ballot: **900**

A copy of the proxy form(s) authorizing the undersigned to vote by proxy as above is attached to this ballot.

Hugh Hardy
(signature)

Hugh Hardy
(name printed)

KEEPING RECORDS

The **Minutes** of the shareholders' meeting are the official memory of what happened. (See the discussion of minutes in Chapter 3.) Examples of minutes relating to shareholder meetings follow.

sample of form 5: **Minutes of Annual meeting of the Shareholders**

Minutes of the Annual Meeting of the Shareholders of Scrupulous Corporation

The annual meeting of the Shareholders of the Corporation was held on the date and at the time and place set forth in the written notice of meeting, or waiver of notice signed by shareholders, and attached to the minutes of this meeting.

The following shareholders were present:

Shareholder	No. of Shares
Henry Hardy	**20,000**
Raymond Rodriguez	**15,000**
Della Driskell	**15,000**
Calvin Collier	**15,000**
Hugh Hardy	**20,000**
Roberta Moore	**15,000**

The meeting was called to order and it was moved, seconded, and carried that **Raymond Rodriguez** act as Chairman and that **Roberta Moore** act as Secretary.

A roll call was taken and the Chairman noted that all of the outstanding shares of the Corporation were represented in person or by proxy. Any proxies are attached to these minutes.

Minutes of the preceding meeting of the Shareholders, held on **January 7, 2006** were read and approved.

Upon motion duly made, seconded, and carried, the following were elected directors for the following year:

Calvin Collier   Hugh Hardy

Della Driskell   Roberta Moore

The President welcomed those present and introduced the following guests:

Representing Bean-Counter Associates: **Tex A. Voydence**

Representing Dewey, Cheatham & Howe: **Sue M. Goode**

(See Continuation Sheets)

There being no further business, the meeting adjourned.

Roberta Moore
Secretary

Approved: *Raymond Rodriguez*

Also as in the case of **MINUTES** of directors meetings, corporate secretaries are occasionally asked to produce official copies of the minutes. Form 12 in Appendix C is for certification of the minutes. (For certification of a particular resolution adopted by shareholders, use form 14.) The following are examples of these forms.

sample of form 12: **CERTIFIED COPY OF MINUTES OF MEETING OF THE SHAREHOLDERS**

Certified Copy of Minutes of Meeting of the Shareholders of Scrupulous Corporation

I HEREBY CERTIFY that I am the Corporate Secretary of **Scrupulous Corporation**, and that the attached is an accurate copy of the minutes of the meeting of the Shareholders of the corporation, held on **April 7, 2006**.

Signed and the seal of the Corporation affixed, **July 20, 2006**.

Seal of Scrupulous Corporation

20✳06

State of West Carolina

Roberta Moore
Roberta Moore,
Secretary

---

sample of form 14: **CERTIFIED COPY OF RESOLUTIONS ADOPTED BY THE SHAREHOLDERS**

Certified Copy of Resolutions Adopted by the Shareholders of Scrupulous Corporation

I HEREBY CERTIFY that I am the Corporate Secretary of **Scrupulous Corporation**, that the following is an accurate copy of resolution(s) adopted by the Shareholders of the corporation, effective **April 7, 2006**, and that such resolutions continue in effect as of the date of this certification:

"RESOLVED, that the appointment by the board of directors of Bean-Counter Associates, Certified Public Accountants, as independent auditors for the company in connection with the fiscal year ended February 28, 2006, is hereby approved, ratified, and confirmed."

Signed and the seal of the Corporation affixed, **July 20, 2006**.

Seal of Scrupulous Corporation

20✳06

State of West Carolina

Roberta Moore
Roberta Moore,
Secretary

Dividends

Chapter 6 mentioned that shareholders have two important rights. Chapter 7 dealt with voting, the first of those rights. This chapter deals with the second important right—the right to a share of the profits of the business. A *dividend* is a division of the corporation's profits among the shareholders.

ACCOUNTING ISSUES— MONEY FOR THE DIVIDEND

States have tried various financial tests for a corporation to determine whether it has enough cash, assets, or both to safely declare and pay a dividend. The MBCA forbids a dividend, if, after the dividend is paid, the company cannot pay its debts as they become due, or if its liabilities are greater than its assets. (MBCA, Sec. 6.40.)

NOTE: *For this purpose, liabilities include preferences owed to any preferred shareholders if the company were dissolved. Check with your accountant.*

The calculation may not be as straightforward as you imagine and the penalties for a director who votes for an illegal dividend—one that does not meet the test—are severe. The director may be personally liable for restoring the money to the corporation.

Dividends need not be paid in cash. They can be paid in property belonging to the corporation or in corporate shares.

THE ROLE OF DIRECTORS IN DECLARING DIVIDENDS

The right to receive a share of the company's profits is one of the basic rights of shareholders. You might think that it would be something the shareholders could vote on, but they cannot. Only the board of directors can declare a dividend for fear that, given the power to raid the corporate treasury, the shareholders might take more than is wise.

Record Date

As is the case with deciding who is entitled to vote shares of stock, there must be a way of determining the shareholders who are entitled to receive a dividend. The list is established as a *record date* chosen by the directors. (see Chapter 7.)

Cash Dividends— Common Stock

Common shareholders have a right as shareholders to share in the company's profits, but they do not have a right to a particular dividend. They only get a dividend when the directors decide it is time and pass a resolution declaring one. The directors can do this at irregular intervals. Many companies establish a policy of declaring regular dividends that the shareholders come to rely on. Nevertheless, the directors are free to forego a *regular dividend*, if they wish, by simply not declaring it.

The following are two resolutions, one in which the directors establish a policy of regular dividend payments, and one in which a single dividend is declared.

sample of form 64: **DIRECTORS' CONSENT TO ACTION**
ESTABLISHING A REGULAR QUARTERLY CASH DIVIDEND

Consent to Action without Formal Meeting by the Directors of

Scrupulous Corporation

The undersigned directors of the corporation hereby adopt the following resolution:

RESOLVED, that to the extent permitted by law, it is the intent of the board of directors that the corporation shall henceforth pay regular quarterly dividends on the common shares of the corporation in the amount of $0.25 per share of common stock issued and outstanding, and further

RESOLVED, that the declaration and payment of such regular dividends shall in every case be subject to the board's reasonable judgment as to their advisability at the time of such declaration.

This resolution shall be effective at **10 a.**m. on the **30th** of **June, 2006**.

Henry Hardy   *Roberta Moore*   *Raymond Rodriguez*
Henry Hardy,   Roberta Moore,   Raymond Rodriguez,
Director   Director   Director

---

sample of form 65: **DIRECTORS' CONSENT TO ACTION**
DECLARING A CASH DIVIDEND ON COMMON STOCK

Consent to Action without Formal Meeting by the Directors of

Scrupulous Corporation

The undersigned directors of the corporation hereby adopt the following resolution:

RESOLVED, that there is declared a cash dividend on the common shares of the corporation in the amount of $0.25 per share issued and outstanding, payable on October 15, 2006 to shareholders of record on October 1, 2006, and further

RESOLVED, that officers of the corporation are authorized and directed to take such actions as may be necessary or desirable to give effect to the above resolution and to properly record the payment of the dividend in the accounts of the company.

This resolution shall be effective at **10 a.**m. on the **30th** of **June 2006**.

Henry Hardy   *Roberta Moore*   *Raymond Rodriguez*
Henry Hardy, Director   Roberta Moore, Director   Raymond Rodriguez,
Director   Director   Director

Cash Dividends— Preferred Stock

The dividends paid on preferred shares are usually expressed as a percentage of the issue price.

Example:

If preferred shares with an annual dividend of $1.00 were sold by the corporation for $10 per share, the shares have a 10% annual dividend ($1.00 per share per year is 10% of the $10.00 purchase price). The resolution declaring the first quarterly dividend on those shares would declare a dividend of $0.25, as in the following example.

NOTE: *Remember that even preferred dividends may not be paid until each dividend is declared by the board of directors.*

sample of form 66: **DIRECTORS' CONSENT TO ACTION DECLARING A CASH DIVIDEND ON PREFERRED STOCK**

Consent to Action without Formal Meeting by the Directors of

Scrupulous Corporation

The undersigned directors of the corporation hereby adopt the following resolution:

RESOLVED, that there is declared a cash dividend on the preferred shares of the corporation in the amount of $0.25 per share issued and outstanding, payable on October 15, 2006 to shareholders of record on October 1, 2006, and further

RESOLVED, that officers of the corporation are authorized and directed to take such actions as may be necessary or desirable to give effect to the above resolution and to properly record the payment of the dividend in the accounts of the company.

This resolution shall be effective at **10:00 a**.m. on the **30th** of **June, 2006.**

Henry Hardy	*Roberta Moore*	*Raymond Rodriguez*
Henry Hardy, Director	Roberta Moore, Director	Raymond Rodriguez, Director

---

Stock Dividends

Dividends payable in stock of the corporation, rather than in cash or other property, do not affect the ownership of the company. Each existing shareholder gets new shares of stock and the shares are distributed among the shareholders *pro rata* (proportionally). So, if you own 10% of the outstanding shares of the corporation before the stock dividend, you own 10% after. There are just more shares outstanding.

Why do it then? Shareholders of publicly traded corporations usually do see a slight increase in the total market value of their shares after a stock dividend. A stock dividend reduces the per share market value of the stock, which may increase the number of investors who can afford to purchase the company's stock. If the number of potential investors increases, then so will the demand for the stock. For small companies with no market for their shares, there is little reason to do it unless you just want there to be more outstanding shares. It is a simple process, provided there are enough shares authorized in the Articles of Incorporation. If there are not enough authorized, then the articles must be amended by the shareholders to increase the number authorized. Because the shareholders do not own any more after the stock dividend than they did before, it should have no income tax effect.

A *stock split* may have the same effect as a stock dividend, but it is conceptually different. The effect is that the shareholders own more shares than they did before, but their percentage ownership of the company does not change. But rather than new shares being issued, the old outstanding shares are divided or *split* by some factor so that there are more than there were. Again, there is no tax effect.

The mechanism for effecting a split is more complicated than that for a stock dividend in most states. If the shares are par value shares, usually the Articles of Incorporation must be amended to reduce the par value. If the shares are *no par*, an amendment may not be necessary, depending on whether state law requires the articles to include the *stated capital per share*.

Logically, a *reverse stock split* is the opposite. The old outstanding shares become fewer. If a stock split or reverse stock split involves a change in par value, it may be advisable to retrieve the old share certificates (because they will state the old par value) and replace them with new certificates.

If your company is in need of a stock split or reverse stock split (or if you do not have enough authorized shares for a stock dividend), you should consult your lawyer and accountant about the undoubtedly unique factors that will affect the process. One such factor you will have to consider is whether you have enough authorized shares to issue the new shares required by the dividend or stock split. (see Chapter 6.)

Following is an example of a resolution declaring a stock dividend.

sample of form 67: **Directors' Consent to Action Declaring a Stock Dividend**

Consent to Action without Formal Meeting by the Directors of Scrupulous Corporation

The undersigned directors of the corporation hereby adopt the following resolution:

RESOLVED, that there is declared a stock dividend on the common shares of the corporation at the rate of 1.5 share(s) of common stock for each share issued and outstanding, payable on October 15, 2006 to shareholders of record on October 1, 2006, and further

RESOLVED, that officers of the corporation are authorized and directed to take such actions as may be necessary or desirable to issue new stock certificates, to otherwise give effect to the above resolution, and to properly record the payment of the dividend and issuance of stock in the accounts and records of the corporation.

This resolution shall be effective at **3:00 p**.m. on the **30th** of **June, 2006.**

Henry Hardy
Henry Hardy, Director

Roberta Moore
Roberta Moore, Director

Raymond Rodriguez
Raymond Rodriguez, Director

Dividends Paid in Property Other than Cash or Shares of the Company

Sometimes a corporation will own property that it would like to give to its shareholders. The way to do it is with a *dividend in kind*. The property could be anything from land to paper clips, but most frequently it is paid in stock of some company *other than* the company paying the dividend.

Example:

Suppose your company owns a subsidiary it no longer wants. It could sell the subsidiary, or it could spin it off by giving it to the shareholders.

The following example of a resolution accomplishes such a dividend, but can be used for other kinds of property dividends by changing the description of the property as appropriate. Unlike a stock dividend or split, a dividend in kind may have very significant tax effects.

sample of form 68: **DIRECTORS' CONSENT TO ACTION DECLARING A DIVIDEND IN KIND**

Consent to Action without Formal Meeting by the Directors of

Scrupulous Corporation

The undersigned directors of the corporation hereby adopt the following resolution:

RESOLVED, that there is declared a dividend on the common shares of the corporation payable in shares of Honor Corporation, a wholly owned subsidiary of Scrupulous Corporation at the rate of 2.0 share(s) of common stock for each share of this corporation issued and outstanding, payable on August 30, 2006 to shareholders of record on August 15, 2006, and further

RESOLVED, that officers of the corporation are authorized and directed to take such actions as may be necessary or desirable to issue stock certificates, to otherwise give effect to the above resolution, and to properly record the payment of the dividend and issuance of stock in the accounts and records of the appropriate corporation.

This resolution shall be effective at **10:00 a**.m. on the **30th** of **June, 2006.**

Henry Hardy
Henry Hardy, Director

Roberta Moore
Roberta Moore, Director

Raymond Rodriguez
Raymond Rodriguez, Director

Officers

Unlike shareholders and directors, officers *are* agents of the corporation and *do* represent the corporation with the power to bind it in contractual relationships. They carry out their function as individuals rather than through group decisions. As *executives*, they execute the policies of the directors.

NUMBER OF OFFICERS

How many officers does a corporation need? Modern corporate statutes allow wide flexibility in creating corporate offices. There is no requirement to have an officer bearing any specific title. However, there is little reason for a corporation to deviate from the standard list and many good reasons for sticking with it. The standard list includes a president, a vice president, and a secretary.

Often the secretary also holds the title and duties of the vice president and treasurer. It is common for one person to hold more than one office, but the same person should not be both president and secretary. Many documents require the signature of both and may not be signed twice by the same person.

State laws and contracting parties often presume (and in some cases require) that documents (notably deeds) will be signed by the president (or vice president) and attested (i.e., have the corporate seal attached) by the secretary.

Any corporation will soon find that these two offices are a practical necessity. Any other arrangement, although legal, would require unending explanation and justification to outsiders. (The next most useful office is that of an assistant secretary who can fill in to sign corporate documents when the secretary is not conveniently available.)

Beyond these basics, the possibilities are endless. Corporations have invented any number of imaginative titles such as first assistant vice president for public information. Among very large corporations, titles such as Chief Executive Officer (CEO), Chief Financial Officer (CFO), and Chief Operating Officer (COO) have gained popularity. Ordinarily they have duties similar to those of a president or treasurer.

DUTIES OF OFFICERS

In addition to signing documents, the officers may be assigned a long list of general duties and, as agents of the company, may be assigned specific, temporary responsibilities as the need arises. The following five examples of bylaw provisions describe the standard duties for the officers indicated. They are written as they might appear in the company's **BYLAWS** (or a resolution to amend the bylaws, see Chapter 12) but the same job descriptions might also be used to describe an officer's duties in an employment contract (to be used on form 71).

Sample of **BYLAW PROVISION ESTABLISHING THE DUTIES OF THE PRESIDENT**

The President shall be the Chief Executive Officer of the corporation and, subject to the direction and control of the Board of Directors, shall supervise and manage the business affairs of the corporation and perform all duties incident to the office of President and other duties as may be assigned by the Board of Directors from time to time. The President shall have authority to sign, with the Secretary, an Assistant Secretary, or any other officer of the corporation duly authorized by the Board of Directors. The President may also share certificates of the corporation, deeds, deeds of trust, mortgages, bonds, contracts, or other instruments authorized by the Board of Directors to be executed by the corporation, unless authority to sign such instruments shall have been expressly delegated by the Board of Directors or required by law to be signed by some other officer or agent. The President shall, when present, preside at meetings of the Shareholders.

Sample of **BYLAW PROVISION ESTABLISHING THE DUTIES OF THE VICE PRESIDENT**

Any Vice President shall perform the duties of the President when the President is absent, unable, or unwilling to act. When so acting, a Vice President shall have the same powers and be subject to the same limitations as the President. Any Vice President shall have authority to sign, with the Secretary, an Assistant Secretary, or any other officer of the corporation duly authorized by the Board of Directors. The Vice President may also share certificates of the corporation, deeds, deeds of trust, mortgages, bonds, contracts, or other instruments authorized by the Board of Directors to be executed by the corporation, unless authority to sign such instruments shall have been expressly delegated by the Board of Directors or required by law to be signed by some other officer or agent. The Vice President shall also have and perform other duties as may be assigned by the Board of Directors from time to time.

Sample of **BYLAW PROVISION ESTABLISHING THE DUTIES OF THE SECRETARY**

The Secretary shall have such duties as may be assigned by the President or the Board of Directors from time to time and shall perform all duties incident to the office of Secretary including but not limited to the following: (1) Having custody and maintenance of the records of the corporation, including the stock transfer books, and authenticating the same when requested or required to do so. (2) Having custody of the seal of the corporation and affixing it to documents which are duly authorized to be executed under seal. (3) With the President or a Vice President, the signing of certificates for shares of the corporation, the issuance of which have been duly authorized. (4) Giving notice of all meetings of shareholders, directors, and committees as required by law and the bylaws of the corporation. (5) Preparing minutes of all such meetings in properly organized and maintained books. (6) Preparing shareholder lists prior to each shareholders' meeting as required by law and the bylaws of the corporation.

Sample of **Bylaw Provision Establishing**
the Duties of the Assistant Secretary

Any Assistant Secretary shall perform the duties of the Secretary when the Secretary is absent, unable, or unwilling to act. When so acting, an Assistant Secretary shall have the same powers and be subject to the same limitations as the Secretary. Any Assistant Secretary, with the President or a Vice President, may sign certificates for shares of the corporation, the issuance of which have been duly authorized. An Assistant Secretary shall perform such other duties as may be assigned by the President or the Board of Directors from time to time.

Sample of **Bylaw Provision Establishing the Duties of the Treasurer**

The Treasurer shall have such duties as may be assigned by the President or the Board of Directors from time to time and shall perform all duties incident to the office of Treasurer including but not limited to the following: (1) Having custody of and responsibility for all funds and securities belonging to the corporation. (2) Receiving and giving receipts for moneys paid to the corporation from whatever source and the deposit of the same, in the name of the corporation, in depositories duly authorized by the corporation. (3) Maintaining appropriate accounts and records for the corporation as required by law. (4) Having charge of the preparation of financial statements of the corporation according to Generally Accepted Accounting Principles (GAAP).

The following is a *catch all* provision for the bylaws that allows the board of directors to create new offices without the need of amending the bylaws.

Sample of **Bylaw Provision Allowing for the Appointment**
of Additional Officers as the Board Sees Fit

In addition to the offices established pursuant to these bylaws, the board of directors may create additional offices and appoint additional officers from time to time.

APPOINTMENT AND TERMINATION OF OFFICERS

Officers are often appointed by the board of directors upon the recommendation of current officers, although recommendation is not necessary.

NOTE: *Directors are* **elected** *and officers are* **appointed**.

Following are two resolutions. The first appoints an officer, while the second appoints a whole slate of officers at once—a frequent occurrence when a corporation is organized or is acquired by new owners.

sample of form 69: **DIRECTORS' CONSENT TO ACTION APPOINTING A NEW OFFICER**

Consent to Action without Formal Meeting by the Directors of

Scrupulous Corporation

The undersigned directors of the corporation hereby adopt the following resolution:

RESOLVED, that Calvin Collier is appointed to the office of Vice President of the corporation effective **July 1, 2006** to hold such office until his death, resignation, retirement, removal, disqualification, or the appointment of a successor.

This resolution shall be effective at **10:00 a.**m. on the **19th** of **June, 2006**.

Henry Hardy
Henry Hardy, Director

Roberta Moore
Roberta Moore, Director

Raymond Rodriguez
Raymond Rodriguez, Director

---

sample of form 70: **DIRECTORS' CONSENT TO ACTION
APPOINTING A SLATE OF OFFICERS**

Consent to Action without Formal Meeting by the Directors
of
Scrupulous Corporation

The undersigned directors of the corporation hereby adopt the following resolution:

RESOLVED, that the following individuals are appointed to the offices indicated opposite their names, each of them to hold such office beginning on the effective date of appointment and until his or her death, resignation, retirement, removal, disqualification, or the appointment of a successor:

Name:	Office:	Effective date of appointment:
Raymond Rodriguez	President	February 1, 2006
Roberta Moore	Vice-President & Secretary	February 1, 2006
Henry Hardy	Treasurer	February 1, 2006

This resolution shall be effective at **3:00 p.**m. on the **16th** of **January, 2006**.

Henry Hardy *Roberta Moore* *Raymond Rodriguez*

Henry Hardy,	Roberta Moore,	Raymond Rodriguez,
Director	Director	Director

The Officer as Employee

An officer is always an agent of the corporation, but it is not always true that an officer is an employee of the corporation. For example, an officer may be the employee of a parent corporation who serves as an officer of a subsidiary as a convenience to the employer parent. Or the corporation may be a small family company in which a spouse serves as secretary or assistant secretary as a convenience to the person who runs the business.

If the officer is an employee, it may be desirable to have a written employment contract. There is a simple **EMPLOYMENT AGREEMENT** for a company officer in Appendix C. (see form 71, p.315.) Space is provided to fill in the appropriate job description for each officer. (To add an **INDEMNIFICATION AGREEMENT**, see form 92 and Chapter 11.)

Many employment agreements are, of course, much more elaborate. Following is an example of form 71 completed for the office of president.

sample of form 71: **Employment Agreement (President)**

Employment Agreement

This employment agreement is made by between **Raymond Rodriguez** (the "Employee") and **Scrupulous Corporation** (the "Corporation"). It is agreed by the Employee and the Corporation as follows:

1. The Board of Directors of the corporation has duly appointed the Employee to the office of **President** subject to the terms and conditions of this agreement.

2. Such appointment shall be effective on **January 1, 2006** at which time the Employee shall begin employment and assume the duties and authorities of **President**.

3. The duties of the **President** shall be as follows:

To act as Chief Executive Officer of the corporation and, subject to the direction and control of the Board of Directors, to supervise and manage the business affairs of the corporation, and to perform other duties as stated in the bylaws of the corporation. The President shall, when present, preside at meetings of the shareholders.

4. The Employee's salary and benefits during the term of this agreement shall be as stated in this paragraph and may be adjusted from time to time by action of the Board of Directors of the Corporation.

$50,000 per year, plus group life insurance, and health insurance for the employee and his wife and minor children.

5. Employment pursuant to this agreement shall be:

- ☒ for a period of **3** years beginning on the effective date stated above.

- ❏ at will and may be ended by the Employee or by action of the Board of Directors of the corporation at any time and for any reason.

This agreement was executed by the Employee and by the Corporation by authority of its Board of Directors on **December 18, 2005**.

Corporation: Employee:

By: *Henry Hardy*   *Raymond Rodriguez*
    Henry Hardy, President   Raymond Rodriguez, Director

The following is a directors' resolution authorizing the execution of the employment contract.

sample of form 72: **DIRECTORS' CONSENT TO ACTION AUTHORIZING AN OFFICER'S EMPLOYMENT AGREEMENT**

Consent to Action without Formal Meeting by the Directors of Scrupulous Corporation

The undersigned directors of the corporation hereby adopt the following resolution:

WHEREAS, the management of the corporation has presented to the board of directors a proposed employment contract between the corporation and **Raymond Rodriguez** as **President** of the corporation, which contract is incorporated into this resolution by reference (management storage file no. 00-35) and has recommended the approval of such contract, it is, after due consideration

RESOLVED, that the referenced employment contract between the corporation and **Raymond Rodriguez** as **President** of the corporation is approved and ratified, and further

RESOLVED, that the appropriate officers of the corporation are authorized and directed to execute such contract.

This resolution shall be effective at **10:00 a.**m. on the **18th** of **December, 2005**.

Henry Hardy
Henry Hardy, Director

Roberta Moore
Roberta Moore, Director

Raymond Rodriguez
Raymond Rodriguez, Director

It is not required that there be a written employment contract, but as a minimum there should be a resolution of the directors establishing a salary and any other conditions of employment that are pertinent. An example of such a resolution follows. (See Chapter 10 for other director actions that may be useful.)

sample of form 73: DIRECTORS' CONSENT TO ACTION
ESTABLISHING AN OFFICER'S SALARY

Consent to Action without Formal Meeting by the Directors of

Scrupulous Corporation

The undersigned directors of the corporation hereby adopt the following resolution:

RESOLVED, that the corporation shall pay to Roberta Moore, for services rendered as Vice President and Secretary of the corporation, an annual salary of $48,000 in equal monthly payments (subject to requirements for withholding amounts for taxes, etc.), such salary to be effective on February 1, 2006, and further

RESOLVED, that as Vice President and Secretary, Roberta Moore shall be entitled to receive coverage under the corporation's health plan for executive employees during the period of her employment by the corporation.

This resolution shall be effective at **3:00 p.**m. on the **16th** of **January, 2006**.

Henry Hardy
Henry Hardy, Director

Roberta Moore
Roberta Moore, Director

Raymond Rodriguez
Raymond Rodriguez, Director

Resignation and Termination

Officers serve at the pleasure of the board of directors. An employment agreement with an officer may be for a specific term (say, five years), but that does not mean that the corporation must keep an officer it does not want. If the corporation removes the officer, it is not necessarily the same as firing him or her. The former officer could continue as an employee or hold another office. But depending on the employment contract, the corporation could be liable for damages caused to the officer/employee as a result of such removal.

Similarly, an officer with a contract can resign at any time. If the resignation violates the agreement, the officer could be liable for damages. An example of an officer's resignation follows. It should be addressed to the board of directors that appointed him or her.

sample of form 74: **DIRECTORS' CONSENT TO ACTION ACCEPTING AN OFFICER'S RESIGNATION**

Consent to Action without Formal Meeting by the Directors of

Scrupulous Corporation

The undersigned directors of the corporation hereby adopt the following resolution:

RESOLVED, that the resignation of **Henry Hardy** as **Vice President** of the corporation, effective **January 27, 2006** is accepted.

This resolution shall be effective at **10:00 a.**m. on the **16th** of **January, 2006**.

Henry Hardy
Henry Hardy, Director

Roberta Moore
Roberta Moore, Director

Raymond Rodriguez
Raymond Rodriguez, Director

The board may formally accept the resignation by a resolution. This should remove any possibility that the employee could later revoke the resignation.

The removal of an officer, whatever its legal consequences in the context of an **EMPLOYMENT AGREEMENT**, is also easily accomplished by a resolution such as the following.

sample of form 75: **DIRECTORS' CONSENT TO ACTION TERMINATING AN OFFICER'S APPOINTMENT**

Consent to Action without Formal Meeting by the Directors of Scrupulous Corporation

The undersigned directors of the corporation hereby adopt the following resolution:

RESOLVED, that **Absentia Morgen** is removed from the office of **Vice President** for Public Relations of the corporation effective **March 31, 2006**.

This resolution shall be effective at **10:00 a.m.** on the **16th** of **January, 2006**.

| *Henry Hardy* | *Roberta Moore* | *Raymond Rodriguez* |
| Henry Hardy, Director | Roberta Moore, Director | Raymond Rodriguez, Director |

Incumbency

As is the case with the board of directors (see form 12), the secretary is occasionally asked to certify the names of persons currently holding corporate offices. A **CERTIFICATION OF OFFICERS BY THE SECRETARY** is in Appendix C. (see form 76, p.320.) An example follows.

sample of form 76: **CERTIFICATION OF OFFICERS BY THE SECRETARY**

Certification of Officers by the Secretary of Scrupulous Corporation

I hereby certify that I am the Corporate Secretary of the Corporation, that the individuals listed below have been duly elected to the offices of the Corporation appearing opposite their names, and that they continue to hold such offices on the date of this certification:

President: **Raymond Rodriguez**   Vice President: **Hugh Hardy**

Secretary: **Roberta Moore**   Treasurer: **Calvin Collier**

Other: _____   Other: _____

Signed and the seal of the corporation affixed on **September 18, 2006**.

Seal of Scrupulous Corporation

20✳06

State of West Carolina

Roberta Moore
Roberta Moore,
Corporate Secretary

Employees, Independent Contractors, and Agents

An *agent* is someone who has authority to act in the place of another. An *employee* is someone who is long-term hired to perform services for his or her employer. An *independent contractor* is someone who provides services, but who is not hired and who acts with minimal supervision. Employees and independent contractors may also be agents.

EMPLOYEE VS. INDEPENDENT CONTRACTOR

The difference between an *employee* and an *independent contractor* is an important distinction. An employer owes significant legal duties to an employee that it may not owe to an independent contractor. Perhaps even more importantly, an employer owes duties to the government on account of an employee such as taxes, workers' compensation, and the like. An employer may be liable to a third party for the negligence of an employee in instances when it would not be liable for the negligence of an independent contractor.

It is not always easy to tell which is which. Just because you and someone you hire explicitly agree between yourselves at the time of the hire that it will be an independent contractor relationship, that does not mean a court or the IRS will agree with you if the issue comes up later.

There is a list of factors to be considered. A "yes" answer to all or most of the following questions will likely mean that the person hired is an independent contractor rather than an employee.

- ❒ Does the person hired exercise independent control over the details of the work, such as the methods used to complete the job?

- ❒ Is the person hired in a business different from that of the person hiring? (For example, a plumber is hired by a lawyer.)

- ❒ Does the person hired work as a specialist without supervision by the person hiring?

- ❒ Does the person hired supply his or her own tools?

- ❒ Is the person hired for only a short period of time rather than consistently over a relatively long period?

- ❒ Does the job require a relatively high degree of skill?

- ❒ Is the person paid *by the job* rather than *by the hour*?

Employees It is not necessary to have a written **Employment Agreement** for employees, although, contracts for employment that cannot be completed within a year may not be enforceable unless they are in writing. Some corporations have a policy against it and hire their employees *at will*, meaning that they can be fired or can quit at any time. Often though, the law limits the conditions under which even an *at-will* employee can be fired.

Independent Contractors Contracts with independent contractors do not have to be in writing either, but it is often even more important that they are written than it is for an **Employment Agreement**. For one thing, the writing is an opportunity to state clearly that you intend it to be an independent contractor arrangement. Also, since by definition you have relatively little control over the way an independent contractor does the work, the writing may be your last chance to influence important matters like exactly what the job is and when it must be completed.

EMPLOYEE PAY

The management of personnel is an art form this book cannot help you with, but keeping track of compensation, especially for the higher-paid employees, is one of the duties of the board of directors. As always, their actions must be recorded. The following are directors' resolutions giving a raise to a single employee, giving a bonus to another employee, and setting salaries for a group of employees for the new year. These may be easily adapted for other employees and specific situations.

sample of form 77: **DIRECTORS' CONSENT TO ACTION AUTHORIZING A RAISE**

Consent to Action without Formal Meeting by the Directors
of
Scrupulous Corporation

The undersigned directors of the corporation hereby adopt the following resolution:

RESOLVED, that effective **August 1, 2006**, the annual salary of **Henry Hardy** shall be increased from its present rate to **$75,000** per year payable monthly, subject to customary withholding requirements.

This resolution shall be effective at **10 a.**m. on the **1st** of **April, 2006**.

Henry Hardy	*Roberta Moore*	*Raymond Rodriguez*
Henry Hardy, Director	Roberta Moore, Director	Raymond Rodriguez, Director

---

sample of form 78: **DIRECTORS' CONSENT TO ACTION AUTHORIZING A BONUS**

Consent to Action without Formal Meeting by the Directors
of
Scrupulous Corporation

The undersigned directors of the corporation hereby adopt the following resolution:

RESOLVED, that on or before **December 31, 2006**, the appropriate officer of the corporation is authorized and directed to pay to **Raymond Rodriguez**, on behalf of the corporation, a bonus in the amount of **$5,000.00** in addition to his regular salary.

This resolution shall be effective at **10 a.**m. on the **28th** of **April, 2006**.

Henry Hardy	*Roberta Moore*	*Raymond Rodriguez*
Henry Hardy, Director	Roberta Moore, Director	Raymond Rodriguez, Director

---

sample of form 79: **DIRECTORS' CONSENT TO ACTION
AUTHORIZING A NEW SALARY SCHEDULE**

Consent to Action without Formal Meeting by the Directors of

Scrupulous Corporation

The undersigned directors of the corporation hereby adopt the following resolution:

RESOLVED, that beginning **October 1, 2006**, the annual salaries of the individuals named below shall be the amounts stated opposite their names (subject to customary withholding requirements) payable in the manner indicated, and that such salaries shall remain in effect until changed or superseded by action of the board of directors:

Name:	Annual salary:	Payment period:
Raymond Rodriguez	**$85,000.00**	**Monthly**
Roberta Moore	**$55,000.00**	**Monthly**
Henry Hardy	**$48,500.00**	**Monthly**

This resolution shall be effective at **10:00 a.**m. on the **15th** of **September, 2006**.

Henry Hardy   *Raymond Rodriguez*
Henry Hardy, Director   Raymond Rodriguez, Director

Roberta Moore
Roberta Moore, Director

INDEPENDENT CONTRACT CONSULTANTS

Consultants are a category of independent contractors. Frequently they are hired without any sort of written agreement, but it is hard to imagine a situation in which having a written agreement is not better. Many consultants will have their own standard agreement forms for you to sign.

Accountants

Accountants provide a variety of services, from bookkeeping and preparation of tax forms to the formal audit of a company's financial statements. Audits are expensive and, for most corporations, not necessary. An audit may be required by some regulatory agency or by contract with some institution. Be careful that you do not lightly sign an agreement with a lender or some other party that requires the production of *audited financial statements*. You may be getting into more than you bargained for. The example that follows is a directors' resolution authorizing the engagement of accountants to do the job.

sample of form 80: **DIRECTORS' CONSENT TO ACTION HIRING OUTSIDE AUDITORS**

Consent to Action without Formal Meeting by the Directors of Scrupulous Corporation

The undersigned directors of the corporation hereby adopt the following resolution:

WHEREAS, management has presented to the board of directors a proposed engagement letter between **Bean-Counters Associates PLLC** and the corporation pursuant to which such firm will provide auditing services to the corporation for the fiscal year ended **December 31, 2006** (the engagement letter is located in management storage file no. **06-351**), and

WHEREAS, after discussion, the board of directors believes it to be in the best interests of the corporation to enter into such agreement, it is therefore

RESOLVED, that the proposed engagement letter for auditing services between the corporation and Bean-Counters Associates is hereby approved and ratified, and further

RESOLVED, that the corporation shall seek the ratification of such appointment by the shareholders of the corporation at its next annual meeting of shareholders, and further

RESOLVED, that the appropriate officers of the corporation are authorized and directed to execute the referenced agreement and to take such actions as are necessary to obtain ratification of the engagement by shareholders.

This resolution shall be effective at **3:00 p.**m. on the **22nd** of **December, 2006**.

Henry Hardy   *Raymond Rodriguez*
Henry Hardy, Director   Raymond Rodriguez, Director

Roberta Moore
Roberta Moore, Director

Lawyers   Lawyers are predictably creative about the ways in which you can pay them. Usually contracts for legal services provide for payment by the hour or, when the client is a plaintiff in a lawsuit asking for money damages, on a contingent basis. A *contingent fee* is an arrangement in which the lawyer gets a share of the client's recovery, whatever that may be. The following is a resolution for the hiring of a lawyer.

sample of form 81: **DIRECTORS' CONSENT TO ACTION HIRING A LAW FIRM**

Consent to Action without Formal Meeting by the Directors of Scrupulous Corporation

The undersigned directors of the corporation hereby adopt the following resolution:

WHEREAS, management has presented to the board of directors a proposed engagement letter between **Dewey, Cheatham & Howe LLP** and the corporation pursuant to which the firm will provide legal services to the corporation in connection with general business matters (the engagement letter is located in management storage file number **06-25**), and

WHEREAS, after discussion, the board of directors believes it to be in the best interests of the corporation to enter into such agreement, it is therefore

RESOLVED, that the proposed engagement letter for legal services between the corporation and **Dewey, Cheatham & Howe LLP** is approved, ratified, and confirmed.

This resolution shall be effective at **10:00 a.**m. on the **1st** of **February, 2006**.

Henry Hardy
Henry Hardy, Director

Raymond Rodriguez
Raymond Rodriguez, Director

Roberta Moore
Roberta Moore, Director

EMPLOYEE BENEFITS

At some point, you may want to set up various benefit programs for employees. In setting up some of these benefit programs, tax ramifications to both the corporation and the recipient may be important considerations. Due to such tax and other possible complications, the corporation would be well advised to seek outside professional assistance in developing the details of the plan.

Also, in order to adopt some of these benefit programs, the **BYLAWS** or **ARTICLES OF INCORPORATION** may need to be amended. You will need to read your corporation's **ARTICLES OF INCORPORATION** to determine whether these programs can be established by the board of directors or may only be established by the shareholders, by amendment to the **BYLAWS**, or by amendment to the **ARTICLES OF INCORPORATION**. The following are basic resolutions for various types of benefit plans.

sample of form 82: **SHAREHOLDERS' CONSENT TO ACTION ESTABLISHING A HEALTH CARE PLAN**

Consent to Action without Formal Meeting by the Shareholders of
Scrupulous Corporation

The undersigned shareholders of the corporation hereby adopt the following resolution:

RESOLVED, that the employee health care plan, a copy of which is attached to this Consent to Action (the Plan), is adopted and approved, and further

RESOLVED, that the officers of the corporation are authorized and directed to take such action as is necessary or desirable to implement the Plan.

This resolution shall be effective at **10 a.**m. on the **4th** of **January, 2006**.

Raymond Rodriguez
Raymond Rodriguez, Shareholder

Roberta Moore
Roberta Moore, Shareholder

Hugh Hardy
Hugh Hardy, Shareholder

Della Driskell
Della Driskell, Shareholder

Henry Hardy
Henry Hardy, Shareholder

Calvin Collier
Calvin Collier, Shareholder

sample of form 83: **SHAREHOLDERS' CONSENT TO ACTION ESTABLISHING A GROUP LIFE INSURANCE PROGRAM**

Consent to Action without Formal Meeting by the Shareholders of
Scrupulous Corporation

The undersigned shareholders of the corporation hereby adopt the following resolution:

RESOLVED, that the officers of the corporation are authorized and directed to contract with an insurance provider for a group life insurance program with the following basic provisions:

1. Life insurance shall be provided to all employees with **5** or more years of service with the corporation;

2. Each employee's life insurance policy shall be in an amount equal to one year's salary of the employee;

3. The entire cost of the group life insurance program shall be paid by the corporation.

This resolution shall be effective at **3 p.**m. on the **4th** of **January, 2006**.

Roberta Moore
Roberta Moore, Shareholder

Hugh Hardy
Hugh Hardy, Shareholder

Henry Hardy
Henry Hardy, Shareholder

Raymond Rodriguez
Raymond Rodriguez, Shareholder

Della Driskell
Della Driskell, Shareholder

Calvin Collier
Calvin Collier, Shareholder

NOTE: *You might also want to include such other provisions as may be advised by your insurance carrier, as well as an option for employees to obtain higher amounts of coverage at their own expense. You can also use the format of the other employee benefit program resolutions by simply referring to a more detailed plan to be attached to the minutes of the meeting.*

sample of form 84: **SHAREHOLDERS' CONSENT TO ACTION ESTABLISHING A RETIREMENT PLAN**

Consent to Action without Formal Meeting by the Shareholders of Scrupulous Corporation

The undersigned shareholders of the corporation hereby adopt the following resolution:

RESOLVED, that the employee retirement plan, a copy of which is attached to this Consent to Action (the Plan), is hereby adopted and approved, and further

RESOLVED, that the officers of the corporation are authorized and directed to take whatever action they deem necessary or desirable to implement the Plan, including but not limited to retaining legal counsel or other financial professionals to ensure that the Plan complies with any federal or state requirements for registration and to obtain any tax classification or benefits as may be directed in the Plan.

This resolution shall be effective at **10 a.**m. on the **4th** of **January, 2006**.

Raymond Rodriguez
Raymond Rodriguez, Shareholder

Roberta Moore
Roberta Moore, Shareholder

Hugh Hardy
Hugh Hardy, Shareholder

Della Driskell
Della Driskell, Shareholder

Henry Hardy
Henry Hardy, Shareholder

Calvin Collier
Calvin Collier, Shareholder

---

sample of form 85: **SHAREHOLDERS' CONSENT TO ACTION ESTABLISHING A PROFIT SHARING PLAN**

Consent to Action without Formal Meeting by the Shareholders of Scrupulous Corporation

The undersigned shareholders of the corporation hereby adopt the following resolution:

RESOLVED, that the profit sharing plan, a copy of which is attached to this Consent to Action (the Plan), is adopted and approved, subject to the receipt of assurances regarding legal and tax treatment of the Plan as provided in this resolution below, and further

RESOLVED, that the President and Secretary of the corporation, or their designees, are authorized and directed to take any action reasonably necessary to implement the Plan, including but not limited to executing a trust agreement pursuant to the Plan, and further

RESOLVED, that the officers of the corporation are authorized and directed to retain legal counsel to provide whatever services the officers deem necessary or desirable in order to receive legal assurance that the Plan is qualified under applicable provisions of the Internal Revenue Code for the tax treatment contemplated by the Plan and to provide the board of directors with an opinion satisfactory to the board as to legal compliance of the plan with the Internal Revenue Code and other applicable law, and further

RESOLVED, that the officers of the corporation are authorized and directed to take such actions as may be necessary or desirable to put the profit sharing plan into operation.

This resolution shall be effective at **3 p.**m. on the **4th** of **January, 2006**.

Raymond Rodriguez	*Roberta Moore*
Raymond Rodriguez, Shareholder	Roberta Moore, Shareholder
Hugh Hardy	*Della Driskell*
Hugh Hardy, Shareholder	Della Driskell, Shareholder
Henry Hardy	*Calvin Collier*
Henry Hardy, Shareholder	Calvin Collier, Shareholder

sample of form 86: **Shareholders' Consent to Action Establishing a Stock Option Plan**

Consent to Action without Formal Meeting by the Shareholders of Scrupulous Corporation

The undersigned shareholders of the corporation hereby adopt the following resolution:

RESOLVED, that the stock option plan, a copy of which is attached to this Consent to Action (the Plan), is adopted and approved, and further

RESOLVED, that a total number **50,000** shares of the common stock of this corporation shall be set aside for sale pursuant to the terms of the Plan.

This resolution shall be effective at **3 p.**m. on the **4th** of **January, 2006**.

Raymond Rodriguez	*Roberta Moore*
Raymond Rodriguez, Shareholder	Roberta Moore, Shareholder
Hugh Hardy	*Della Driskell*
Hugh Hardy, Shareholder	Della Driskell, Shareholder
Henry Hardy	*Calvin Collier*
Henry Hardy, Shareholder	Calvin Collier, Shareholder

NOTE: *In order to accomplish implementation of the stock option plan, it may also be necessary for the shareholders to make a resolution increasing the total number of shares of stock (see the sample on page 154). This will probably require an amendment to the* ARTICLES OF INCORPORATION.

sample of form 87: SHAREHOLDERS' CONSENT TO ACTION
ESTABLISHING A COMPREHENSIVE BENEFIT PLAN

Consent to Action without Formal Meeting by the Shareholders of
Scrupulous Corporation

The undersigned shareholders of the corporation hereby adopt the following resolution:

RESOLVED, that the comprehensive employee benefit plan, a copy of which is attached to this Consent to Action (the Plan), is adopted and approved, and further

RESOLVED, that the officers of the corporation are authorized and directed to take whatever action they deem reasonably necessary to implement the Plan, including but not limited to retaining legal counsel or other professional advisors to ensure that the Plan complies with applicable federal or state requirements and to obtain any tax classification or tax benefits as may be contemplated by the Plan.

This resolution shall be effective at **10 a.**m. on the **4th** of **January, 2006.**

Raymond Rodriguez	*Roberta Moore*
Raymond Rodriguez, Shareholder	Roberta Moore, Shareholder
Hugh Hardy	*Della Driskell*
Hugh Hardy, Shareholder	Della Driskell, Shareholder
Henry Hardy	*Calvin Collier*
Henry Hardy, Shareholder	Calvin Collier, Shareholder

NONCOMPETITION AND NONDISCLOSURE AGREEMENTS

A common headache for employers is the unfaithful employee who quits and goes to work for a competitor, taking with him or her confidential information and techniques belonging to the former employer. One reason for the headache is that there is a bias in the law protecting employees and their right to make a living. While an employee may have no right to steal your confidential information, he or she does have a right to find a job in the field for which they are trained.

Noncompetition agreements can work, and you can have a contract that will give you more protection from a disloyal employee than you get with no contract at all. But it is not easy. A noncompete agreement has to be *reasonable* as to the geographical area it covers and as to the period of its effectiveness. It is not reasonable to insist that a former employment can never compete against you anywhere in the world. A contract like that would be ignored by the courts. What is reasonable is more difficult to say. To be safe, you should get some advice from your lawyer about the courts' views in your state. If you push too hard, you may find that a court will simply not enforce your agreement.

Another problem with a **NONCOMPETITION AND NONDISCLOSURE AGREEMENT** is consideration. (see form 111, p.362.) For a contract to be enforced, it must be *supported by consideration*. In other words, what are you giving to the employee in exchange for his or her promise not to compete? You cannot just add a noncompete provision to an existing contract. It will not be enforceable. You must pay something for the employee's promise. Ideally, the noncompetiton and nondisclosure promises will be included in the employee's first employment agreement with the company. That way, there is little doubt about consideration. If the issue comes up later, as often happens, after the employee proves his or her value to the company, the problem gets more complicated.

The following example presumes that the employee is not a new employee. Similar provisions could be included in a first time employment contract.

sample of form 111: **NONCOMPETITION AND NONDISCLOSURE AGREEMENT**

This agreement is made between Raymond Rodriguez (the "Employee") and Scrupulous Corporation (the "Corporation"). The Employee agrees to the terms of this agreement in consideration of the Employee's continued employment by the Corporation and additional consideration consisting of an increase in annual salary of $10,000.00 (Ten Thousand Dollars and 00 Cents) payable monthly, which the Employee acknowledges is consideration paid by the Corporation over and above the consideration due to the Employee pursuant to his or her usual terms of employment. The Employee also acknowledges the receipt and sufficiency of such consideration to support his or her promises made in this agreement.

1. The Employee agrees that upon termination of employment for any reason, he or she will not enter into competition with the Corporation, its successors, or assigns in the area and for the period of time stated below.

2. For purposes of this agreement, the term "competition" shall mean any activity of the Employee consisting of or related to (a) soliciting orders for any product or service competitive with the Corporation, (b) contracting, for the purpose of soliciting business, any customer, client, or account of the Corporation in existence during the term of his or her employment by the corporation, (c) disclosing confidential information of the Corporation, including but not limited to trade secrets, customer lists, supplier lists and prices, and pricing schedules, or without in any way limiting the foregoing, (d) disclosing the contents of or removing from Employer's place of business any document marked "secret" or "confidential."

Any such activity shall be considered "competition" whether undertaken directly or indirectly, as an owner, officer, director, employee, consultant, stockholder, partner, or in any other relationship with a competing business.

3. The period of time referred to in paragraph 1 shall be twenty-four months following the termination of the Employee's employment by the Corporation, and the area referred to in paragraph 1 shall be limited to the following:

The state of West Carolina.

4. Violation of this agreement by the Employee will entitle the Corporation to an injunction to prevent any such competition or disclosure, without posting of any bond by the Corporation; and will entitle the Corporation to other legal remedies, including attorney's fees and costs.

5. This agreement may not be modified except in writing signed by both parties.

This agreement was executed by the Employee and by the Corporation by authority of its Board of Directors on February 25th, 2006.

Employee: Corporation:

Raymond Rodriguez   By: *Calvin Collier*

Raymond Rodriguez   Calvin Collier, Vice President

POWERS OF ATTORNEY

A *power of attorney* is a written authority for someone to act as your *agent*. The person who acts as your agent is called an *attorney in fact*. (This is not the same as your agent for legal matters, who is called an *attorney at law*.) An attorney in fact is usually not an employee of the company. If you want the vice president to perform some task on behalf of the company, you can simply have the board of directors authorize the act in a resolution. You do not need a separate document such as the ones on pages 159 and 160. But you may want someone who is not already an agent to undertake some duty.

NOTE: *Remember that a director is not an agent of the company. If for some reason you want a director to undertake the job of negotiating or executing a contract, the corporation might make him or her its attorney in fact for that purpose.*

A power of attorney can be for a particular duty and expire when that duty is done. It is then called a **LIMITED POWER OF ATTORNEY**. (see form 88, p.332.) It can also authorize a wide range of activity and last for an indefinite period of time, called a **GENERAL POWER OF ATTORNEY**. (see form 89, p.333.) A power of attorney can usually be revoked at any time by the person giving it with a **REVOCATION OF POWER OF ATTORNEY**. (see form 90, p.334.) Examples of specific and general powers of attorney and a revocation follow.

sample of form 88: **LIMITED POWER OF ATTORNEY**

Limited Power of Attorney

Scrupulous Corporation (the "Corporation") hereby grants to **James Bond** (the "Agent") a limited power of attorney. As the Corporation's attorney in fact, the Agent shall have full power and authority to undertake and perform the following on behalf of the Corporation:

Execute a contract and financing documents for the purchase and financing of a 2005 Dodge Ram delivery van.

By accepting this grant, the Agent agrees to act in a fiduciary capacity consistent with the reasonable best interests of the Corporation. This power of attorney may be revoked by the Corporation at any time; however, any person dealing with the Agent as attorney in fact may rely on this appointment until receipt of actual notice of termination.

IN WITNESS WHEREOF, the undersigned corporation has executed this power of attorney under seal and by authority of its board of directors on **May 9, 2006**.

```
+----------------------------------+
|   Seal of Scrupulous Corporation |
|                                  |
|              20✷06               |
|                                  |
|      State of West Carolina      |
+----------------------------------+
```

By: _Raymond Rodriguez_____
      Raymond Rodriguez, President

Attest:

_Roberta Moore_____
Roberta Moore, Secretary

STATE OF
COUNTY OF

I certify that **Roberta Moore** personally appeared before me on **May 10, 2006** and acknowledged that (s)he is Secretary of **Scrupulous Corporation** and that by authority duly given and as the act of the corporation, the foregoing instrument was signed in its name by its President, sealed with its corporate seal and attested by him/her as its Secretary.

_Penny Moneypenny_____
Penny Moneypenny
Notary Public
Notary's commission expires: **August 30, 2008**

I hereby accept the foregoing appointment as attorney in fact on **May 10, 2006**

_James Bond_____
James Bond, Attorney in Fact

sample of form 89: **GENERAL POWER OF ATTORNEY**

General Power of Attorney

Scrupulous Corporation (the "Corporation") hereby grants to **James Bond** (the "Agent") a general power of attorney. As the Corporation's attorney in fact, the Agent shall have full power and authority to undertake any and all acts that may be lawfully undertaken on behalf of the corporation including but not limited to the right to buy, sell, lease, mortgage, assign, rent, or otherwise dispose of any real or personal property belonging to the Corporation; to execute, accept, undertake, and perform contracts in the name of the Corporation; to deposit, endorse, or withdraw funds to or from any bank depository of the Corporation; to initiate, defend, or settle legal actions on behalf of the Corporation; and to retain any accountant, attorney, or other advisor deemed by the Agent to be necessary to protect the interests of the Corporation in relation to such powers.

By accepting this grant, the Agent agrees to act in a fiduciary capacity consistent with the reasonable best interests of the Corporation. This power of attorney may be revoked by the Corporation at any time; however, any person dealing with the Agent as attorney in fact may rely on this appointment until receipt of actual notice of termination.

IN WITNESS WHEREOF, the undersigned corporation has executed this power of attorney under seal and by authority of its board of directors as of the date stated above.

Scrupulous Corporation

Seal of Scrupulous Corporation

20✳06

State of West Carolina

By: *Raymond Rodriguez*

Raymond Rodriguez, President

Attest:

Roberta Moore

Roberta Moore, Secretary

STATE OF
COUNTY OF

I certify that **Roberta Moore** personally appeared before me on **May 10, 2006** and acknowledged that (s)he is Secretary of **Scrupulous Corporation** and that by authority duly given and as the act of the corporation, the foregoing instrument was signed in its name by its President, sealed with its corporate seal and attested by him/her as its Secretary.

Penny Moneypenny

Penny Moneypenny,
Notary Public
Notary's commission expires: August 30, 2008

I hereby accept the foregoing appointment as attorney in fact on **May 10, 2006**.

James Bond

James Bond, Attorney in Fact

sample of form 90: **Revocation of Power of Attorney**

Revocation of Power of Attorney

The appointment of **James Bond** as the attorney in fact of the undersigned Corporation (the "Corporation") made on **May 10, 2006** is hereby revoked and terminated by the Corporation effective on this date.

Signed and the corporate seal affixed on **October 25, 2006**.

Seal of Scrupulous Corporation
20✳06
State of West Carolina

Scrupulous Corporation

By: *Raymond Rodriguez*
Raymond Rodriguez, President

Attest:

Roberta Moore
Roberta Moore, Secretary

AGENTS FOR SERVICE OF PROCESS

A corporation must, by law, have at least one kind of *agent*. There must be a person designated to receive official notice of lawsuits and other official documents, known as an *agent for service of process* or *registered agent*. If the corporation is sued, it is usually the registered agent who first receives delivery of the complaint. There must be such an agent located in the state where the company is incorporated and in any other state where the company is registered to do business. The registered agent is first designated in the **ARTICLES OF INCORPORATION**, so no further action need be taken unless it becomes necessary to appoint a new agent.

The registered agent may be anyone competent to receive important documents and see that they are delivered to the appropriate person within the corporate organization. The agent should be selected with some care, because once the agent receives the notice, the corporation is presumed by law to know about its contents. Even if the agent tosses the notice in the trash and no one else at the corporation ever hears about it, the notice is still considered effective and the corporation is expected to respond accordingly.

The agent does not have to be an employee of the corporation or even a real human being. It could be the company's lawyer, or it could be a corporation that provides such services for a fee.

Changing Registered Agents

It is the board of directors that chooses new registered agents. Following is a resolution for adoption by the board of directors designating a new registered agent for service of process.

sample of form 91: **DIRECTORS' CONSENT TO ACTION DESIGNATING A NEW REGISTERED AGENT FOR SERVICE OF PROCESS**

**Consent to Action without Formal Meeting by the Directors
of
Scrupulous Corporation**

The undersigned directors of the corporation hereby adopt the following resolution:

WHEREAS, the corporation's current designated registered agent for service of process has resigned, it is therefore

RESOLVED, that the person named below is appointed to serve as the corporation's registered agent for service of process

**Dewey Howe, attorney
Dewey, Cheatham & Howe LLP
4 Chancery Lane
Pleasant Cove, West Carolina 30006**

and further

RESOLVED, that the officers of the corporation are authorized and directed to file such documents and notices as may be necessary or desirable to give effect to this resolution.

This resolution shall be effective at **10:00 a.**m. on the **6th** of **January, 2006**.

Henry Hardy   *Raymond Rodriguez*
Henry Hardy, Director   Raymond Rodriguez, Director

Roberta Moore
Roberta Moore, Director

In order to give effect to the change of registered agent, the corporation must give official notice to the state, ordinarily to the office of the Secretary of State. Your state will have a preferred form for that purpose, obtainable from the Secretary of State's office or website. You should use that form. Following is a typical **STATEMENT OF CHANGE OF REGISTERED OFFICE AND/OR REGISTERED AGENT** form completed for Scrupulous Corporation. (see form 126, p.381.)

sample of form 126: **STATEMENT OF CHANGE OF REGISTERED OFFICE AND/OR REGISTERED AGENT**

Statement of Change of Registered Office and/or Registered Agent

Pursuant to the laws of this State, the undersigned corporation submits the following for the purpose of changing its registered office and/or registered agent.

The name of the corporation is: **Scrupulous Corporation**.

The mailing address, street address, and county of the corporation's registered office **currently on file** is:

> **Roberta Moore**
> **No. 4 Beach Place, South Coast County, West Carolina 27000**

The name of the current registered agent is: **Roberta Moore**.

1. The mailing address, street address and county of the new registered office of the corporation is: (*to be completed only if the registered office is being changed*)

> **239 Surf Street**
> **Pleasant Cove, South Coast County, W. Carolina 27000**

2. The name of the new registered agent and the new agent's consent to appointment appears below: (*to be completed only if the registered agent is being changed*)

> **Raymond Rodriguez**   *Raymond Rodriguez*

3. The address of the corporation's registered office and the address of the business office of its registered agent, as changed, will be identical.

4. This statement will be effective upon filing, unless a date and/or time is specified: _____.

This is the **20th** day of **August, 2006**.

> Scrupulous Corporation
>
> *Raymond Rodriguez*
>
> Raymond Rodriguez, President

Protecting the Officers and Directors from Liability

There is a tension in the law between two strong public policy goals. On the one hand, we would like boards of directors to be populated by intelligent, experienced people who are willing to provide their judgment and expertise at low cost to the company. On the other hand, we would like the law to strictly scrutinize the activities of directors and severely punish those who, by being negligent or dishonest, wind up costing the company money. If we push the latter policy, we risk making the potential liability of directors too great and discouraging good people from serving. If we are too lenient, in the hope of making it easier for people to serve, we place corporations in danger from unscrupulous or incompetent directors. From time to time, the legal pendulum swings from one policy goal to the other.

AVOIDING AND COMPENSATING FOR LIABILITY

There are several ways to protect directors and officers from liability. One is a rule of law called the *business judgment rule* that protects management from liability for damages resulting from a decision that turns out badly for the corporation. The rule protects management so long as the decision, even though a bad one, was made in good faith, on adequate information, and within management's authority.

Beyond the protection afforded by the business judgment rule, corporations may, and in some cases must, provide additional protection by *indemnifying* (compensating) officers and directors for liability and expenses they incur while performing their duties. Generally it is possible to afford greater protection to directors than to officers. Corporations may be able to buy insurance to pay such indemnification.

Some states now allow the **ARTICLES OF INCORPORATION** to relieve directors from much potential liability by including an *exculpation* (removal of guilt) *clause* in the articles. Such clauses usually provide that, to the extent permitted by law, the directors will not be personally liable to the corporation or shareholders for monetary damages for breach of the director's duty. A director will not be relieved of liability if his or her breach resulted in a personal profit or was the result of dishonesty. Such a provision preserves the company's right to obtain an injunction from a court ordering the director to stop whatever he or she is doing that is in breach of the director's duty.

INDEMNIFICATION OF OFFICERS AND DIRECTORS

An **INDEMNIFICATION AGREEMENT** between a corporation and a director is included in Appendix C. (see form 92, p.336.) On the following page is an example of such an agreement completed, followed by a provision for indemnification that could possibly be included in an officer's **EMPLOYMENT AGREEMENT**. The intent is to require the corporation to indemnify the director or officer to the greatest extent allowed by law.

A corporation should not lightly agree to such an arrangement, as it could subject the company to considerable expense at the hands of a director or officer who turns out to be less than the best.

sample of form 92: **INDEMNIFICATION AGREEMENT (FOR DIRECTOR)**

Indemnification Agreement

This indemnification agreement is entered into by and between **Scrupulous Corporation** (the "Corporation") and **Della Driskell** (the "Director").

In consideration of the Director's consent to serve or to continue serving as a director of the Corporation and other valuable consideration, the parties agree for themselves, their successors, and assigns, as follows.

1. Subject to the terms and limitations provided in this agreement, the Corporation hereby agrees to indemnify and hold the Director harmless to the fullest extent permitted by law against the expenses, payments, and liabilities described in this agreement and incurred by the Director by reason of the fact that the Director is or was a director, officer, employee, or agent of the Corporation or serves or served, at the request of the Corporation, as a director, officer, partner, trustee, employee, or agent of any other enterprise or as a trustee or administrator under an employee benefit plan.

   1.1. The expenses, payments, and liabilities referred to above are:

      1.1.1. Reasonable expenses, including attorney's fees, incurred by the Director in connection with any threatened, pending, or completed inquiry, proceeding, action, suit, investigation, or arbitration, whether civil, criminal, or administrative, and any appeal therefrom, whether or not brought by or on behalf of the Corporation.

      1.1.2. Any payment made by the Director in satisfaction of any judgment, money decree, fine, excise tax, penalty, or reasonable settlement for which the Director became liable in any matter described in subparagraph 1.1.1 above.

      1.1.3. Reasonable expenses, including legal fees, incurred by the Director in enforcing his or her rights under this paragraph.

   1.2. To the fullest extent allowed by law, the Corporation shall pay the expenses and payments described in paragraph 1.1 above in advance of the final disposition of any matter.

2. The rights of the Director hereunder shall inure to the benefit of the Director and his or her heirs, legal representative, and assigns.

3. The Director shall have the rights provided for in this agreement whether or not he or she is an officer, director, employee, or agent at the time such liabilities or expenses are imposed or incurred and whether or not the claim asserted against the Director is based on matters that predate the execution of this agreement.

4. The rights of the Director under this agreement are in addition to and not exclusive of any other rights to which he or she may be entitled under any statute, agreement, insurance policy, or otherwise.

5. The Corporation agrees to use its best reasonable efforts to obtain and pay for a policy of insurance to protect and insure the Director's rights under this agreement.

IN WITNESS WHEREOF, the parties have executed this agreement under seal and by authority of its board of directors on **February 16, 2006**.

> Seal of Scrupulous Corporation
>
> 20✳06
>
> State of West Carolina

Corporation:

By: *Raymond Rodriguez*
    President

Attest: *Roberta Moore* , Secretary

Della Driskell
Director

Sample EMPLOYMENT CONTRACT PROVISION REGARDING INDEMNIFICATION OF AN OFFICER

Subject only to the terms and limitations provided in this paragraph, the Corporation hereby agrees to indemnify and hold Della Driskell harmless to the fullest extent permitted by law against the expenses, payments, and liabilities described in this paragraph and incurred by Della Driskell by reason of the fact that Della Driskell is or was an officer, director, employee, or agent of the Corporation or serves or served, at the request of the Corporation, as a director, officer, partner, trustee, employee, or agent of any other enterprise or as a trustee or administrator under an employee benefit plan.

1. The expenses, payments, and liabilities referred to above are:

1.1. Reasonable expenses, including attorney's fees, incurred by Della Driskell in connection with any threatened, pending, or completed inquiry, proceeding, action, suit, investigation, or arbitration, whether civil, criminal, or administrative, and any appeal therefrom, whether or not brought by or on behalf of the Corporation.

1.2. Any payment made by Della Driskell in satisfaction of any judgment, money decree, fine, excise tax, penalty, or reasonable settlement for which Della Driskell became liable in any matter described in subparagraph 1.1 above.

1.3. Reasonable expenses, including legal fees, incurred by Della Driskell in enforcing her rights under this paragraph.

2. To the fullest extent allowed by law, the Corporation shall pay the expenses and payments described in paragraph 1 above in advance of the final disposition of any matter.

3. The rights of Della Driskell under this paragraph shall inure to the benefit of Della Driskell and her heirs, legal representative, and assigns.

4. Della Driskell shall have the rights provided for in this paragraph whether or not she is an officer, director, employee, or agent at the time such liabilities or expenses are imposed or incurred, and whether or not the claim asserted against Della Driskell is based on matters that predate the execution of this agreement.

5. The rights of Della Driskell under this provision are in addition to and not exclusive of any other rights to which she may be entitled under any statute, agreement, insurance policy, or otherwise.

6. The Corporation agrees to use its best reasonable efforts to obtain and pay for a policy of insurance to protect and insure Della Driskell's rights under this agreement.

Indemnification in the Bylaws

The provision below takes a different approach. It is a provision to be included in the **BYLAWS** and grants indemnification rights to all directors. It is possible to include officers in such a plan, but many corporations find it wiser to deal with the officers on a case-by-case basis, picking and choosing the ones to receive the benefits of such an arrangement. It is best to have a provision such as this adopted (or later approved or ratified) by the shareholders. If the directors adopt such a provision benefiting themselves, it is likely to be more open to challenge than if the shareholders had approved it.

Sample BYLAW PROVISION REQUIRING BROAD INDEMNIFICATION OF OFFICERS AND DIRECTORS

The Corporation shall indemnify and hold harmless to the fullest extent permitted by law any person who at any time serves or has served as a director of the corporation and any such director who, at the request of the corporation, serves or served as a director, officer, partner, trustee, employee, or agent of any other enterprise or as a trustee or administrator under an employee benefit plan, against the expenses, payments, and liabilities described in this paragraph below which were incurred by such person by reason of the fact that he or she served in any such capacities.

The expenses, payments, and liabilities referred to above are: (1) reasonable expenses, including attorney's fees, incurred by the Director in connection with any threatened, pending, or completed inquiry, proceeding, action, suit, investigation, or arbitration, whether civil, criminal, or administrative, and any appeal therefrom, whether or not brought by or on behalf of the Corporation; (2) any payment made by the Director in satisfaction of any judgment, money decree, fine, excise tax, penalty, or reasonable settlement for which the Director became liable in any matter described in this paragraph above; and (3) reasonable expenses, including legal fees, incurred by the Director in enforcing his or her rights under this paragraph.

To the fullest extent allowed by law, the Corporation shall pay the expenses and payments allowed pursuant to this paragraph in advance of the final disposition of any matter. The rights of any Director hereunder shall inure to the benefit of the Director and his or her heirs, legal representative, and assigns. A Director shall have the rights provided for in this paragraph whether or not he or she is a director at the time such liabilities or expenses are imposed or incurred, and whether or not the claim asserted against the Director is based on matters that predate the adoption of this bylaw provision. The rights of a Director hereunder are in addition to and not exclusive of any other rights to which he or she may be entitled under any statute, agreement, insurance policy, or otherwise. Any person who at any time after adoption of this bylaw serves or has served in a capacity so as to allow him or her indemnification hereunder shall be deemed to have done so in reliance upon, and as consideration for, the indemnification rights provided in this bylaw.

The Board of Directors of the corporation shall take all such action and make all such determinations as may be necessary or desirable under the law to properly authorize the payment of the indemnification provided by this bylaw, including, without limitation, establishing special committees of the board of directors, hiring special counsel, and/or obtaining shareholder approval of such indemnification.

The Corporation shall obtain a policy of insurance to protect and insure the Directors' rights under this agreement.

INSURANCE

The indemnification agreements discussed are of use only if the corporation has funds to pay the indemnification when it is due. It is the nature of things that lawsuits against directors and officers are rare when times are good and all too frequent when the corporation is in trouble. A corporation in so much trouble that the directors are being sued by the shareholders may not have money to pay indemnification.

Insurance policies to protect directors and officers in case they are sued for a breach of their duties to the corporation, called *errors and omissions* coverage, can fill that gap. However, errors and omissions coverage can be difficult to get and, where available, impossibly expensive for many corporations. Following is an example of a resolution for purchasing such insurance in the event it is available.

sample of form 93: **Directors' Consent to Action Approving the Purchase of Directors' and Officers' Liability Insurance**

Consent to Action without Formal Meeting by the Directors
of
Scrupulous Corporation

The undersigned directors of the corporation hereby adopt the following resolution:

WHEREAS, the management of the corporation has presented to the board of directors a proposed policy of insurance providing errors and omissions coverage for the officers and directors of the corporation and insuring the company's obligations to pay indemnification to its officers and directors pursuant to the articles of incorporation and/or bylaws of the company and various contractual arrangements, and

WHEREAS, management has recommended the approval to the purchase of the policy, it is, after due consideration

RESOLVED, that the policy of insurance negotiated with American Chance Insurance Co. and titled Directors' and Officers Liability Policy; Scrupulous Corporation presented to the board of directors (the Policy), which Policy is incorporated by reference into this Consent to Action by reference (management storage file no **06-258**), is approved and ratified, and further

RESOLVED, that the appropriate officers are authorized and directed to take such actions and execute such documents as are necessary or desirable to place such policy in effect and to make premium payments from corporate funds so as to keep such policy in force until further action by the board of directors.

This resolution shall be effective at **10:00 a.**m. on the **18th** of **January, 2006**.

Henry Hardy   *Roberta Moore*   *Raymond Rodriguez*
Henry Hardy,   Roberta Moore,   Raymond Rodriguez,
Director   Director   Director

CONFLICTS OF INTEREST

Corporations often enter into contracts with individual officers or directors. For example, a small company may want to borrow money from a director, buy real estate, or lease office space from a director. If such a contract is unfair to the corporation, an unhappy shareholder may ask a court to declare the contract void. In such cases, the company may recover damages from the officer or director who takes unfair advantage of the corporation.

The MBCA makes it clear that a contract between the corporation and one of its officers or directors is enforceable so long as the facts of the conflict are known to the board of directors who approve the contract by majority vote of disinterested (unconflicted) directors. Such a contract is also enforceable if the facts are made know to the shareholders and they approve it by a majority of disinterested shareholders, or if the contract is demonstrably unfair to the corporation in any case. (MBCA, Sec. 8.31.)

What can be done to avoid or minimize conflicts of interest? Here is when properly recorded **MINUTES** of a directors meeting can be very valuable. The following example of **MINUTES** records the action of directors in approving a contract between one of the directors and the company.

Sample **PARTIAL MINUTES OF DIRECTORS MEETING AUTHORIZING THE PURCHASE OF PROPERTY FROM A DIRECTOR**

Mr. Rodriguez next reported on the company's need for additional office space, explaining that the number of employees has expanded greatly since its present location was first occupied. Mr. Rodriguez explained that the report he was about to present involved a potential conflict of interest between the corporation and Mr. Henry Hardy, one of the company's directors.

Mr. Hardy stated that he was aware of the potential conflict and that he wished therefore to avoid taking part in any discussion of the matter. He asked that he be excused from the meeting and assured the directors that he would be available to answer any questions that might arise during the board's deliberations.

After Mr. Hardy left the meeting, the President's report was distributed to the remaining directors. A copy of the report is filed in management storage file No. 06-56. The directors noted that figures presented by Mr. Rodriguez in his report predicted that the company would gain substantial savings over a five year period by purchasing and expanding onto the vacant lot adjacent to the company's present location compared to the renting of additional needed space or relocation of the company's operation elsewhere.

Such property, it was noted, belonged to Mr. Henry Hardy. Mr. Rodriguez reported that the property had belonged to the Hardy family for many years. Mr. Rodriguez reported that, while Mr. Hardy was reluctant to sell the property, the company, through its general counsel had succeeded in negotiating its purchase for $145,000 under the terms of a proposed contract included in the President's report. The property had been appraised by an independent professional appraiser whose report was also included in the President's report and showed the proposed purchase price to be within the range of values reported by the appraiser.

The Board then reviewed the appraisal report and the proposed purchase contract in detail. After discussion, the following resolutions, moved for adoption by Ms. Driskell, seconded by Ms. Moore, were adopted.

RESOLVED, that the proposed contract for the purchase of the lot adjacent to the company's headquarters as described in the President's report presented to this meeting (management storage file No. 06-56) for a cash purchase price of $145,000 is hereby approved and ratified, and further

RESOLVED, that the board of directors, noting that such property belongs to Mr. Hugh Hardy, a member of the board of directors and shareholder of the company, specifically finds that the proposed contract and purchase price is reasonable and fair to the corporation, and further

RESOLVED, that the officers of the corporation are authorized to execute such contract together with such other documents as may be necessary or desirable to complete the described purchase within 120 days of the date of this resolution.

chapter 12

Amending Bylaws and Articles of Incorporation

From time to time, it may become apparent that a corporation's **BYLAWS** or **ARTICLES OF INCORPORATION** no longer exactly fit the company's needs. **BYLAWS** and **ARTICLES OF INCORPORATION** can be *amended* (changed) by the directors and/or the shareholders.

AMENDING BYLAWS

BYLAWS are easier to amend than the **ARTICLES OF INCORPORATION**. In almost all cases, the shareholders must vote to change the articles and file them at the office of the Secretary of State or other appropriate agency. In most cases, when you want to make a change in the **BYLAWS**, it will be the directors who do it, but the shareholders also have the power to do so.

Amendment by Shareholders

When should the shareholders amend the **BYLAWS**? For most corporations (depending on the way your articles and **BYLAWS** read, there will be a section in the **BYLAWS** on amendments), the rule is that the shareholders can amend the **BYLAWS** by majority vote as long as the changes are consistent with state law. However, once the shareholders have adopted or amended a provision of the **BYLAWS**, the law may limit the power of the directors to change it later.

As a practical matter, you do not want the shareholders to amend the **BYLAWS** except to enact a provision that the shareholders do not want the directors to be able to change without shareholder permission. Provisions specifying important rights having to do with the shareholders are the most common examples, for instance, limitations on the rights of shareholders to dispose of their shares. There are special statutory rules about amending quorum and voting requirements for shareholders and directors. (MBCA, Secs. 10.21 and 10.22.)

Amendment by Directors

When should the directors amend the **BYLAWS**? In most cases, if the **BYLAWS** need amending, it is the directors who should do it. Of course, if the provision to be amended is one that was adopted or previously amended by the shareholders, it may be that the directors *cannot* do it. And, if it is a provision that the shareholders do not want the directors to be able to change later, then the directors *should not* do it.

Following are Consents to Actions by directors amending the **BYLAWS**. In these examples and other forms contained in this book when a document is amended, the amended provision is to be restated in full in the resolution. It is not absolutely necessary to do so, but it does reduce the possibility that someone will misread the amendment in the context of the provision, thus defeating the intent of the amendment.

sample of form 94: **DIRECTORS' CONSENT TO ACTION AMENDING BYLAWS BY CHANGING AN EXISTING PROVISION**

Consent to Action without Formal Meeting by the Directors of

Scrupulous Corporation

The undersigned directors of the corporation hereby adopt the following resolution:

RESOLVED, that pursuant to Article **6**, Section **5** of the bylaws of the corporation, Article **6**, Section **4** of such bylaws is amended to read in its entirety as follows:

Section 4. Fiscal year. The fiscal year of the corporation shall end on December 31 of each calendar year.

This resolution shall be effective at **10:00 a.**m. on the **17th** of **November, 2006.**

Henry Hardy
Henry Hardy, Director

Raymond Rodriguez
Raymond Rodriguez, Director

Roberta Moore
Roberta Moore, Director

---

sample of form 95: **DIRECTORS' CONSENT TO ACTION AMENDING BYLAWS BY ADDING A NEW PROVISION**

Consent to Action without Formal Meeting by the Directors of

Scrupulous Corporation

The undersigned directors of the corporation hereby adopt the following resolution:

RESOLVED, that pursuant to Article **6**, Section **5** of the bylaws of the corporation, the bylaws are amended by the addition of a new provision at Article **2**, Section **8** to read in its entirety as follows:

Section 8. Shareholder proposals. When giving notice of an annual or special meeting of shareholders, the corporation shall give notice of a matter a shareholder intends to raise at the meeting if a request to do so is received by the secretary of the corporation at least 10 days before the corporation gives notice of the meeting.

This resolution shall be effective at **3:00 p.**m. on the **17th** of **November, 2006**.

Henry Hardy
Henry Hardy, Director

Roberta Moore
Roberta Moore, Director

Raymond Rodriguez
Raymond Rodriguez, Director

AMENDING ARTICLES OF INCORPORATION

Most state statutes allow some simple changes to be made in the **ARTICLES OF INCORPORATION** by the directors acting alone. (MBCA, Secs. 10.02 and 10.05.) In most cases it takes both directors and shareholders to amend the articles. The directors recommend the change to the shareholders, and the shareholders either approve or disapprove the proposed change.

Under the statute, the only occasion on which a proposed amendment may be presented to the shareholders without the directors' positive recommendation is when the directors have a conflict of interest or when some other special circumstance makes it inappropriate to make a recommendation. In that case, the directors must explain why there is no recommendation.

If there is to be a shareholders' meeting (remember the vote can be made by unanimous written consent), the company must give notice to the shareholders stating the purpose of the meeting and enclosing a copy of the proposed amendment. (MBCA, Sec. 10.03.)

After the amendment has been adopted by the shareholders, **ARTICLES OF AMENDMENT** must be filed with the state. (MBCA, Sec. 10.08.) (see form 120, p.371.)

Dissenters' Rights

Some changes in a corporation so seriously affect the existing rights of shareholders that shareholders who *dissent from* (vote against) the action are allowed to opt out and have their shares purchased by the corporation at *fair market value*. (MBCA, Chapter 13.) Many of these actions arise in the context of amending the **ARTICLES OF INCORPORATION**.

– Warning –

Dissenters' rights is a complicated issue that reaches beyond the scope of this book. Failure to follow the statutory procedures exactly may undo any amendment you attempt, in addition to creating substantial liability. For that reason, you should consult your attorney before attempting to do more than the most innocuous of amendments to the articles. A corporation with more than one class of shareholders may also encounter special difficulties in amending its articles, in which case a lawyer's advice would be particularly useful.

The following is a directors' resolution recommending an amendment to the **ARTICLES OF INCORPORATION** to the shareholders. Next is a shareholders' resolution approving the amendment. Your state may have a fill-in-the-blank form that must be used for the amendment of **ARTICLES OF INCORPORATION**. If not, you can use form 120. An example of form 120 completed may be found in Chapter 13. The amendment usually becomes effective when the **Articles of Amendment** are filed.

sample of form 96: **Directors' Consent to Action Recommending an Amendment to the Articles of Incorporation**

Consent to Action without Formal Meeting by the Directors of

Scrupulous Corporation

The undersigned directors of the corporation hereby adopt the following resolution:

RESOLVED, that pursuant to the laws of the state of **West Carolina** and the articles and bylaws of the corporation, the board of directors recommends to the shareholders of the corporation that its articles of incorporation be amended by changing Article **2** to read in its entirety as follows:

2. The number of shares the corporation shall have authority to issue is 200,000 no par value.

and further

RESOLVED, that the directors recommend to the shareholders that they vote in favor of the proposed amendment, and further

RESOLVED, that the submission of the proposed amendment to the shareholders for approval shall be on the condition that the directors, by majority vote, may withdraw and cancel the amendment at any time prior to its effective date, and further

RESOLVED, that the appropriate officers of the corporation are authorized and directed to call a special meeting of the shareholders, giving appropriate notice, on **November 30, 2006** for the purpose of approving or disapproving such proposed amendment, or to obtain shareholder approval of the amendment by Consent to Action without Formal Meeting of the Shareholders; and, upon approval by the shareholders, to execute and file articles of amendment and to take such other actions as may be necessary or desirable to give effect to the proposed amendment and the foregoing resolution.

This resolution shall be effective at **10:00 a.**m. on the **17th** of **November, 2006**.

Henry Hardy
Henry Hardy, Director

Roberta Moore
Roberta Moore, Director

Raymond Rodriguez
Raymond Rodriguez, Director

sample of form 97: **SHAREHOLDERS' CONSENT TO ACTION ADOPTING THE RECOMMENDED AMENDMENT**

Consent to Action without Formal Meeting by the Directors of

Scrupulous Corporation

The undersigned shareholders of the corporation hereby adopt the following resolution:

WHEREAS, the directors of the corporation have proposed that its articles of incorporation be amended in the manner set out below and have recommended to the shareholders that such amendment be adopted by its shareholders, it is therefore

RESOLVED, that the proposal and recommendation by the directors is ratified and approved and that the articles of incorporation is of the corporation are amended by changing Article **2** to read in its entirety as follows:

2. The number of shares the corporation shall have authority to issue is 200,000 no par value.

This resolution shall be effective at **10:00 a.**m. on the **17th** of **November, 2006**.

Roberta Moore	*Hugh Hardy*
Roberta Moore, Shareholder	Hugh Hardy, Shareholder
Henry Hardy	*Raymond Rodriguez*
Henry Hardy, Shareholder	Raymond Rodriguez, Shareholder
Della Driskell	*Calvin Collier*
Della Driskell, Shareholder	Calvin Collier, Shareholder

Changing the Corporate Name

Many people incorrectly believe that, because a corporation has incorporated under a certain name, that name cannot be used by any other business. When your corporation was created, it is very likely your lawyer asked you to suggest several possible names for it. The lawyer then checked with the state to see if the names you liked were available. That is, the lawyer checked whether there were any already existing corporations with the same or very similar names.

However, for a name to be available for use, it is sufficient that it differs only slightly from existing names—maybe only a spelling difference. Even so, the fact that a name has been used by a corporation does not mean that the same name could not be adopted by a partnership or sole proprietorship, or by a corporation in another state.

Just because a name is *available* according to the standards of your Secretary of State does not mean you may legally use it. It may be that the name is the registered *trademark* or *service mark* of another company and that your use of the name would violate the rights of the mark's owner. Only a trademark search will discover whether this is true. (See Chapter 2 for more information on corporate names.)

ADOPTING A CORPORATE ALIAS

One way to change the name of your business is to adopt an *assumed* or *fictitious name*. This method is simple and quick. Usually, it does not require that you check with the state to see if a name is available. However, if you adopt as an alias a name that is someone else's trademark, you may be liable for *infringement*. So that people dealing with your company have fair notice of your company's true identity, it is required that you file a formal declaration of the alias. These filing requirements vary quite a bit from state to state.

Sometimes the filing must be done with a state agency, sometimes with the city or county where the corporation conducts its business, and sometimes both. A company could have several different assumed names. For example, it may conduct a fast food business under one name and sell television sets at a different location under another.

Below is a directors' resolution authorizing the use of an assumed name, followed by an example of a typical formal declaration that lets the public know who they are dealing with. This form may vary substantially from the one required in your state. The statute dealing with the filing requirement may well be located somewhere other than in your state's corporations act since partnerships and sole proprietorships, which adopt aliases, are also required to make such a filing.

sample of form 98: **DIRECTORS' CONSENT TO ACTION AUTHORIZING THE ADOPTION OF AN ASSUMED NAME**

Consent to Action without Formal Meeting by the Directors of

Scrupulous Corporation

The undersigned directors of the corporation hereby adopt the following resolution:

RESOLVED, that the corporation shall assume and henceforth conduct its home safety consulting business under the name **CarefulCo.**, and further

---

RESOLVED, that the appropriate officers of the corporation are authorized and directed to execute and file such certificates and declarations as may be required by law and to take such other acts as may be necessary or desirable to give effect to the foregoing resolution.

This resolution shall be effective at **10:00 a.**m. on the **27th** of **March, 2006**.

Henry Hardy
Henry Hardy, Director

Raymond Rodriguez
Raymond Rodriguez, Director

Roberta Moore
Roberta Moore, Director

CHANGING THE CORPORATION'S NAME IN THE ARTICLES OF INCORPORATION

A corporation's name is officially adopted in the **ARTICLES OF INCORPORATION**. In order to change the official name, therefore, the **ARTICLES OF INCORPORATION** must be amended. (See the discussion of the procedure for amending articles of incorporation in Chapter 12.) Examples of a directors resolution to recommend a name change, a shareholders resolution adopting the name change, and on Articles of Amendment changing the name of the corporation follow on p.184.

Name Changes and Stock Certificates

After the corporation has a new name, it will still have stock certificates circulating bearing the old name. There is no harm in this, and frequently the corporation will allow the old certificates to remain outstanding. When shares are traded, the new shareholder may ask to have new certificates issued bearing the new name.

The company may want to call in the old certificates and issue new ones in their place. It is difficult to get shareholder corporation in this effort, but it helps to make the process as simple as possible. A letter requesting such cooperation from a shareholder is on p.185.

sample of form 99: **Directors' Consent to Action**
Recommending a Name Change to the Shareholders

Consent to Action without Formal Meeting by the Directors of Scrupulous Corporation

The undersigned directors of the corporation hereby adopt the following resolution:

RESOLVED, that pursuant to the laws of the state of **West Carolina** and the articles and bylaws of the corporation, the board of directors recommends to the shareholders of the corporation that its articles of incorporation be amended to change the name of the corporation from its current name to **Scrupulous America, Inc.**, and further

RESOLVED, that such change be accomplished by amending Article **1** to read in its entirety as follows:

1. The name of the corporation is Scrupulous America, Inc.

and further

RESOLVED, that the directors recommend to the shareholders that they vote in favor of the proposed amendment, and further

RESOLVED, that the submission of the proposed amendment to the shareholders for approval shall be on the condition that the directors, by majority vote, may withdraw and cancel the amendment at any time prior to its effective date, and further

RESOLVED, that the appropriate officers of the corporation are authorized and directed to call a special meeting of the shareholders, giving appropriate notice, on **a date between May 1 and May 31, 2006**, for the purpose of approving or disapproving such proposed amendment or to obtain shareholder approval of the proposed amendment by Consent to Action without Formal Meeting of the Shareholders; and, upon approval by the shareholders, to execute and file articles of amendment and to take such other actions as may be necessary or desirable to give effect to the proposed amendment and the foregoing resolution.

This resolution shall be effective at **3:00 p.**m. on the **17th** of **April, 2006**.

Henry Hardy
Henry Hardy, Director

Raymond Rodriguez
Raymond Rodriguez, Director

Roberta Moore
Roberta Moore, Director

sample of form 100: **Shareholders' Consent to Action Adopting the Name Change**

Consent to Action without Formal Meeting by the Directors of Scrupulous Corporation

The undersigned shareholders of the corporation hereby adopt the following resolution:

WHEREAS, the directors of the corporation have proposed that its articles of incorporation be amended to change the name of the corporation and have recommended to the shareholders that such amendment be adopted by its shareholders, it is therefore

RESOLVED, that the proposal and recommendation by the directors is ratified and approved and that the articles of incorporation is of the corporation are amended by changing **Article 1** to read in its entirety as follows:

1. The name of the corporation is Scrupulous America, Inc.

This resolution shall be effective at **10:00 a.**m. on the **17th** of **April, 2006**.

Roberta Moore	*Hugh Hardy*
Roberta Moore, Shareholder	Hugh Hardy, Shareholder
Henry Hardy	*Raymond Rodriguez*
Henry Hardy, Shareholder	Raymond Rodriguez, Shareholder
Della Driskell	*Calvin Collier*
Della Driskell, Shareholder	Calvin Collier, Shareholder

---

sample of form 120: **Articles of Amendment Changing the Name of the Corporation**

Articles of Amendment of Scrupulous Corporation

The Articles of Incorporation of **Scrupulous Corporation** are hereby amended as follows:

1. The name of the corporation is **Scrupulous Corporation**.

2. The following amendment to the company's articles of incorporation was adopted by its shareholders on **December 14th, 2006** as prescribed by law:

The articles of incorporation of the corporation are hereby amended by changing Article **6** to read in its entirety as follows:

ARTICLE **6** The name of the corporation is **Scrupulous American, Inc.**

3. At the time of such adoption, the number of shares of the corporation outstanding was **100,000** and the number of votes entitled to be voted on the adoption was **100,000** and the number of votes indisputably represented at the meeting of shareholders was **100,000** shares at the meeting in person and by proxy whose voting rights were uncontested.

4. The number of undisputed votes cast for the amendment was **100,000**, a number sufficient for adoption of the proposed amendment.

5. These articles will become effective at the date and time of their filing.

The date of these Articles of Amendment is **December 28, 2006**.

Scrupulous Corporation

By: *Raymond Rodriguez*

Raymond Rodriguez, President

Sample **LETTER TO SHAREHOLDERS TO EXCHANGE OLD CERTIFICATES**

Scrupulous America, Inc.

No. 4 Beach Place, Pleasant Cove, West Carolina 27000

January 4, 2006

Henry Hardy
1440 Enterprise Blvd.
New York, NY 10033

Re: Share certificate(s) number(s): 000005

Dear Mr. Hardy:

Recently the shareholders of Scrupulous Corporation voted to change the company's name to Scrupulous America, Inc. The name change is now official, and your corporation would like to exchange your share certificate(s) for new certificates bearing the company's new name.

Enclosed for your convenience is an envelope addressed to the corporate secretary. Please place your certificates in the envelope and return them to the company. No postage is required. The secretary will issue new share certificates in the same name or names as the old ones and send them to you by return mail to the address listed above. If you would like the certificates sent to a different address, please so indicate by changing the above address as appropriate and returning this letter to us along with your old shares.

Thank you for your cooperation.

Scrupulous America, Inc.

By: *Calvin Collier*

Calvin Collier, Treasurer

Doing Business in Another State

A corporation acting in the state where it is incorporated is called a *domestic corporation*. When that corporation does business in another state, it is a *foreign corporation* in that state. Before a foreign corporation is permitted to *do business* in a state, it must apply for and receive a *certificate of authority* from the Secretary of State in the state in which the foreign corporation plans to do business. This process is somewhat confusingly called *domestication*; that is, becoming domestic in a state where the company is not incorporated.

Many corporations do most of their business as a foreign corporation. For example, a great many large corporations are incorporated under the laws of Delaware but have their principal offices—and most of their business—in other states. Such corporations are Delaware domestic corporations and foreign corporations in the states where they have their principal offices.

When is it necessary to apply for a **CERTIFICATE OF AUTHORITY**? Sometimes *doing business* in a state is not a clear-cut issue. It is clear that corporations can do some things in a state and still not meet the requirements for domestication.

Example:

An Arizona corporation sells goods by mail order. A citizen of Texas places an order through the mail, and the Arizona company fills the order. The Arizona corporation has no offices or employees resident in Texas. The Arizona corporation is not *doing business* in Texas and does not have to apply for a certificate of authority.

But suppose the Arizona corporation leases a warehouse in Texas and uses it as a distribution center for its mail order goods. It employs workers to manage the Texas warehouse. The Arizona corporation would very likely be required to domesticate in Texas.

Some kinds of business have special obligations with regard to operating in other states. For example, before an insurance company can sell a policy to a citizen of another state, even if the company has no sales people or offices resident in that state, it must be licensed by the Insurance Department of that state.

Failing to Domesticate

If a company is required to domesticate but fails to do so, the sanctions can be severe. There may be fines on the corporation or its management. There may be additional taxes or interest on fees that would have been imposed had the company properly domesticated. The foreign corporation may be denied the right to bring law suits in the state where it has failed to obtain a certificate of authority. The state may seek an injunction to prevent the corporation from doing business in the state.

Domestication Procedure

Obtaining a CERTIFICATE OF AUTHORITY bears some resemblance to incorporation. The application has some of the same information that would be found on ARTICLES OF INCORPORATION. It is also necessary to choose a name in the new state that does not conflict with the name of a corporation already doing business in that state. The standards are the same that apply when a company is incorporated. (see Chapter 2.)

If the foreign corporation is incorporated under a name that is not available in the new state, it may be necessary for the company to choose a new name for use only in the state where it is domesticating. It may be necessary to adopt an assumed name or alias in the new state. (see Chapter 13, "Changing the Corporate Name.") It will also be necessary to obtain a Certificate of Existence from the Secretary of State where the company is incorporated. This is a certification that the company is incorporated and in good standing with its home state. There is a fee for filing an Application for Certificate of Existence, which is usually about $250.

It is also necessary to designate a registered agent in the new state. The registered agent must be a person or corporation resident in the new state who is appointed to receive important official documents, such as lawsuit complaints. (see Chapter 10, "Employees and Agents.")

A resolution for adoption by the board of directors authorizing the officers of a company to apply for a **CERTIFICATE OF AUTHORITY** follows.

sample of form 101: **DIRECTORS' CONSENT TO ACTION AUTHORIZING APPLICATION FOR A CERTIFICATE OF AUTHORITY TO DO BUSINESS IN A FOREIGN STATE**

Consent to Action without Formal Meeting by the Directors of Scrupulous Corporation

The undersigned directors of the corporation hereby adopt the following resolution:

WHEREAS, management of the corporation has recommended to the board of directors that the corporation undertake business activities in the state of **New State** and have advised the board that, in order to do so, it is necessary to obtain a certificate of authority to engage in business in that state, it is therefore

RESOLVED, that the officers of the corporation are authorized and directed to apply for and obtain a certificate of authority to carry on business in the state of **New State,** and further

RESOLVED, that **Calvin Collier** at 234 **Start Up Place, Beginning County, Fresh City, New State 30800** is appointed to serve as the corporation's registered agent for service of process in the state of **New State**, and further

RESOLVED, that the officers of the corporation are authorized to file such applications and other documents and to take such further actions as may be necessary or desirable to give effect to this resolution.

This resolution shall be effective at **10:00 a.**m. on the **4th** of **December, 2006.**

Henry Hardy	*Roberta Moore*	*Raymond Rodriguez*
Henry Hardy, Director	Roberta Moore, Director	Raymond Rodriguez, Director

Following is a typical **APPLICATION FOR CERTIFICATE OF AUTHORITY** seeking permission for Scrupulous Corporation to engage in business in New State. (see form 127, p.382.) The Secretary of State where your company intends to do business will more than likely have a standard form for this application that you should use.

sample of form 127: **APPLICATION FOR CERTIFICATE OF AUTHORITY**

Application for Certificate of Authority

Pursuant to the laws of the state of New State, the undersigned corporation hereby applies for a Certificate of Authority to transact business in the State of New State and for that purpose submits the following:

1. The name of the corporation is **Scrupulous Corporation** and if the corporate name is unavailable for use in the state of New State, the name the corporation wishes to use is **Scrupulous Carolina Corporation**.

2. The state or country under whose laws the corporation was organized is: **West Carolina**.

3. The date of incorporation was **June 30, 2006** its period of duration is: **perpetual**.

4. The street address of the principal office of the corporation is:

1 Scrupulous Plaza
Pleasant Cove, West Carolina 27000

5. The mailing address if different from the street address of the principal office of the corporation is:

PO Box 0000
Pleasant Cove, West Carolina 27000

6. The street address and county of the registered office in the State of New State is:

234 Start Up Place
Beginning County
Fresh City, New State 30800

---

7. The mailing address, if different from the street address, of the registered office in the State of New State is: _____
_____.

8. The name of the registered agent in the State of New State is: **Calvin Collier**.

9. The names, titles, and usual business addresses of the current officers of the corporation are:

Name	Title	Business Address
Raymond Rodriguez	**Pres.**	**1 Scrupulous Plaza, Pleasant Cove, WC 27000**
Henry Hardy	**V. Pres.**	**1 Scrupulous Plaza, Pleasant Cove, WC 27000**
Roberta Moore	**V. Pres.**	**1 Scrupulous Plaza, Pleasant Cove, WC 27000**

10. Attached is a certificate of existence (or document of similar import), duly authenticated by the Secretary of State or other official having custody of corporate records in the state or country of incorporation.

11. If the corporation is required to use a fictitious name in order to transact business in this state, a copy of the resolution of its board of directors, certified by its secretary, adopting the fictitious name is attached.

12. This application will be effective upon filing, unless a delayed date and/or time is specified: _____.

This the **10th** day of **July 2006**.

Name of Corporation: **Scrupulous Corporation**

Signature: *Raymond Rodriguez*

Type or Print Name and Title: **Raymond Rodriguez, President**

OTHER BUSINESS REQUIREMENTS

Any time a company engages in business in a new location, it must comply with the local laws. There may be many requirements with regard to taxes, employment law, business licensing laws, etc., which must be considered just as they had to be considered when the company began business in its home state. The Secretary of State's website, or other state government websites, often provide useful information about local requirements.

Mergers

There are many different ways one business can acquire another. One company could buy the shares of another, after which the acquired company would be a subsidiary of the acquiring company. One company could buy the business assets of another, leaving behind a shell corporation that continues to be owned by its old shareholders. Or there could be a *merger* in which the acquired corporation becomes a part of, and disappears into, the acquiring corporation.

Each acquisition method has advantages and disadvantages. Depending on the type of business and the separate (often conflicting) concerns of the acquiring entity, the acquisition target, and their various owners, some method should be chosen that best serves the interests of the parties. The successful negotiation of an acquisition is not an easy task. Too often business people begin the process with insufficient experience or advice. They reach an advanced stage in the process of agreement only to find that they have overlooked some wrinkle in tax law, securities law, or corporate law that frustrates the deal or greatly devalues it. Get the professional advice you need early enough to make it effective.

STATUTORY METHODS FOR MERGING CORPORATIONS

Mergers between corporations, or between corporations and other types of entities, can occur only because there are statutes that allow it to happen. In order for a merger to occur, the steps laid out in the statute must be followed carefully and completely or else the merger may not be effective. It can be a complex procedure and should not be attempted without competent legal advice.

There are many different kinds of mergers, differing chiefly in the number and relationships of the companies involved and the payment for shares given up by the shareholders whose company disappears into another company.

Example:

In a cash merger, the shareholders of the acquired (nonsurviving) corporation receive cash in exchange for their shares. Often the shareholders of the acquired corporation receive shares of the acquiring (surviving) corporation in exchange for their shares.

In a *triangular merger*, the acquired (target) corporation disappears into a subsidiary of the acquiring corporation. The subsidiary survives and the target's shareholders receive shares of the subsidiary's parent or some other consideration for their shares of the target corporation.

In a *reverse triangular merger*, the acquired corporation survives as a subsidiary of the parent and its former shareholders receive shares of the parent in exchange for the shares of the acquired company. One form is frequently chosen over another for its tax consequences.

In recent years, many states have amended their statutes to facilitate mergers between corporations and other entities such as limited liability companies and limited partnerships. (See Chapter 1 for more information about these entities.) These mergers are called *cross-species* mergers or *inter-species* mergers, and they are very similar to mergers between corporations. Many states have standard forms, similar to articles of merger between corporations, to assist with cross-species mergers. Check the website of your state's Secretary of State.

CORPORATIONS OF DIFFERENT STATES

What if the corporations are organized in different states? A corporation organized under the laws of one state may merge with a corporation organized under the laws of another state. In that case, the laws and procedures of both states must be followed exactly. Sometimes this leads to curious and annoying contradictions. For example, the merger may become *effective* in one state before it does in the other.

Each state may require similar but slightly different forms to be filed. If the surviving corporation wishes to continue conducting business in the state where the nonsurviving corporation conducted its business, it will be necessary for the surviving corporation to *domesticate* in that state by filing additional forms. These forms, among other things, designate a person in that state to be the agent on whom notice of lawsuits and other forms of process may be served. (see Chapter 14.)

MERGER OF A SUBSIDIARY CORPORATION INTO ITS PARENT

The usual procedure for a merger is similar to the procedure for amending the **ARTICLES OF INCORPORATION**. That is, the directors propose and recommend the merger and the shareholders then either approve or disapprove it. Also, as in the case of some amendments, some mergers may be accomplished by a short cut.

When the merger is between a parent corporation and a wholly owned subsidiary (i.e., the parent owns 100% of the shares), the directors can do it alone without shareholder approval. (MBCA, Sec. 11.04.) That makes sense because the shareholders own the same thing after the merger that they owned before—it is just arranged in a different set of boxes. Provided the laws of both states allow it, you can accomplish a short form merger of this type between two corporations incorporated under the laws of different states.

In a merger, the directors of the parent corporation adopt a plan of merger and file **ARTICLES OF MERGER** with the state incorporating the plan. There is a short form and a long form in Appendix C. (see form 103 and 106, respectively.)

sample of form 102: **Directors' Consent to Action**
Adopting a Plan of Merger for Merging with a Subsidiary Corporation

---

Consent to Action without Formal Meeting by the Directors of

Scrupulous Corporation

The undersigned directors of the corporation hereby adopt the following resolution:

WHEREAS the directors of the corporation have determined that it is in the best interests of the corporation that it merge with its wholly owned subsidiary (the Merging Corporation), it is therefore

RESOLVED, that the following plan of merger between this corporation and its wholly owned subsidiary, Honor Corporation, is hereby approved and adopted:

Plan of Merger

A. The name of the parent corporation into which the subsidiary shall merge is Scrupulous Corporation, which shall be the Surviving Corporation, and the name of the subsidiary corporation which shall merge into the parent is Honor Corporation, which shall be the Merging Corporation.

B. On the effective date of the merger, the Merging Corporation shall merge into the Surviving Corporation and the corporate existence of the Merging Corporation shall cease. The shares of the Merging Corporation shall not be converted into shares, obligations, or other securities of the Surviving Corporation or any other corporation or into cash or other property in whole or in part. The outstanding shares of the Surviving Corporation will not be converted, exchanged, or altered in any manner, but shall remain outstanding shares of the Surviving Corporation.

C. The directors of the Surviving Corporation may, in their discretion, abandon this merger at any time before its effective date.

D. The effective date of this merger shall be the close of business on the date articles of merger relating to this merger are filed as required by law.

Further RESOLVED, that the corporation, as shareholder of the Merging Corporation, waives all notice of the proposed merger, and further

RESOLVED, that the appropriate officers of the corporation are authorized and directed to execute and file articles of merger and to take such other actions as may be necessary or desirable to give effect to the above resolution.

This resolution shall be effective at **10:00 a.**m. on the **30th** of **March, 2006.**

Henry Hardy	*Roberta Moore*	*Raymond Rodriguez*
Henry Hardy, Director	Roberta Moore, Director	Raymond Rodriguez, Director

sample of form 103: **Articles of Merger (Short Form)**

Articles of Merger of

Honor Corporation

into

Scrupulous Corporation

These Articles of Merger are submitted by **Scrupulous Corporation** organized under the laws of **West Carolina** (the "Surviving Corporation") for the purpose of merging its subsidiary corporation **Honor Corporation** organized under the laws of **New State** (the "Merging Corporation")into the Surviving Corporation.

1. The following Plan of Merger has been duly approved by the board of directors of the surviving corporation.

Plan of Merger

A. The name of the parent corporation into which the subsidiary shall merge is **Scrupulous Corporation** which shall be the Surviving Corporation, and the name of the subsidiary corporation which shall merge into the parent is **Honor Corporation** which shall be the Merging Corporation.

B. On the effective date of the merger, the Merging Corporation shall merge into the Surviving Corporation and the corporate existence of the Merging Corporation shall cease. The shares of the Merging Corporation shall not be converted into shares, obligations, or other securities of the Surviving Corporation, or any other corporation, or into cash, or other property in whole or in part. The outstanding shares of the Surviving Corporation will not be converted, exchanged, or altered in any manner, but shall remain outstanding shares of the Surviving Corporation.

C. The directors of the Surviving Corporation may, in their discretion, abandon this merger at any time before its effective date.

D. The effective date of this merger shall be the close of business on the date articles of merger relating to this merger are filed as required by law.

2. Shareholder approval of the merger was not required because the Surviving Corporation was the owner of 100% of the outstanding shares of the Merging Corporation, and the Plan of Merger does not provide for any amendment to the articles of incorporation of the Surviving Corporation.

These articles of merger were signed by the corporation on **April 1, 2006**.

Scrupulous Corporation

By: *Raymond Rodriguez*

Raymond Rodriguez, President

MERGER OF CORPORATIONS WITH DIFFERENT OWNERS

As you would expect, when the corporations intending to merge have different owners, the owners must have a chance to approve or disapprove the proposal.

Board of Directors and Shareholders

In a merger of independent corporations, the shareholders are acquiring and disposing of property—not just rearranging it. So the directors of the corporations must recommend the proposed merger to the shareholders, and then the shareholders of each corporation must approve the proposed plan of merger. If the directors, because of a conflict of interest or for some other sufficient reason, believe they should not favorably recommend the proposed merger, they must explain to the shareholders why they cannot take a position.

The complexities must be carefully considered in the merger of two or more corporations with different owners. The plan of merger will very likely be a much more complex document than the one in the previous example. In fact, when the corporations are any more than shell corporations, there will likely be a separate merger agreement that covers the many details inherent in combining two unique and ongoing business operations.

The three forms on the following pages illustrate the kind of basic documents that would accomplish such a merger (i.e., a directors' resolution recommending a merger plan, a shareholders' resolution adopting the plan, and the long form **ARTICLES OF MERGER**). (see form 106, p.351.) In the examples, one share of the surviving corporation will be issued for each share of the merging corporation. After the merger is complete, the shareholders of the merging corporation will be new shareholders of the surviving corporation. As usual, your state will have standard forms for **ARTICLES OF MERGER**, available from the Secretary of State's or the Secretary's website.

An infinite number of other arrangements are possible, including some other ratio for issuing shares (e.g., two shares of the survivor for each share of the merging corporation) or cash given in exchange for shares of the merging corporation.

The samples of shareholders' and directors' resolutions authorizing mergers are given in the form of Consents to Action. Mergers and acquisitions are serious matters for any corporation and should be undertaken only after due consideration and possibly debate. This may be an issue you want to discuss in a real meeting rather than trying to accomplish the procedure with Consents to Action. Remember, you want to be able to prove that your directors carefully considered the issues before making the decision. A way to do that is with the carefully drafted minutes of a real meeting. (see Chapter 3.)

sample of form 104: **Directors' Consent to Action Recommending a Plan of Merger to the Shareholders**

Consent to Action without Formal Meeting by the Directors of

Scrupulous Corporation

The undersigned directors of the corporation hereby adopt the following resolution:

WHEREAS, the directors of the corporation, after due consideration, have determined that it is in the best interests of the corporation that it enter into a merger with **Home Safety Systems, Inc.** under the terms of a plan of merger set out below, it is therefore

RESOLVED, that pursuant to the laws of the state of **West Carolina** and the articles and bylaws of the corporation, the board of directors recommends to the shareholders of the corporation that the following Plan of Merger be adopted by the shareholders:

Plan of Merger

A. ***Home Safety Systems, Inc.***, *which shall be the Merging Corporation, shall merge into **Scrupulous Corporation**, which shall be the Surviving Corporation.*

B. *On the effective date of the merger, the Merging Corporation shall merge into the Surviving Corporation, and the corporate existence of the Merging Corporation shall cease. On the effective date of the merger, each outstanding share of the Merging Corporation shall be converted into **one** share of the Surviving Corporation. The outstanding shares of the Surviving Corporation will not be converted, exchanged, or altered in any manner, but shall remain outstanding shares of the Surviving Corporation.*

C. Each shareholder of the Merging Corporation holding a certificate representing share(s) of such corporation shall surrender the certificate and shall be entitled to receive certificate(s) representing the shares of the Surviving Corporation to which the Shareholder is entitled under this Plan of Merger. After the effective date of the merger and before such surrender, each certificate representing shares of the Merging Corporation shall be deemed for all purposes to evidence ownership of the shares of the Surviving Corporation to which the Shareholder is entitled under this Plan of Merger.

D.   The directors of the Surviving Corporation or the Merging Corporation may, in their discretion, abandon this merger at any time before its effective date.

E. The effective date of this merger shall be the close of business on the date articles of merger relating to this Plan of Merger are filed as required by law.

Further RESOLVED, that the submission of the Plan of Merger to the shareholders for approval shall be on the condition that the directors, by majority vote, may withdraw and cancel such proposed merger at any time before its effective date, and further

RESOLVED, that the appropriate officers of the corporation are hereby authorized and directed to call a special meeting of the shareholders, giving appropriate notice, on **a date selected by the President during the month of May** for the purpose of approving or disapproving the Plan of Merger, or to obtain shareholder approval of the Plan of Merger by Consent to Action without Formal Meeting; and, upon approval by the shareholders of the corporations participating in the proposed merger to execute and file articles of merger and to take such other actions as may be necessary or desirable to give effect to the Plan of Merger and this resolution.

This resolution shall be effective at **10:00 a.**m. on the **17th** of **April, 2006**.

Henry Hardy
_____
Henry Hardy, Director

Roberta Moore
_____
Roberta Moore, Director

Raymond Rodriguez
_____
Raymond Rodriguez, Director

sample of form 105: **SHAREHOLDERS' CONSENT TO ACTION ADOPTING A PLAN OF MERGER**

Consent to Action without Formal Meeting by the Shareholders of

Scrupulous Corporation

The undersigned shareholders of the corporation hereby adopt the following resolution:

WHEREAS, the directors of the corporation have proposed the adoption of a Plan of Merger accomplishing the merger of **Home Safety Systems, Inc.** into **Scrupulous Corporation** and have recommended to the shareholders that the Plan of Merger be adopted, it is therefore

RESOLVED, that such proposal and recommendation by the directors is ratified and approved and that the following Plan of Merger is adopted:

Plan of Merger

A. ***Home Safety Systems, Inc.**, which shall be the Merging Corporation, shall merge into **Scrupulous Corporation**, which shall be the Surviving Corporation.*

B. *On the effective date of the merger, the Merging Corporation shall merge into the Surviving Corporation, and the corporate existence of the Merging Corporation shall cease. On the effective date of the merger, each outstanding share of the Merging Corporation shall be converted into **one** share of the Surviving Corporation. The outstanding shares of the Surviving Corporation will not be converted, exchanged, or altered in any manner, but shall remain outstanding shares of the Surviving Corporation.*

C. *Each shareholder of the Merging Corporation holding a certificate representing share(s) of such corporation shall surrender the certificate and shall be entitled to receive certificate(s) representing the shares of the Surviving Corporation to which the Shareholder is entitled under this Plan of Merger. After the effective date of the merger and before such surrender, each certificate representing shares of the Merging Corporation shall be deemed for all purposes to evidence ownership of the shares of the Surviving Corporation to which the Shareholder is entitled under this Plan of Merger.*

D. *The directors of the Surviving Corporation or the Merging Corporation may, in their discretion abandon this merger at any time before its effective date.*

E. *The effective date of this merger shall be the close of business on the date articles of merger relating to this Plan of Merger are filed as required by law.*

This resolution shall be effective at **3:00 p.**m. on the **17th** of **April, 2006**.

Roberta Moore	*Hugh Hardy*
Roberta Moore, Shareholder	Hugh Hardy, Shareholder
Henry Hardy	*Raymond Rodriguez*
Henry Hardy, Shareholder	Raymond Rodriguez, Shareholder
Della Driskell	*Calvin Collier*
Della Driskell, Shareholder	Calvin Collier, Shareholder

sample of form 106: **Articles of Merger (Long Form)**

Articles of Merger of

Home Safety Systems, Inc.

into

Scrupulous Corporation

These Articles of Merger are submitted by **Scrupulous Corporation** organized under the laws of **West Carolina** (the "Surviving Corporation") for the purpose of merging **Home Safety Systems, Inc.**, organized under the laws of **New State** (the "Merging Corporation") into the Surviving Corporation.

1. The following Plan of Merger has been duly approved by the boards of directors of the Surviving Corporation and the Merging Corporation:

Plan of Merger

A. Home Safety Systems, Inc., which shall be the Merging Corporation, shall merge into Scrupulous Corporation, which shall be the Surviving Corporation.

B. On the effective date of the merger, the Merging Corporation shall merge into the Surviving Corporation and the corporate existence of the Merging Corporation shall cease. On the effective date of the merger, each outstanding share of the Merging Corporation shall be converted into one share of the Surviving Corporation. The outstanding shares of the Surviving Corporation will not be converted, exchanged, or altered in any manner, but shall remain outstanding shares of the Surviving Corporation.

C. Each shareholder of the Merging Corporation holding a certificate representing share(s) of such corporation shall surrender such certificate and shall be entitled to receive certificate(s) representing the shares of the Surviving Corporation to which the Shareholder is entitled under this Plan of Merger. After the effective date of the merger and before such surrender, each certificate representing shares of the Merging Corporation shall be deemed for all purposes to evidence ownership of a like number of shares of the Surviving Corporation.

D. The directors of the Surviving Corporation or the Merging Corporation may, in their discretion, abandon this merger at any time before its effective date.

E. The effective date of this merger shall be the close of business on the date articles of merger relating to this Plan of Merger are filed as required by law.

2. The designation and number of outstanding shares and the number of votes entitled to be cast by each voting group entitled to vote separately on such Plan as to the Merging Corporation were:

Designation:	Shares outstanding:	Votes entitled to be cast:
Common shares	1,000,000	1,000,000

The number of votes cast for such Plan by shareholders of the Merging Corporation was **89,000** which was sufficient for approval of the Plan by the shareholders of the Merging Corporation.

3. The designation and number of outstanding shares and the number of votes entitled to be cast by each voting group entitled to vote separately on such Plan as to the Surviving Corporation were:

Designation:	Shares outstanding:	Votes entitled to be cast:
Common shares	1,000,000	1,000,000

The number of votes cast for such Plan by shareholders of the Surviving Corporation was **100,000** which was sufficient for approval of the Plan by the shareholders of the Surviving Corporation.

These articles of merger were signed by the corporation on **November 10, 2006**.

By: *Raymond Rodriguez*

Raymond Rodriguez, President

Dissenting Shareholders

See the discussion of dissenters' rights in Chapter 12. The merger of a corporation is one of those fundamental changes that will give rise to dissenters' rights, and it must be dealt with carefully and cautiously for the reasons discussed earlier.

Exchanging Stock Certificates

When the shareholders of the merging corporation will be getting shares of the surviving corporation in connection with the merger, you will want to retrieve their old certificates and replace them with certificates for the correct number of shares of the surviving corporation. You will note in the plan of merger that, even if the shareholders do not cooperate, the old share certificates nevertheless represent shares of the surviving corporation once the merger is effective.

UNAVOIDABLE COMPLEXITIES

Mergers and other forms of acquisition can have very serious tax effects and should not be undertaken without ample expert advice. If one or the other of the corporations involved has a substantial number of shareholders, the same securities regulations discussed in Chapter 6 will apply. (In a merger, the shares of one or both of the corporations involved are bought and sold.) A vote of the shareholders may be required, in which case the securities regulations mentioned in Chapter 7 will apply. The advice of an experienced securities lawyer may be indispensable.

chapter 16

Other Methods of Acquiring a Business

Other than mergers, stock purchases and asset purchases are the usual methods of acquiring a business. In a stock purchase, the acquirer will simply purchase most or all of the outstanding shares of a corporation. Usually this means that the purchaser will negotiate the purchase of each individual shareholder's stock. It works well if there is only one or a few shareholders, but presents obvious difficulties if there are many. For instance, if the corporation has 300 or 3,000 shareholders—how do you negotiate that many individual stock purchase deals?

SHARE EXCHANGE

Most states now allow a *share exchange* procedure in which the shareholders of the target corporation vote on whether to sell all their shares as a group to an acquiring corporation. The procedure is very much like a merger. That is, the directors of the two corporations involved in the acquisition recommend to their respective shareholders that they adopt a *plan of share exchange*.

The principal practical difference between a merger and a share exchange is that, in a merger, the acquired (target) corporation loses its separate identity. That is, it disappears into the acquiring corporation. In a share exchange, both the acquiring corporation and the target corporation continue to exist as separate corporations. Just as there can be mergers between corporations and other entities such as limited liability companies (cross-species, see Chapter 15), there can be share exchanges involving corporations and other entities.

The plan may provide for the target shareholders giving up their shares in exchange for cash, or shares of the acquiring corporation, or some other combination. If the shareholders of the two corporations approve the plan, then the acquiring corporation becomes the owner of the shares of the target corporation. Shareholders of the target corporation, like shareholders of a merging corporation, have dissenters' rights. If they follow the procedures correctly, shareholders of the target corporation may force the new corporation to buy their shares for *fair value* as that may ultimately be determined by a court. Another way to acquire the shares of a corporation through purchase is by way of a tender offer. (see page 208.)

In an asset purchase, the acquirer buys most or all of the things owned by the target business and uses the assets to continue the business, more or less leaving behind a shell. The great thing about an asset purchase is that the buyer can pick and choose what it wants and leave behind the undesirable parts—including liabilities.

Stock purchases and asset purchases may sound simpler than mergers, but do not be deceived. The tax implications are at least as complex, and although you *may* avoid a shareholders vote in a stock or asset transaction, you *may not*. A share exchange will require the same sort of vote that a merger would. And, if a corporation sells all (or substantially all) its assets except *in the ordinary course of business*, that too requires shareholder approval. Because selling all a company's assets is almost by definition not in the ordinary course of business, shareholder approval of an asset sale is almost always required.

STOCK TRANSACTIONS

The usual stock transaction involves one corporation buying all the outstanding shares of another from one or several shareholders. The procedure is not different in concept from the procedure you would use to buy a house. After looking over the purchase and deciding it is what you want, you negotiate a deal.

Frequently there is a *letter of intent*, a sort of preliminary agreement, sometimes called an *agreement in principle*, laying out the basic terms of the deal. This serves as a sort of verbal handshake. It may be a legally binding contract even though it is short and informal, so treat it with respect. It may have legal consequences, so do not sign it unless you mean it. Once there is an agreement to agree embodied in the letter of intent, your lawyers will negotiate a more detailed definitive agreement which will cover the items mentioned in the letter of intent and many others.

The final decision to buy will have to be made by the board of directors in a resolution. Of course, management will have kept the directors fully informed of the negotiations throughout the process and may want the directors to specifically authorize each step by appropriate resolutions.

sample of form 107: **DIRECTORS' CONSENT TO ACTION AUTHORIZING AN ACQUISITION OF STOCK**

Consent to Action without Formal Meeting by the Directors of

Scrupulous Corporation

The undersigned directors of the corporation hereby adopt the following resolution:

WHEREAS, management of the corporation has entered into negotiations with **Homer M. Safety** for the sale and purchase of the outstanding shares of **Home Safety Systems, Inc.** by this company, and after due consideration the directors have determined that such transaction under the terms and conditions expressed in the **Corporate Acquisition Agreement** presented to the directors (the Agreement) (a copy of the Agreement is located in management Storage file No. 07-57) is in the best interests of the Corporation, it is therefore

RESOLVED, that the purchase of the outstanding shares of **Home Safety Systems, Inc.** by this corporation under the terms and conditions of the Agreement executed by management dated **June 15, 2007**, is approved, ratified, and confirmed, and further

RESOLVED, that the appropriate officers of the corporation are authorized and directed to take such actions as may be necessary or desirable to give effect the above resolution and the Agreement.

This resolution shall be effective at **3:00 p.**m. on the **30th** of **November, 2006**.

Henry Hardy
Henry Hardy, Director

Roberta Moore
Roberta Moore, Director

Raymond Rodriguez
Raymond Rodriguez, Director

Tender Offers   When there are too many shareholders to negotiate a stock transaction with each of them, a *tender offer* may be a workable alternative. A tender offer is really a package of offers made simultaneously by a potential buyer to each individual shareholder on a take it or leave it basis, conditioned on there being enough takers to satisfy the buyer. Each shareholder decides whether or not to sell. If enough of them agree to sell, the buyer will have the number of shares it wants.

However, when there are so many shareholders that individual negotiations are impractical, the tender offer procedure may become an expensive proposition richly complicated in its own right. Tender offers are highly regulated by the Securities and Exchange Commission and by state governments. If you are contemplating a tender offer, be sure to consult your lawyer.

ASSET TRANSACTIONS

In an asset transaction, instead of buying a batch of identical things—shares of stock—you are buying a list of individual items—

desks, computers, paper clips, trucks, etc. It may be that some of these assets are transferable only by way of special documentation.

Example:

If you are buying the target's fleet of automobiles, you have to deal with the title documents peculiar to motor vehicles. If you are buying the target's real estate, deeds must be recorded. If you are buying shares of stock that the target owns, the share certificates must be endorsed and the transfer recorded by the issuing corporation.

So an asset transaction may involve a formidable stack of documents. Nevertheless, the same basic documents involved in a typical stock transaction will be somewhere in the stack.

If the seller is a corporation disposing of all or substantially all of its assets, the transaction will have to be approved by the seller's shareholders in much the same way that they would have to approve a merger or share exchange. The example that follows demonstrates the directors' authorization to purchase assets.

sample of form 108: **DIRECTORS' CONSENT TO ACTION AUTHORIZING PURCHASE OF ASSETS OF ANOTHER BUSINESS**

Consent to Action without Formal Meeting by the Directors of

Scrupulous Corporation

The undersigned directors of the corporation hereby adopt the following resolution:

WHEREAS, management of the corporation has entered into negotiations with for the sale and purchase of substantially all of the assets of **Home Safety Systems, Inc.** by this company, and after due consideration the directors have determined that such transaction under the terms and conditions expressed in the **Asset Acquisition Agreement** presented to the directors (the Agreement) (a copy of the Agreement is located in management Storage file No. 07-87) is in the best interests of the Corporation, it is therefore

RESOLVED, that the purchase of the assets of **Home Safety Systems, Inc.** by this corporation under the terms and conditions of the Agreement executed by management dated **June 1, 2006**, is approved, ratified, and confirmed, and further

RESOLVED, that the appropriate officers of the corporation are authorized and directed to take such actions as may be necessary or desirable to give effect the above resolution and the Agreement.

This resolution shall be effective at **3:00 p.**m. on the **30th** of **November, 2006**.

Henry Hardy　　　　　　　　　*Roberta Moore*
Henry Hardy, Director　　　　　　Roberta Moore, Director

Raymond Rodriguez
Raymond Rodriguez, Director

Bulk Sales　　One of the advantages of an asset transaction mentioned above is that the buyer can leave undesirable assets and liabilities of the seller behind and purchase only the assets the buyer really wants. This is in contrast to a merger or stock acquisition in which the buyer becomes responsible for the target's liabilities at the same time it acquires the target's assets. There is a danger then, that in an asset deal, a corporation might keep its debts while giving up all the assets it could use to pay the debts, thus cheating its creditors.

Many states have enacted *bulk sales statutes* as a safeguard for creditors in such situations. The statutes require that a company selling most of its assets must give fair notice to its creditors so they can take steps to protect themselves. If the requirements of the statute are not followed precisely, the buyer will find itself responsible for the seller's debts whether it wants them or not.

In recent years, bulk sales statutes have received considerable criticism and some states have repealed them. If your state has a bulk sales statute, it will probably be found in Article 6 of the state's Uniform Commercial Code. Compliance with this statute can be tricky, and you should consult your lawyers.

As with mergers and share exchanges, shareholders of a corporation selling substantially all of its assets will have dissenters' rights. (see Chapter 12.)

Financial Transactions

The purchase and financing of major assets is a complicated but necessary fact of life for most businesses. This chapter summarizes the procedures for several typical transactions.

BORROWING MONEY

Like other people, corporations sometimes need more money than they have and must borrow money from a bank or a friend. The procedure is not much different from the procedure for an individual.

Borrowing from an Institution

When the corporation goes to a bank for a loan, the bank will usually insist on using its own standard form documents right down to a standard form resolution for the directors to vote on authorizing the loan. The forms given next are much shorter and less formal than standard bank forms are likely to be and are more suitable for smaller loans such as ones that might be obtained by a small company from one of its shareholders.

Possible Conflicts

When a corporation borrows from a *friend*, that is, a shareholder or director, some potential conflicts arise. The company and the director or shareholder must be careful to avoid potential liability. (see

Chapter 11.) With the right context, such as that provided with the purchase of property from a director (see Chapter 11), the following resolution may be used in borrowing from a director, shareholder, or other person.

sample of form 112: **DIRECTORS' CONSENT TO ACTION AUTHORIZING THE BORROWING OF MONEY**

Consent to Action without Formal Meeting by the Directors of

Scrupulous Corporation

The undersigned directors of the corporation hereby adopt the following resolution:

RESOLVED, that the corporation shall borrow from **The Bank of Care** the sum of **$100,000.00 (One Hundred Thousand Dollars and 00 cents)** at the rate of interest and payable according to the terms of a promissory note presented to the directors for their approval (the Note) (located in management Storage File no. 07-98), and further

RESOLVED, that the president or vice president and secretary or assistant secretary of the corporation are authorized and directed to execute the Note under the seal of the corporation, to receive the proceeds of the loan, to deposit the loan proceeds into the depository accounts of the corporation, and to take such other actions as may be necessary or desirable to give effect to this resolution.

This resolution shall be effective at **10:00 a.**m. on the **30th** of **November, 2006**.

Henry Hardy
Henry Hardy, Director

Roberta Moore
Roberta Moore, Director

Raymond Rodriguez
Raymond Rodriguez, Director

LOANING MONEY

The primary lending done by small corporations is the lending of money to officers and directors. Such lending should not be undertaken lightly. Lending money to a shareholder may be considered a distribution of corporate assets and may be subject to the same limitations as dividends. (see Chapter 8.) Moreover, it is an unequal distribution (that is, some shareholders get it and some do not) and may be subject to legal limitations for that reason. Such distributions may also have surprising and unwelcome tax effects. Lending to officers and directors may be a conflict of interest and subject the borrowers to liability for a breach of their fiduciary duty to the corporation. Therefore, it would be a good idea to consult an attorney and tax accountant before making such loans.

sample of form 113: **DIRECTORS' CONSENT TO ACTION AUTHORIZING A LOAN TO AN OFFICER OR DIRECTOR**

Consent to Action without Formal Meeting by the Directors of

Scrupulous Corporation

The undersigned directors of the corporation hereby adopt the following resolution:

RESOLVED, that the corporation shall lend to **Hugh Hardy** the sum of **$5,000.00 (Five Thousand Dollars and 00 cents)** and further

RESOLVED, that the **Treasurer** of the corporation is authorized to issue a check to **Hugh Hardy** for the sum of **$5,000.00** upon receipt of a promissory note signed by the borrower providing for the repayment of the principle of the loan and payment of interest at the rate of **06.5** per cent per annum in **48 equal monthly installments**.

This resolution shall be effective at **3:00 p.**m. on the **30th** of **November, 2006**.

Henry Hardy
Henry Hardy, Director

Roberta Moore
Roberta Moore, Director

Raymond Rodriguez
Raymond Rodriguez, Director

BUYING AND SELLING REAL ESTATE

Unless the business of your corporation is the purchase, development, and resale or leasing of real property, it is likely that the decision to buy or sell land or buildings represents a significant step. It will follow careful, and possibly quite lengthy, consideration including a period of investigation, appraisal, and thought about the future of the business. The issue may be visited several times by the board of directors, which may want to be involved at every step.

Eventually the final decision will be made and the authority of the board of directors to complete the transaction will be needed. Following is a directors' resolution authorizing the purchase of real property with the proceeds of a bank loan. It presumes that the directors have previously authorized the company's officers to negotiate the purchase and enter into contracts subject to the board's final approval. On page 216 is a resolution authorizing the sale of real property.

sample of form 114: DIRECTORS' CONSENT TO ACTION
AUTHORIZING THE PURCHASE OF REAL PROPERTY

Consent to Action without Formal Meeting by the Directors of

Scrupulous Corporation

The undersigned directors of the corporation hereby adopt the following resolution:

WHEREAS, management of the corporation, under authority previously given by this board of directors, have entered into negotiations for the purchase of real property located at **No. 6 Beach Place, Pleasant Cove, West Carolina** (the Property) and have recommended to the directors that the corporation agree to the purchase of the Property for the sum of **$250,000.00** under the terms of a "Contract for the Sale and Purchase of Real Property" dated **September 10, 2006**, (a copy of the contract is located in management storage file no. 06-54), and

WHEREAS, management has recommended that the corporation purchase the Property using the proceeds of a loan negotiated by management from **The Bank of Care** under the terms of a "loan

Agreement" dated **September 10, 2006** (management storage file no. 06-54), and

WHEREAS, after due consideration, the board of directors believes such transactions to be in the best interests of the corporation, it is therefore,

RESOLVED, that the "Contract for the Sale and Purchase of Real Property" dated **September 10, 2006** between **WC Beach Properties, Inc.** and the corporation and the "Loan Agreement" dated **September 10, 2006**, between **The Bank of Care** and the corporation presented to this board for its consideration are approved, ratified, and confirmed, and further

RESOLVED, that the appropriate officers of the corporation are authorized and directed, with the advice of corporate legal counsel, to execute other documents, including without limitation notes, mortgages, and deeds of trust, in order to complete the described borrowing of money and purchase of real property according to the terms of such agreements, and to take such further actions as may be necessary or desirable to give effect to this resolution.

This resolution shall be effective at **10:00 a.**m. on the **1st** of **September, 2006**.

Henry Hardy
Henry Hardy, Director

Roberta Moore
Roberta Moore, Director

Raymond Rodriguez
Raymond Rodriguez, Director

sample of form 115: DIRECTORS' CONSENT TO ACTION
AUTHORIZING THE SALE OF REAL PROPERTY

Consent to Action without Formal Meeting by the Directors of

Scrupulous Corporation

The undersigned directors of the corporation hereby adopt the following resolution:

WHEREAS, management of the corporation, under authority previously given by this board of directors, have entered into negotiations for the sale of real property belonging to the corporation located at **416 Swamp Boulevard** and have recommended to the directors that the corporation agree to the sale of such property for the amount of **$350,000** under the terms and conditions contained in a "Contract for the Sale and Purchase of Real Property" dated **August 30, 2006** (a copy of such contract is located in management storage file no. 06-53), and

WHEREAS, after due consideration, the board of directors believes the transaction to be in the best interests of the corporation, it is therefore,

RESOLVED, that the "contract for the Sale and Purchase of Real Property" dated **August 30, 2006** between the corporation and **WC Swamp Properties LLC** presented to this board for its consideration is approved, ratified, and confirmed, and further,

RESOLVED, that the appropriate officers of the corporation are authorized and directed, with the advice of corporate legal counsel, to execute other documents, including without limitation a deed for the transfer of such property, in order to complete the sale of the property according to the terms of the approved agreement, and to take such further actions as may be necessary or desirable to give effect to this resolution.

This resolution shall be effective at **10:00 a.**m. on the **30th** of **August, 2006**.

Henry Hardy
Henry Hardy, Director

Roberta Moore
Roberta Moore, Director

Raymond Rodriguez
Raymond Rodriguez, Director

Contracts, Deeds, and Lawyers

Buying and selling real estate has been going on for thousands of years. One of the reasons we developed law in the first place was to protect the ownership of real estate without the need for armed combat. So the laws are detailed and, like the lands they deal with, are uniquely tied to and vary with the jurisdiction. A lawyer who knows the applicable state law and even the recording customs at the local court house will be indispensable even for small real estate transactions. He or she will know what to do about title searches, insurance, and countless little details that will nevertheless loom large if not handled correctly.

Closing the Sale

A real estate closing can be a monumental paper shuffle, especially if the property is complex commercial property. Once again the value of an attorney experienced in the procedure will be indispensable. But you have a part, too.

Keep an eye on the detail. Before the closing, become as familiar as you can with the documents that will pass under your nose. You know what is important to you better than your lawyer does. There will not be much time for reading and explanations at the closing, and what there is you will likely be paying for by the hour.

LEASING REAL ESTATE

Leasing real property is a lot like buying it. In fact, you are buying it for a period of time, so the process is in some ways similar. Commercial real estate leases are usually quite long and vary considerably with the nature of the property involved. As with a purchase, any lease of real property is going to be an important event for the company that will require the directors' approval.

sample of form 116: **Directors' Consent to Action Authorizing the Lease of Real Property**

Consent to Action without Formal Meeting by the Directors of

Scrupulous Corporation

The undersigned directors of the corporation hereby adopt the following resolution:

WHEREAS, management of the corporation, under authority previously given by this board of directors, have entered into negotiations for the long term lease of real property located at **No. 5 Beach Place, Pleasant Cove, West Carolina** and have recommended to the directors that the corporation agree to the lease of such property under the terms and conditions contained in a "Contract for the Lease of Real Property" dated **September 1, 2006**, (a copy of such contract is located in management storage file no. 06-55), and

WHEREAS, after due consideration, the board of directors believes such transaction to be in the best interests of the corporation, it is therefore,

RESOLVED, that the "Contract for the Lease of Real Property" dated **September 1, 2006**, between **Samantha Surfcomb** and the corporation presented to this board for its consideration is approved, ratified, and confirmed, and further,

RESOLVED, that the appropriate officers of the corporation are authorized and directed, to take such further actions as may be necessary or desirable to give effect to this resolution.

This resolution shall be effective at **10:00 a.**m. on the **4th** of **September, 2006**.

Henry Hardy _____   _Roberta Moore_ _____
Henry Hardy, Director   Roberta Moore, Director

Raymond Rodriguez _____
Raymond Rodriguez, Director

SELLING AND PURCHASING EQUIPMENT

This, and the following section, are written mostly for the benefit of the business that occasionally purchases or leases equipment for its own use and occasionally disposes of such equipment. The implications of selling and leasing equipment as a business are beyond the scope of this book.

Not every purchase or sale of equipment requires formal authorization by a company's board of directors. It depends on the size of the corporation compared to the size of the transaction being considered. It is not likely that the board of directors of a multi-million dollar corporation would concern itself with the purchase of one copy machine. It depends on the customary relationship between the board and management. What does the board expect? Would it be surprised to hear that management had made the proposed purchase without consulting the board? It may also depend simply on whether or not the other party to the contract wants assurance of the board's approval.

A resolution granting the board's approval follows. Remember that directors can approve of management's actions after the fact. If it is only after a transaction takes place that management gets around to asking permission, and if the board is of a mind to give belated permission, the same form works. In addition to *approving*, the board also *ratifies*.

There is really no conceptual difference between the board's approval of equipment sales and purchases, and approval of sales and purchases of real estate. Equipment transactions are ordinarily smaller than real estate transactions, so a simpler form may be in order. But if a particular equipment deal is as important to the company as buying and selling real estate would ordinarily be, then you may want to use the more elaborate forms as guides.

sample of form 117: **Directors' Consent to Action Authorizing the Sale/Purchase of Equipment**

Consent to Action without Formal Meeting by the Directors of

Scrupulous Corporation

The undersigned directors of the corporation hereby adopt the following resolution:

WHEREAS, management of the corporation have recommended to the directors that the corporation agree to the **purchase of one JCN DataDriver 3000 Computer** for the sum of **$5,000** under the terms of a contract dated **March 13, 2006**, (a copy of such contract is located in management storage file no. 06-78), and

WHEREAS, after due consideration, the board of directors believes such transaction to be in the best interests of the corporation, it is therefore,

RESOLVED, that the contract dated **March 13, 2006**, between **Pleasant Cove Computers, Inc**. and the corporation presented to this board for its consideration are approved, ratified, and confirmed, and further,

RESOLVED, that the appropriate officers of the corporation are authorized and directed to take such further actions as may be necessary or desirable to give effect to this resolution.

This resolution shall be effective at **3:00 p.**m. on the **17th** of **March, 2006**.

Henry Hardy
Henry Hardy, Director

Roberta Moore
Roberta Moore, Director

Raymond Rodriguez
Raymond Rodriguez, Director

LEASING EQUIPMENT

Sometimes equipment leasing arrangements are really an alternative method of financing the purchase of equipment. The lessee *leases* the equipment but expects that at the end of the lease term, *ownership* of the property will transfer to the lessee. The tax treatment of such arrangements is a complicated subject that cannot be dealt with here. The transactions discussed here are relatively short-term rental arrangements of needed equipment, which the renter will, after the rental term, return to its owner.

The decision about whether or not director approval of a rental agreement is needed is based on the same considerations discussed in connection with the sale and purchase of equipment.

sample of form 118: DIRECTORS' CONSENT TO ACTION
AUTHORIZING THE LEASE OF EQUIPMENT

Consent to Action without Formal Meeting by the Directors of

Scrupulous Corporation

The undersigned directors of the corporation hereby adopt the following resolution:

WHEREAS, management of the corporation have recommended to the directors that the corporation agree to the **rental** of one **JCN DataDriver 3000 Computer** under the terms of a lease agreement dated **March 13, 2006** (a copy of such contract is located in management storage file no. **06-78**), and

WHEREAS, after due consideration, the board of directors believes such transaction to be in the best interests of the corporation, it is therefore,

RESOLVED, that the contract dated **March 13, 2006**, between **Pleasant Cove Computers, Inc.** and the corporation presented to this board for its consideration are approved, ratified, and confirmed, and further,

RESOLVED, that the appropriate officers of the corporation are authorized and directed to take such further actions as may be necessary or desirable to give effect to this resolution.

This resolution shall be effective at **3:00 p.**m. on the **17th** of **March, 2006**.

Henry Hardy
Henry Hardy, Director

Roberta Moore
Roberta Moore, Director

Raymond Rodriguez
Raymond Rodriguez, Director

ASSIGNMENT OF ASSETS FROM SHAREHOLDER

Sometimes a shareholder will contribute assets, instead of cash, to the corporation. An **ASSIGNMENT OF ASSETS** form to accomplish such a transfer is included in Appendix C. (see form 119, p.370.) Of course, if the property being transferred is of a certain nature, you may also need to take whatever steps are necessary to legally transfer title. Also, before engaging in any such transfer, you may want to obtain the advice of your tax adviser.

sample of form 119: **ASSIGNMENT OF ASSETS**

Assignment of Assets

This agreement is made the **10th** day of **May, 2006**, by **Della Driskell** ("Shareholder") and **Scrupulous Corporation**, a **West Carolina** corporation ("Corporation"), who agree as follows:

1. The Shareholder hereby transfers and assigns the assets listed on the attached Exhibit "A" to the Corporation.

2. In consideration for said transfer and assignment of assets, the Corporation shall issue to the Shareholder **100** shares of the **common** stock of the Corporation, with a par value of **(no par)** per share.

Shareholder: Corporation:

Della Driskell   By: *Calvin Collier*
Della Driskell   Calvin Collier, Vice President

CERTIFIED DOCUMENTS

At various stages in the transactions described in this chapter, the corporation may be asked to provide certified lists of officers (form 76) or directors (form 24), and certified copies of shareholder or director resolutions (forms 11–14). Occasionally, parties to one of the transactions described in this chapter will ask the corporation to provide a copy of some other document, such as a promissory note or a contract, certified by the corporation to be an accurate copy. The corporate secretary may use form 53 for this purpose.

Dissolution

Once you have a corporation, how do you get rid of it? The process for *voluntarily* terminating the existence of a corporation has two parts—dissolution and liquidation. *Dissolution* is the legal step of filing articles of dissolution with the Secretary of State formally declaring that the corporation no longer exists for the purpose of carrying on a business. *Liquidation* is the process of winding up the company's affairs, selling its assets, paying its debts, and distributing whatever is left to its shareholders.

Corporations can also be dissolved *involuntarily*. Following a judicial process, a corporation can be dissolved at the instigation of one or more shareholders when the directors or shareholders are deadlocked, or occasionally when a majority of the shareholders have treated a minority unfairly. A corporation may also be dissolved at the instigation of a state agency if the corporation has consistently refused to follow the law.

EFFECTS OF DISSOLUTION

A dissolved corporation does not really cease to exist. Even after articles of dissolution have been filed, a corporation can still be the defendant in a lawsuit. It can still own, buy, and sell property and do most things it did before the dissolution. What it cannot do is carry on its normal business as it did before the dissolution. After dissolution, the corporation may only engage in the process of winding up.

DISSOLUTION BEFORE SHARES ARE ISSUED

Before a corporation issues shares, the directors (or, if there are no directors, the incorporators) may dissolve a corporation by adopting an appropriate resolution and filing articles of dissolution with the Secretary of State. Following are resolutions appropriate for dissolving a corporation that has not issued shares.

sample of form 128: **DIRECTORS' CONSENT TO ACTION DISSOLVING A CORPORATION BEFORE THE ISSUANCE OF SHARES**

Consent to Action without Formal Meeting by the Directors of

Scrupulous Corporation

The undersigned directors of the corporation hereby adopt the following resolution:

RESOLVED, that pursuant to the laws of the state of **West Carolina** the corporation shall be dissolved and that any officer or director of the corporation is hereby authorized and directed to complete, execute, and file with the Secretary of State of **West Carolina** Articles of Dissolution accomplishing such dissolution, and further

RESOLVED, that such dissolution shall be effective on the effective date of such Articles of Dissolution.

This resolution shall be effective at **3:00 p.**m. on the **20th** of **January, 2006**.

Henry Hardy　　　　　　　　　　　*Roberta Moore*
Henry Hardy, Director　　　　　　　Roberta Moore, Director

Raymond Rodriguez
Raymond Rodriguez, Director

DISSOLUTION AFTER SHARES ARE ISSUED

Once a corporation has shareholders, a corporation cannot voluntarily dissolve without permission of the shareholders. The process is similar to the process for amending the **Articles of Incorporation** described in Chapter 12, "Amending Bylaws and Articles of Incorporation."

First, the directors adopt a resolution recommending dissolution to the shareholders, and then the shareholders adopt a resolution approving the dissolution. Ordinarily, the dissolution must be approved by a majority of the shares entitled to be voted. The company then files the **Articles of Dissolution of a Business Corporation** with the Secretary of State. (see form 131, p.387.)

Following are directors' and shareholders' resolutions for the dissolution of a corporation that has issued shares.

sample of form 129: **Directors' Consent to Action Recommending Dissolution of a Corporation**

Consent to Action without Formal Meeting by the Directors of

Scrupulous Corporation

The undersigned directors of the corporation hereby adopt the following resolution:

RESOLVED, that pursuant to the laws of the state of **West Carolina**, the board of directors recommends to the shareholders of the corporation that the corporation be dissolved and that the shareholders approve the recommendation, and further

RESOLVED, that the appropriate officers of the corporation are authorized and directed to call a special meeting of the shareholders, to give appropriate notice, or to arrange for approval of the recommendation by consent to action without formal meeting of the shareholders, and further

RESOLVED, that upon approval by the shareholders and at such time as he/she deems in the best interests of the corporation, the President or his/her designee shall have authority to execute and file articles of dissolution and to take such other actions as may be necessary or desirable to give effect to the proposed dissolution and this resolution.

This resolution shall be effective at **10:00 a.**m. on the **6th** of **February, 2006**.

Henry Hardy
Henry Hardy, Director

Roberta Moore
Roberta Moore, Director

Raymond Rodriguez
Raymond Rodriguez, Director

sample of form 130: **SHAREHOLDERS' CONSENT TO ACTION APPROVING THE DISSOLUTION OF A CORPORATION**

Consent to Action without Formal Meeting by the Shareholders of

Scrupulous Corporation

The undersigned shareholders of the corporation hereby adopt the following resolution:

WHEREAS, the directors of the corporation have proposed that the corporation be dissolved and have recommended to the shareholders that they approve such dissolution, it is therefore

RESOLVED, that the proposal of the directors that the corporation be dissolved is ratified and approved, and that the corporation shall be dissolved.

This resolution shall be effective at **10:00 a.**m. on the **6th** of **February, 2006**.

Roberta Moore
Roberta Moore, Shareholder

Hugh Hardy
Hugh Hardy, Shareholder

Henry Hardy
Henry Hardy, Shareholder

Raymond Rodriguez
Raymond Rodriguez, Shareholder

Della Driskell
Della Driskell, Shareholder

Calvin Collier
Calvin Collier, Shareholder

FILING ARTICLES OF DISSOLUTION

The office of the Secretary of State probably furnishes a preferred form for articles of dissolution. You should use that form. There will also be a filing fee, typically $100 or less. Following are typical **ARTICLES OF DISSOLUTION OF A BUSINESS CORPORATION** completed for Scrupulous Corporation.

sample of form 131: **ARTICLES OF DISSOLUTION OF A BUSINESS CORPORATION**

Articles of Dissolution of a Business Corporation

Pursuant to the laws of this State, the undersigned corporation hereby submits the following Articles of Dissolution for the purpose of dissolving the corporation.

1. The name of the corporation is: **Scrupulous Corporation**.

2. The names, titles, and addresses of the officers of the corporation are:

Raymond Rodriguez	**Henry Hardy**	**Roberta Moore**
President	**V. President & Treasurer**	**V. President & Secretary**
1 Scrupulous Plaza	**1 Scrupulous Plaza**	**1 Scrupulous Plaza**
Pleasant Cove, WC 27000	**Pleasant Cove, WC 27000**	**Pleasant Cove, WC 27000**

3. The names and addresses of the directors of the corporation are:

Raymond Rodriguez	**Henry Hardy**	**Roberta Moore**
1 Scrupulous Plaza	**1 Scrupulous Plaza**	**1 Scrupulous Plaza**
Pleasant Cove, WC 27000	**Pleasant Cove, WC 27000**	**Pleasant Cove, WC 27000**

4. The dissolution of the corporation was authorized on the **15th** day of **November, 2006**.

5. Shareholder approval for the dissolution was obtained as required by law.

6. These articles will be effective upon filing, unless a delayed date and/or time is specified: _____

This the **20th** day of **November, 2006**.

Name of Corporation:	**Scrupulous Corporation**
Signature:	*Raymond Rodriguez*
Typed name and title:	**Raymond Rodriguez, President**

LIQUIDATION

The process of liquidation can be quite lengthy and complex depending on the amount and size of the corporation's assets. The order of priority for distribution of the company's assets is *generally*:

1. payment of corporate debts to persons other than insiders (officers, directors, and shareholders);

2. payment of corporate debts to insiders;

3. payment of dissolution preferences to preferred shareholders, if any; and,

4. distribution of remaining assets to common shareholders.

Directory of State Corporate Statutes

The following information gives the citation to the corporation statutes or code of each state. The names of the statutes or code are those that appear on the books. In some states the name of the publisher is included in the title (such as *West's* Colorado Revised Statutes Annotated or *Vernon's* Annotated Missouri Statutes). For those states that have volume numbers printed on the spine of the books, the volume number is also given below to help you locate the law (however, these are the volume numbers as of the date of publication, and they may change from year to year). If you have any difficulty finding the corporation law for your state, ask a librarian to help you locate it.

Alabama:
Code of Alabama, Title 10-2B

Alaska:
Alaska Statutes, Title 10 (Volume 2)

Arizona:
Arizona Revised Statutes Annotated,
Title 10 (1994 supplement to Volume 3)

Arkansas:
Arkansas Code of 1987 Annotated,
Title 4, Chapter 27 (Volume 2A)

California:
West's Annotated California Code
(look for volume titled "Corporations")

Colorado:
West's Colorado Revised Statutes
Annotated, Title 7

Connecticut:
Connecticut General Statutes Annotated,
Title 33

Delaware:
Delaware Code Annotated, Title 8

District of Columbia:
District of Columbia Code, Title 29

Florida:
Florida Statutes, Chapter 607 (Volume 4)

Georgia:
Official Code of Georgia Annotated, Title 14
(volume 12)
[Note: This is not the "Georgia Code,"
which is a separate, outdated set of
books with a different numbering
system.]

Hawaii:
Hawaii Revised Statutes Annotated,
Title 23, Chapter 415

Idaho:
Idaho Code, Title 30

Illinois:
West's Smith Hurd Illinois Compiled
Statutes Annotated, Chapter 805
(1994 supplement)

Indiana:
West's Indiana Statutes Annotated, Title 23,
Article 1

Iowa:
Iowa Code Annotated, Chapter 490
(Volume 26)

Kansas:
Kansas Statutes Annotated-Official,
Chapter 17 (Volume 2); OR
Vernon's Kansas Statutes Annotated,
Section 17-6001 et seq. (Volume 5
titled "General Corporation Code")

Kentucky:
Kentucky Revised Statutes, Chapter 271B
(Volume 10A)

Louisiana:
West's LSA Revised Statutes,
Section 12-174 et seq. (Volume 5)

Maine:
Maine Revised Statutes Annotated, Title 13

Maryland:
Annotated Code of Maryland (Volume titled
"Corporations and Associations")

Massachusetts:
Annotated Laws of Massachusetts,
Chapter 156

Michigan:
Michigan Statutes Annotated,
Section 21.1 et seq.; OR
Michigan Compiled Laws Annotated,
Section 450.1 et seq.

Minnesota:
Minnesota Statutes Annotated,
Chapter 302A (volume 20)

Mississippi:
Mississippi Code 1972 Annotated, Title 79

Missouri:
Vernon's Annotated Missouri Statutes,
Section 351 (Volume 17A)

Montana:
Montana Code Annotated, Title 35
(Volume 7)

Nebraska:
Revised Statutes of Nebraska, Chapter 21
(Volume 1A)

Nevada:
Nevada Revised Statutes Annotated,
Chapter 78 (Volume 2A)

New Hampshire:
New Hampshire Revised Statutes
Annotated, Chapter 293-A
(ignore "Title" numbers)

New Jersey:
NJSA (for "New Jersey Statutes
Annotated"), Title 14A (Volume 14A
titled "Corporations, General")

New Mexico:
New Mexico Statutes 1978 Annotated,
Chapter 53 (Volume 9)

New York:
McKinney's Consolidated Laws of New
York Annotated (Volume 6 titled
"Business Corporation")

North Carolina:
North Carolina General Statutes,
Chapter 55 (Volume 9)
[Note: The actual title on the cover of
the set of books is "The General
Statutes of North Carolina"]

North Dakota:
North Dakota Century Code Annotated,
Title 10 (Volume 2A)

Ohio:
Anderson's Ohio Revised Code,
Chapter 1701

Oklahoma:
Oklahoma Statutes Annotated, Title 18,
Chapter 22

Oregon:
Oregon Revised Statutes Annotated,
Chapter 60 (Volume 4)

Pennsylvania:
Pennsylvania Code Title 19

Puerto Rico:
Puerto Rico Laws Annotated, Title 14

Rhode Island:
General Laws of Rhode Island, Title 7

South Carolina:
Code of Laws of South Carolina, Title 33
(Volume 10A)

South Dakota:
South Dakota Codified Laws, Title 47
(Volume 14)

Tennessee:
Tennessee Code Annotated, Title 48
(Volume 8B)

Texas:
Vernon's Texas Civil Statutes, Business
Corporation Act (volume 3A)

Utah:
Utah Code Annotated, Title 16 (Volume 2B)

Vermont:
Vermont Statutes Annotated, Title 11A

Virginia:
Code of Virginia 1950, Title 13.1

Washington:
West's Revised Code of Washington
      Annotated, Title 23B

West Virginia:
West Virginia Code, Chapter 31 (Volume 5)

Wisconsin:
West's Wisconsin Statutes Annotated,
      Section 180

Wyoming:
Wyoming Statutes Annotated, Title 17
      (Volume 5)

Website Directory of State Corporate Statutes

NOTE: *These web addresses change from time to time, and some are obviously unwieldy. As an alternative, consider* **www.findlaw.com** *as a resource. From the FindLaw homepage, click on "search cases and codes." Then scroll down to U.S. State Laws and click on your state. From there, go to "resources by jurisdiction" and then look for "state statutes," "state codes," etc. When you arrive at the state's legislative page, you may have to search for "corporations" or "business corporations." Or, consult Appendix A and search for the particular title or chapter number of the statute.*

Alabama: www.legislature.state.al.us/CodeofAlabama/1975/coatoc.htm

Alaska: www.legis.state.ak.us/cgi-bin/folioisa.dll/stattx04/query=*/doc/{t3178}?

Arizona: www.azleg.state.az.us/ArizonaRevisedStatutes.asp?Title=10

Arkansas: www.arkleg.state.ar.us/NXT/gateway.dll?f=templates&fn=default.htm&vid=blr:code

California: http://caselaw.lp.findlaw.com/cacodes/corp.html

Colorado: http://198.187.128.12/colorado/lpext.dll?f=templates&fn=
main.htm&2.0

Connecticut: www.cga.ct.gov/2005/pub/Title33.htm

Delaware: http://198.187.128.12/delaware/lpext.dll/Infobase/acff?fn=
document-frame.htm&f=templates&2.0

District   http://dccode.westgroup.com/toc/default.wl?DocName=
of Columbia: DC10391579&FindType=V&DB=DC-ST-WEB%3BSTADC&RS=
DCC1%2E0&VR=1%2E0

Florida: www.leg.state.fl.us/Statutes/index.cfm?App_mode=Display_Statute
&URL=Ch0607/titl0607.htm&StatuteYear=2004&Title=%2D%3E2
004%2D%3EChapter%20607

Georgia: www.legis.state.ga.us/legis/GaCode/Title14.pdf

Hawaii: www.capitol.hawaii.gov/hrscurrent/?press1=docs
The state corporate statutes are in Chapter 415.

Idaho: www3.state.id.us/idstat/TOC/30001JTOC.html

Illinois: www.ilga.gov/legislation/ilcs2.asp?ChapterID=65

Indiana: www.in.gov/legislative/ic/code/title23/ar1

Iowa: http://nxtsearch.legis.state.ia.us/NXT/gateway.dll/moved%20code/
2005%20Iowa%20Code/1?f=templates&fn=default.htm
(Look for chapter 490)

Kansas: www.kslegislature.org/legsrv-statutes/index.dojjsessionid=
3B9ADBD53601754AF99D07CEA3BC8FAE
(Look for Chapter 17)

Kentucky: http://lrc.ky.gov/krs/titles.htm
(Look for Chapter 271B and following subtitles)

Louisiana: www.legis.state.la.us/lss/lss.asp?doc=76098

Maine: http://janus.state.me.us/legis/statutes/13/title13ch0sec0.html

Maryland: http://mlis.state.md.us/cgi-win/web_statutes.exe
                       (Look for "corporations and associations")

Massachusetts: www.mass.gov/legis/laws/mgl/gl-156-toc.htm

Michigan: www.legislature.mi.gov/mileg.asp?page=getObject&objName=
                       mcl-Act-284-of-1972&highlight=

Minnesota: www.revisor.leg.state.mn.us/bin/getpub.php?pubtype=STAT_CHAP
                       &year=current&chapter=302A

Mississippi: www.mscode.com/free/statutes/79/004/index.htm

Missouri: www.moga.state.mo.us/STATUTES/C351.HTM

Montana: http://data.opi.state.mt.us/bills/mca_toc/35_1.htm

Nebraska: http://statutes.unicam.state.ne.us/corpus/chapall/chap21.html
                       (Scroll down to 21-2001)

Nevada: www.leg.state.nv.us/NRS/NRS-078.html

New Hampshire: www.gencourt.state.nh.us/rsa/html/indexes/293-A.html

New Jersey: http://lis.njleg.state.nj.us/cgi-bin/om_isapi.dll?clientID=24693421
                       &Depth=2&depth=2&expandheadings=on&headingswithhits=
                       on&hitsperheading=on&infobase=statutes.nfo&record={4A52}
                       &softpage=Doc_Frame_PG42

New Mexico: www.conwaygreene.com/nmsu/lpext.dll?f=templates&fn=main-
                       h.htm&2.0

New York: http://assembly.state.ny.us/leg/?cl=13

North Carolina: www.ncleg.net/EnactedLegislation/Statutes/HTML/ByChapter/
                       Chapter_55.html

North Dakota: www.state.nd.us/lr/cencode/t10.html

Ohio: http://onlinedocs.andersonpublishing.com/oh/lpExt.dll?f=templates
                 &fn=main-h.htm&cp=PORC
                 (Click on "TITLE XVII CORPORATIONS-PARTNERSHIP")

Oklahoma: www.oscn.net/applications/oscn/index.asp?ftdb=STOKST18&level=1
                 (Scroll down to §1001)

Oregon: www.leg.state.or.us/ors/060.html

Pennsylvania: www.pacode.com/secure/data/019/019toc.html

Rhode Island: www.rilin.state.ri.us/Statutes/TITLE7/INDEX.HTM

South Carolina: www.scstatehouse.net/code/titl33.htm

South Dakota: http://legis.state.sd.us/statutes/StatutesTitleList.aspx
                 (Look for Title 47)

Tennessee: http://198.187.128.12/tennessee/lpext.dll/Infobase/25cb3?fn=
                 document-frame.htm&f=templates&2.0

Texas: www.capitol.state.tx.us/statutes/ba.toc.htm

Utah: www.le.state.ut.us/~code/TITLE16/16_04.htm

Vermont: www.leg.state.vt.us/statutes/chapters.cfm?Title=11A

Virginia: http://leg1.state.va.us/cgibin/legp504.exe?000+cod+TOC13010000

Washington: www.leg.wa.gov/rcw/index.cfm?fuseaction=title&title=23B

West Virginia: www.legis.state.wv.us/WVCODE/31/masterfrm2Frm.htm

Wisconsin: www.legis.state.wi.us/statutes/Stat0180.pdf

Wyoming: http://legisweb.state.wy.us/statutes/sub17.htm

Blank Forms

This appendix contains the blank forms to use for your corporation. Below is a list of the forms found in this appendix, with the form number (found in the upper, outside corner of the form), the name of the form, and the page on which it can be found. For some of the forms (especially minutes and resolutions) you will need to insert various provisions from the main part of the book.

Table of Forms

Minutes of Regular Meeting of
the Board of Directors of

_____

A meeting of the Board of Directors of the Corporation was held on the date and at the time and place set forth in the written notice of meeting, or waiver of notice signed by directors, and attached to the minutes of this meeting.

The following directors were present:

_____
_____.

The meeting was called to order and it was moved, seconded, and carried that
_____ act as Chairman and that
_____ act as Secretary.

Minutes of the preceding meeting of the Board, held on
_____, were read and approved.

Upon motion duly made, seconded, and carried, the following resolution(s) was/were adopted:

☐ See attached resolutions.

There being no further business, the meeting adjourned.

_____

Secretary

Approved:

_____

**Minutes of Special Meeting of
the Board of Directors of**

_____

A special meeting of the Board of Directors of the Corporation was held on the date and at the time and place set forth in the written notice of meeting, or waiver of notice signed by directors, and attached to the minutes of this meeting.

The following directors were present:

_____
_____.

The meeting was called to order and it was moved, seconded, and carried that _____ act as Chairman and that _____ act as Secretary.

Minutes of the preceding meeting of the Board, held on _____, were read and approved.

Upon motion duly made, seconded, and carried, the following resolution(s) was/were adopted:

☐ See attached resolutions.

There being no further business, the meeting adjourned on _____, 20 _____, at ___ o'clock ___ . m.

_____
Secretary

Approved:

_____

Directors' Meeting Minutes Continuation Sheet

Type & Date of Meeting: _____

Page_____ of _____ pages.

Consent to Action without Formal Meeting of Directors of

_____

The undersigned, being all of the Directors of the Corporation, hereby adopt the following resolutions:

☐ See attached resolutions.

RESOLVED, that these resolutions shall be effective at _____ ____.m., on _____, _____.

_____   _____
Director   Director

_____   _____
Director   Director

_____   _____
Director   Director

Minutes of Annual Meeting of
the Shareholders of

_____

The annual meeting of the Shareholders of the Corporation was held on the date and at the time and place set forth in the written notice of meeting, or waiver of notice signed by shareholders, and attached to the minutes of this meeting.

The following shareholders were present:

Shareholder   No. of Shares

_____   _____

_____   _____

_____   _____

_____   _____

_____   _____

_____   _____

The meeting was called to order and it was moved, seconded, and carried that
_____ act as Chairman and that
_____ act as Secretary.

A roll call was taken and the Chairman noted that all of the outstanding shares of the Corporation were represented in person or by proxy. Any proxies are attached to these minutes.

Minutes of the preceding meeting of the Shareholders, held on
_____, were read and approved.

Upon motion duly made, seconded, and carried, the following were elected directors for the following year:

_____   _____

_____   _____

☐ See attached resolutions.

There being no further business, the meeting adjourned on _____, 20 _____,
at _____ o'clock _____ . m.

_____
Secretary

Approved:

_____

Minutes of Special Meeting of
the Shareholders of

_____

A special meeting of the Shareholders of the Corporation was held on the date and at the time and place set forth in the written notice of meeting, or waiver of notice signed by shareholders, and attached to the minutes of this meeting.

The following shareholders were present:

Shareholder   No. of Shares

_____   _____
_____   _____
_____   _____
_____   _____
_____   _____
_____   _____

The meeting was called to order and it was moved, seconded, and carried that
_____ act as Chairman and that
_____ act as Secretary.

A roll call was taken and the Chairman noted that all of the outstanding shares of the Corporation were represented in person or by proxy. Any proxies are attached to these minutes.

Minutes of the preceding meeting of the Shareholders, held on
_____, were read and approved.

Upon motion duly made, seconded, and carried, the following resolution(s) was/were adopted:

☐ See attached resolutions.

There being no further business, the meeting adjourned on _____, 20 ____, at ___ o'clock __ . m.

_____
                                                                      Secretary

Shareholders:

_____

Shareholders' Meeting Minutes Continuation Sheet

Type & Date of Meeting: _____

Page_____ of _____ pages.

Consent to Action without Formal Meeting of Shareholders of

_____

The undersigned, being all of the Directors of the Corporation, hereby adopt the following resolutions:

☐ See attached resolutions.

RESOLVED, that these resolutions shall be effective at _____ ____.m., on _____, _____.

_____   _____
Shareholder   Shareholder

_____   _____
Shareholder   Shareholder

_____   _____
Shareholder   Shareholder

Resolution of the Board of Directors of

_____

Date: _____

At the meeting referenced above, the Board of Directors hereby adopts the following resolution (which shall be attached to and incorporated by reference in the minutes of said meeting):

Resolution of the Shareholders of

_____

Date: _____

At the meeting referenced above, the Shareholders hereby adopt the following resolution (which shall be attached to and incorporated by reference in the minutes of said meeting):

Certified Copy of Minutes of Meeting
of the Board of Directors of

_____

I HEREBY CERTIFY that I am the Corporate Secretary of _____
_____, that the following is an accurate copy of
minutes of a meeting of the Board of Directors of _____
_____, held on _____, 20_____:

☐ See attached minutes and/or resolutions.

Signed and the seal of the Corporation affixed, _____, 20_____.

_____

Secretary

**Certified Copy of Minutes of Meeting
of the Shareholders of**

_____

I HEREBY CERTIFY that I am the Corporate Secretary of _____

_____, that the following is an accurate copy of

minutes of a meeting of the Shareholders of _____

_____, held on _____, 20_____:

☐ See attached minutes and/or resolutions.

Signed and the seal of the Corporation affixed, _____, 20_____.

_____

Secretary

Certified Copy of Resolutions Adopted by
the Board of Directors of

_____

I HEREBY CERTIFY that I am the Corporate Secretary of _____
_____, that the following is an accurate copy of
resolution(s) adopted by the Board of Directors of _____
_____, effective _____, 20_____, and that
such resolutions continue in effect as of the date of this certification:

☐ See attached minutes and/or resolutions.

Signed and the seal of the Corporation affixed, _____, 20_____.

_____

Secretary

Certified Copy of Resolutions Adopted by
the Shareholders of

_____

I HEREBY CERTIFY that I am the Corporate Secretary of _____
_____, that the following is an accurate copy of
resolution(s) adopted by the Shareholders of _____
_____, effective _____, 20_____, and that
such resolutions continue in effect as of the date of this certification:

☐ See attached minutes and/or resolutions.

Signed and the seal of the Corporation affixed, _____, 20_____.

_____

Secretary

Consent to Action without Formal Meeting by the Directors of

_____

The undersigned directors of the corporation hereby adopt the following resolution:

RESOLVED, that pursuant to _____ of the bylaws of the corporation, the number of directors constituting the board of directors shall be _____, and that such shall be the number of members of the board of directors until changed in a manner authorized by the articles of incorporation and the bylaws of the corporation.

This resolution shall be effective at _____ m. on the _____ of _____, 20____.

_____

_____, Director

_____

_____, Director

_____

_____, Director

Consent to Action without Formal Meeting by the Directors of

_____

The undersigned directors of the corporation hereby adopt the following resolution:

RESOLVED, that the first sentence of _____ of
the bylaws of the corporation is amended to read as follows:

"The number of directors constituting the board of directors shall be _____."

This resolution shall be effective at _____ m. on the _____ of _____,
20_____.

_____

_____, Director

_____

_____, Director

_____

_____, Director

Consent to Action without Formal Meeting by the Shareholders of

_____

The undersigned shareholders of the corporation hereby adopt the following resolution:

RESOLVED, that the following individuals are elected directors of the corporation to serve until their successors are qualified and elected:

This resolution shall be effective at _____ m. on the _____ of _____, 20_____.

_____

_____, Shareholder

_____

_____, Shareholder

_____

_____, Shareholder

_____

_____, Shareholder

_____

_____, Shareholder

Director's Consent to Serve

Date:

TO: The Board of Directors

_____

[name of corporation]

I hereby consent to serve as a director of the Corporation, if elected.

_____

Consent to Action without Formal Meeting by the Directors of

_____

The undersigned directors of the corporation hereby adopt the following resolution:

WHEREAS, management of the corporation has recommended to the board of directors a system for the remuneration of directors for their services, and

WHEREAS, the board of directors, after consideration, has concluded that the recommendations of management are in the best interests of the corporation in maintaining a board of directors the members of which are able and willing to serve diligently, it is therefore,

RESOLVED, that each director of the corporation shall be paid the following fees:

1. For attendance at each meeting or series of meetings lasting fewer than three hours, $_____.

2. For attendance at each meeting or series of meetings lasting three hours or more in one day, $_____.

3. For each overnight stay away from the director's usual residence required by attendance at a meeting or series of meetings, in addition to the fees provided above, $_____ plus reimbursement for lodgings up to $_____ per night.

4. For travel involving distances more than _____ miles to or from a meeting, directors shall be reimbursed for the actual cost of such travel. Travel by private automobile shall be reimbursed at the rate and in the manner provided for reimbursement of employees of the company from time to time.

This resolution shall be effective at _____. m. on the _____ of _____, 20_____.

_____

_____, Director

_____

_____, Director

_____

_____, Director

Consent to Action without Formal Meeting by the Directors of

_____

The undersigned directors of the corporation hereby adopt the following resolution:

WHEREAS, it has been reported by the secretary of the corporation that
_____, a director of the corporation, has
_____
_____
_____
_____, and

WHEREAS, it has been recommended to the shareholders that, for the reason stated
above, _____ should be removed from the
board of directors, it is therefore

RESOLVED, that, at the effective date and time of this resolution,
_____shall be removed from the board of
directors of the corporation, and that there shall be a vacancy on the board of directors.

This resolution shall be effective at _____. m. on the _____ of _____,
20_____.

_____

_____, Director

_____

_____, Director

_____

_____, Director

Date: _____

To: The Board of Directors of _____

I hereby resign as director of _____ effective
_____ at _____. m.

Sincerely,

_____

Consent to Action without Formal Meeting by the Shareholders of

_____

The undersigned shareholders of the corporation hereby adopt the following resolution:

WHEREAS, the _____ of _____
as director of the corporation has created a vacancy on the board of directors, and

WHEREAS, the shareholders wish to fill the vacancy, it is therefore

RESOLVED, that _____ is elected to serve as
director of the corporation for the remainder of the term for which
_____ was elected and until his or her successor is
qualified and elected.

This resolution shall be effective at _____. m. on the _____ of _____,
20_____.

_____

_____, Shareholder

_____

_____, Shareholder

_____

_____, Shareholder

_____

_____, Shareholder

_____

_____, Shareholder

Consent to Action without Formal Meeting by the Directors of

_____

The undersigned directors of the corporation hereby adopt the following resolution:

WHEREAS, the _____ of _____
as a director of the corporation has created a vacancy on the board of directors, and

WHEREAS, the remaining directors, pursuant to _____
of the bylaws of the corporation wish to fill the vacancy, it is therefore

RESOLVED, that _____ is hereby elected to serve as
director of the corporation for the remainder of the term for which
_____ was elected and until his or her successor is
qualified and elected.

This resolution shall be effective at _____. m. on the _____ of _____,
20_____.

_____

_____, Director

_____

_____, Director

_____

_____, Director

Certification of Secretary of

_____

I HEREBY CERTIFY that I am the Corporate Secretary of _____
_____, that the individuals listed below are the duly elected directors of the Corporation, and that they continue to hold the office of director on the date of this certification:

Signed and the seal of the Corporation affixed, _____, 20_____.

_____

                                        Secretary

Consent to Action without Formal Meeting by the Directors of

_____

The undersigned directors of the corporation hereby adopt the following resolution:

RESOLVED, that there is created a/an_____ committee of the board of directors consisting of _____ members, and further

RESOLVED, that to the extent permitted by law and the bylaws of the corporation, the _____ committee shall have the following powers:

Further RESOLVED, that the following individuals are appointed to serve as members of the executive committee of the board of directors until their successors are appointed and qualified:

This resolution shall be effective at _____. m. on the _____ of _____, 20 _____.

_____

_____, Director

_____

_____, Director

_____

_____, Director

Consent to Action without Formal Meeting by the Directors of

_____

The undersigned directors of the corporation hereby adopt the following resolution:

RESOLVED, that the number of members of the _____
committee of the board of directors is increased from _____ to _____,
and further

RESOLVED, that the following individuals are appointed to fill the vacancies created by
the increase in the size of the committee to serve as members of such committee until
their successors are elected and qualified:

This resolution shall be effective at _____. m. on the _____ of _____,
20 ____.

_____

_____, Director

_____

_____, Director

_____

_____, Director

Consent to Action without Formal Meeting by the Directors of

_____

The undersigned directors of the corporation hereby adopt the following resolution:

RESOLVED, that the bylaws of the corporation are amended by the addition of a new Article _____, Section _____ reading in its entirety as follows:

"There shall be an Executive Committee of the board of directors which shall, to the extent permitted by law, and subject to such limitations as may be imposed from time to time by the board of directors, exercise the powers of the board of directors when the board is not in session. The number of members of the Executive Committee shall be established, and may be changed from time to time, by resolution of the Board of Directors. The members of the Executive Committee shall be appointed by a majority of the number of directors in office when the appointment is made and shall serve at the pleasure of a majority of the board in office."

Further RESOLVED, that the initial number of members of the Executive Committee shall be _____, and the initial members of the Executive Committee shall be:

This resolution shall be effective at _____. m. on the _____ of _____, 20_____.

_____

_____, Director

_____

_____, Director

_____

_____, Director

Consent to Action without Formal Meeting by the Directors of

_____

The undersigned directors of the corporation hereby adopt the following resolution:

RESOLVED, that the bylaws of the corporation are amended by the addition of a new Article _____, Section _____ reading in its entirety as follows:

"There shall be an Audit Committee of the board of directors which shall supervise the auditing and examination of the books of account of the corporation by employees and independent auditors of the corporation. The Audit Committee shall meet with the independent auditors not fewer than _____ times during each fiscal year and shall have such other powers and duties as may from time to time be authorized by the board of directors. The number of members of the Audit Committee shall be established, and may be changed from time to time, by resolution of the Board of Directors. The members of the Audit Committee shall be appointed by a majority of the number of directors in office when the appointment is made and shall serve at the pleasure of a majority of the board in office."

Further RESOLVED, that the initial number of members of the Audit Committee shall be _____, and the initial members of the Audit Committee shall be:

This resolution shall be effective at _____. m. on the _____ of _____, 20_____.

_____

_____, Director

_____

_____, Director

_____

_____, Director

Consent to Action without Formal Meeting by the Directors of

_____

The undersigned directors of the corporation hereby adopt the following resolution:

RESOLVED, that the bylaws of the corporation are amended by the addition of a new Article _____, Section _____ reading in its entirety as follows:

"There shall be a Personnel Committee of the board of directors which shall consider and make recommendations to the board of directors regarding recruiting and compensating officers and senior employees of the corporation, the compensation of directors, compliance with applicable laws regarding employment practices, and other matters regarding personnel management, and the Committee shall have such other powers and duties as may from time to time be authorized by the board of directors. The number of members of the Personnel Committee shall be established, and may be changed from time to time, by resolution of the Board of Directors. The members of the Personnel Committee shall be appointed by a majority of the number of directors in office when the appointment is made and shall serve at the pleasure of a majority of the board in office."

Further RESOLVED, that the initial number of members of the Personnel Committee shall be _____, and the initial members of the Personnel Committee shall be:

This resolution shall be effective at _____. m. on the _____ of _____, 20_____.

_____

_____, Director

_____

_____, Director

_____

_____, Director

Consent to Action without Formal Meeting by the Directors of

_____

The undersigned directors of the corporation hereby adopt the following resolution:

RESOLVED, that the bylaws of the corporation are amended by the addition of a new Article _____, Section _____ reading in its entirety as follows:

"There shall be a Nominating Committee of the board of directors which shall consider available candidates for director of the corporation and shall make recommendations to the board of directors regarding the filling of vacancies which may occur from time to time in the membership of the board of directors. The number of members of the Nominating Committee shall be established, and may be changed from time to time, by resolution of the Board of Directors. The members of the Nominating Committee shall be appointed by a majority of the number of directors in office when the appointment is made and shall serve at the pleasure of a majority of the board in office."

Further RESOLVED, that the initial number of members of the Nominating Committee shall be _____, and the initial members of the Nominating Committee shall be:

This resolution shall be effective at _____. m. on the _____ of _____, 20_____.

_____

_____, Director

_____

_____, Director

_____

_____, Director

Notice of Regular Meeting of Board of Directors of

_____

Date:

TO: All Directors

The regular meeting of the board of directors will be held on
_____, _____, at _____ ____.m., at _____
_____.

_____
                                   Corporate Secretary

Notice of Special Meeting of Board of Directors of

_____

Date:

TO: All Directors

There will be a special meeting of the board of directors on _____, _____, at _____   ___.m., at _____ _____.

The purpose(s) of this meeting is/are:

_____

Corporate Secretary

Waiver of Notice of Meeting of Board of Directors of

_____

The undersigned director(s) of the Corporation hereby waive any and all notice required by law or by the articles of incorporation or bylaws of the Corporation, and consent to the holding of a ☐ Regular ☐ Special meeting of the Board of Directors of the Corporation on _____,
at _____ ____.m., at _____
_____.

Name:_____   Date:_____

Name:_____   Date:_____

Name:_____   Date:_____

Name:_____   Date:_____

Name:_____   Date:_____

Name:_____   Date:_____

Agenda of Meeting of the Board of Directors of

_____

Date of Meeting: _____

Certificate No.: _____

No. of Shares: _____

_____

Incorporated under the laws of the State of _____

Authorized Capital Stock:_____ shares.

Par Value: ☐ $_____ per Share   ☐ No Par Value

THIS CERTIFIES THAT _____
is the owner of _____ fully paid and nonassessable shares of
the capital stock of _____
transferable only on the books of the corporation by the holder of this certificate in
person or by the holder's duly authorized attorney upon surrender of this certificate
properly endorsed.

Upon request, and without charge, the corporation will provide written information as to
the designations, preferences, limitations, and relative rights of all classes and series of
shares and the authority of the board of directors to determine the same for future
classes and series.

IN WITNESS WHEREOF, _____
has caused this certificate to be signed by its duly authorized officers and its corporate
seal to be affixed on _____, 20_____.

_____,
President

_____,
Secretary

FOR VALUE RECEIVED, the undersigned hereby sells, assigns, and transfers to
_____,
_____ of the shares represented by the certificate on the reverse side, and
irrevocably appoints _____
attorney, with full power of substitution, to transfer such shares on the books of the
Corporation.

Date: _____, 20_____

_____

Witness:

_____

Social Security Account Number or other Taxpayer Identification Number of the
assignee: _____

Stock Subscription Agreement

_____

In consideration of the mutual promises contained in this agreement and other lawful and sufficient consideration, the receipt of which is hereby acknowledged, _____ (the "Corporation"), a _____corporation, agrees to issue, and the undersigned purchaser agrees to subscribe to and purchase _____ shares of the _____ of the Corporation for cash at the price of $_____. The purchase price for the shares shall be payable in full upon issuance of the shares by the Corporation.

Purchaser:_____
_____
[Name, address, and social security number of taxpayer identification number of purchaser]

Date: _____, 20____

_____
(Signature of Purchaser)

Corporation:

By:_____

Consent to Action without Formal Meeting by the Directors of

_____

The undersigned directors of the corporation hereby adopt the following resolution:

RESOLVED, that for value received, there is granted to _____ (the "Grantee") an option to purchase _____ shares of the _____ of the corporation. The purchase price of the shares will be $_____ per share, payable in cash upon the exercise of the option. The option shall be evidenced by and subject to the terms and conditions of a written Stock Option Agreement in the form presented by management to and now approved by the directors,

Further RESOLVED, that management of the corporation is hereby authorized and directed to take such action and execute such documents as may be necessary or desirable to give effect to the above resolution.

This resolution shall be effective at _____. m. on the _____ of _____, 20_____.

_____

_____, Director

_____

_____, Director

_____

_____, Director

Stock Option Agreement

_____

In consideration of the mutual promises contained in this agreement and other lawful consideration, the receipt and sufficiency of which is hereby acknowledged, _____ (the "Corporation), a _____ corporation, hereby grants to _____ (the "Grantee") an option to purchase shares of the Corporation upon the following terms and conditions:

1. **Consideration of the Grantee.** The grant of an option in this agreement is made in consideration of _____

_____.

2. **Number of shares and price.** The option granted in this agreement (the "Option") is an option of the Grantee to purchase _____ shares of the _____ _____ shares of the Corporation. The purchase price of the shares will be $_____ per share, payable in cash upon the exercise of the option.

3. **Time and method of exercise.** The Option may be exercised in whole or in part by the Grantee at any time and from time to time before _____ by delivery to the Corporation at its principal office written notice of the Grantee's intent to exercise the option stating the number of shares being purchased and accompanied by the purchase price of the shares being purchased. The option may be exercised as to whole numbers of shares only.

4. **Adjustments of the number of shares subject to the Option.** In the event of any share dividend, share split, or other recapitalization affecting the shares of the Company, or a merger of the Corporation in which it is the surviving corporation, the number of shares subject to the Option will be automatically adjusted to equitably reflect such change or merger. In the event of the dissolution of the Corporation, or a merger or other fundamental change following which no shares of the corporation may be issued, the Option will terminate, but the Grantee will have a reasonable opportunity to exercise the Option immediately before such event. Except as provided in this paragraph, the Grantee shall have no rights as a shareholder of the Corporation with respect to the shares subject to the Option until such shares are issued upon exercise of the Option.

5. **No transfer.** The Option may not be transferred by the Grantee other than by will or the laws of inheritance.

The Corporation and the Grantee have executed this Stock Option Agreement under seal on _____, 20____.

Grantee: Corporation:

_____   By: _____
                                                                                                    President
                                                       Attest:

                                                       _____
                                                                                                    Secretary

Consent to Action without Formal Meeting by the Directors of

_____

The undersigned directors of the corporation hereby adopt the following resolution:

WHEREAS, the person(s) named below have agreed to purchase the number of shares stated opposite his or her name, for the consideration indicated, pursuant to a subscription agreement dated _____, 20___, it is therefore

RESOLVED, that the _____ of the corporation, or his or her designee, is authorized and directed, upon receipt by the corporation of the stated consideration, to issue certificates representing the number of _____ shares of the corporation indicated to the persons named below:

Name of purchaser(s):   No. of shares: Consideration received:

This resolution shall be effective at _____. m. on the _____ of _____, 20_____.

_____

_____, Director

_____

_____, Director

_____

_____, Director

Consent to Action without Formal Meeting by the Directors of

_____

The undersigned directors of the corporation hereby adopt the following resolution:

WHEREAS, the person(s) named below have exercised options for the number of shares stated opposite his or her name, for the consideration indicated, pursuant to an option agreement dated _____, 20_____, it is therefore

RESOLVED, that the _____ of the corporation, or his or her designee, is authorized and directed, upon receipt by the corporation of the stated consideration, to issue certificates representing the number of _____ shares of the corporation indicated to the persons named below:

Name of purchaser(s):   No. of shares: Consideration received:

This resolution shall be effective at _____. m. on the _____ of _____, 20_____.

_____

_____, Director

_____

_____, Director

_____

_____, Director

Stock Powers Separate from Certificate

In exchange for valuable consideration, the receipt and sufficiency of which is hereby acknowledged, the undersigned hereby sells, assigns, and transfers to
_____, _____ shares of the stock of _____ registered on the books of the Corporation in the name of the undersigned and represented by Certificate(s) number _____.

The undersigned hereby irrevocably appoints _____, _____, attorney, with full power of substitution, to transfer such shares on the books of the Corporation.

Executed on _____, 20_____.

_____
[Name of person transferring stock]

Witness:

_____

Social Security Account Number of other Taxpayer Identification Number of the assignee: _____

Consent to Action without Formal Meeting by the Directors of

_____

The undersigned directors of the corporation hereby adopt the following resolution:

WHEREAS, _____ has offered to sell to the corporation, and the corporation wishes to purchase _____ shares of the _____ stock of the corporation previously issued to such shareholder, it is therefore

RESOLVED, that the corporation shall purchase _____ shares of the _____ stock of the corporation from _____ for $_____ per share, such transaction to take place on or before _____, and further

RESOLVED, that the articles of incorporation of the corporation shall be amended to reduce the number of authorized shares by the number of shares so purchased, such amendment to be effective on the date such transaction is completed or within a reasonable time thereafter, and further

RESOLVED, that the officers of the corporation are authorized and directed to file articles of amendment with the Secretary of State of _____ giving effect to such amendment in a timely manner, and further

RESOLVED, that the officers of the corporation are authorized and directed to take such actions as may be necessary or desirable to give effect to the above resolutions.

This resolution shall be effective at _____. m. on the _____ of _____, 20_____.

_____

_____, Director

_____

_____, Director

_____

_____, Director

Consent to Action without Formal Meeting by the Directors of

_____

The undersigned directors of the corporation hereby adopt the following resolution:

WHEREAS, _____ has offered to sell to the corporation, and the corporation wishes to purchase _____ shares of the _____ stock of the corporation previously issued to him or her, it is therefore

RESOLVED, that the corporation shall purchase _____ shares of the _____ stock of the corporation for $_____ per share, the transaction to take place on or before _____, 20___, and further

RESOLVED, that the _____ of the corporation or his or her designee is authorized and directed to take such acts as may be necessary or desirable to give effect to the above resolution.

This resolution shall be effective at _____. m. on the _____ of _____, 20_____.

_____

_____, Director

_____

_____, Director

_____

_____, Director

Consent to Action without Formal Meeting by the Directors of

_____

The undersigned directors of the corporation hereby adopt the following resolution:

WHEREAS, the directors have determined to declare a dividend on the common shares payable in shares of stock of the corporation, and

WHEREAS, in order to do so, the number of authorized shares of the corporation must be increased from _____ to _____, it is therefore

RESOLVED, that the articles of incorporation of the corporation be amended to change Article ___ of the articles of incorporation to read in its entirety as follows:

"2. The number of shares the corporation shall have authority to issue is _____."

RESOLVED, that the officers of the corporation are authorized and directed to take such actions, including the filing of Articles of Amendment with the Secretary of State, as may be necessary or desirable to give effect to this resolution.

This resolution shall be effective at _____. m. on the _____ of _____, 20_____.

_____

_____, Director

_____

_____, Director

_____

_____, Director

Shareholders' Agreement

This agreement is made by and among _____
_____ (the "Corporation") and the undersigned shareholders of the corporation (the "Shareholders" collectively, or "Shareholder" individually) on
_____, 20_____.

In consideration of the premises and of the mutual promises and conditions contained in this agreement, the Corporation and the Shareholders agree for themselves, their successors, and assigns, as follows:

1. The number of directors of the corporation shall be _____. So long as he or she shall own shares in the Corporation, each Shareholder shall have the right to serve as a director of the Corporation or to designate a person to serve as director. Any such person named must be reasonably capable of performing the duties of a director.

2. So long as he or she shall own shares in the Corporation, each shareholder shall have the right, but shall not be required, to serve as an officer of the Corporation. The compensation paid to each Shareholder during each calendar year for his or her services as an officer of the Corporation shall be equal to the compensation paid to each other Shareholder of the corporation for services as an officer. The titles and duties of each Shareholder so employed by the Corporation shall be as determined by the Board of Directors from time to time.

3. The Shareholders shall vote their shares in such a way as to give effect to the provisions of this agreement.

4. Every certificate representing shares owned by the parties to this agreement shall prominently bear the following legend: "The shares represented by this certificate are subject to the provisions of a Shareholders' Agreement dated _____, 20_____, a copy of which is on file in, and may be examined at, the principal office of the Corporation."

IN WITNESS WHEREOF, the parties have executed this Agreement under seal on the date indicated above.

By: _____

Attest: _____

_____   _____
Shareholder   Shareholder

_____   _____
Shareholder   Shareholder

_____   _____
Shareholder   Shareholder

Consent to Action without Formal Meeting by the Directors of

_____

The undersigned directors of the corporation hereby adopt the following resolution:

RESOLVED, that pursuant to Article ___ of the articles of incorporation of the corporation, there is created a class of preferred shares, series _____, with the preferences, limitations, and relative rights stated in the following amendment to the articles of incorporation, and further

RESOLVED, that Article ___ of the articles of incorporation is amended to read as follows:

2. The number of shares the corporation shall have authority to issue is _____ divided into _____ classes as follows:

Class	Series	Par Value	Number of Shares Authorized

When and if legally declared by the board of directors, the record holder of each share of Preferred stock, Series _____, shall be entitled to receive cash dividends at the annual rate of $_____ per share payable in equal quarterly installments beginning on _____, 20__. Cash dividends on Preferred shares shall be cumulative from the first dividend payment following the issuance of the share, and shall be declared and paid, or set apart for payment, before any cash dividends shall be paid on the Common stock.

Further RESOLVED, that the President of the corporation and his/her designees are authorized and directed to take such actions, including filing Article of Amendment, as may be necessary or desirable to give effect to this resolution.

This resolution shall be effective at _____. m. on the _____ day of _____, 20 ____.

_____

_____, Director

_____

_____, Director

_____

_____, Director

Certificate No.: _____

No. of Preferred Shares, Series _____: _____

_____

PREFERRED STOCK, SERIES _____

Incorporated under the laws of the State of _____

Authorized Preferred Stock, Series _____: _____ shares, No Par Value.

THIS CERTIFIES THAT _____ is the owner
of _____ fully paid and nonassessable shares of the capital
stock of _____ transferable only on the
books of the corporation by the holder of this certificate in person or by the holder's duly
authorized attorney upon surrender of this certificate properly endorsed.

Upon request, and without charge, the corporation will provide written information as to
the designations, preferences, limitations, and relative rights of all classes and series of
shares and the authority of the board of directors to determine the same for future
classes and series.

IN WITNESS WHEREOF, _____
has caused this certificate to be signed by its duly authorized officers and its corporate
seal to be affixed on _____, 20_____.

_____,
President

_____,
Secretary

FOR VALUE RECEIVED, the undersigned hereby sells, assigns, and transfers to

_____,
_____ of the shares represented by the certificate on the reverse side, and
irrevocably appoints _____
attorney, with full power of substitution, to transfer such shares on the books of the
Corporation.

Date: _____, 20____

_____

Witness:

_____

Social Security Account Number or other Taxpayer Identification Number of the
assignee: _____

Lost or Destroyed Stock Certificate Indemnity Agreement and Affidavit

The undersigned, being duly sworn, hereby affirms the following:

1. The undersigned is record holder of _____ shares (the "Shares") of the stock of _____ (the "Corporation"). The Shares were represented by stock certificate number _____ issued on _____ (the "Certificate").

2. The undersigned is the sole owner of the Shares, having never endorsed, delivered, transferred, assigned, or otherwise disposed of them or the Certificate in such a way as to give any other person any interest in the Shares.

3. The undersigned has duly searched for the Certificate, has been unable to find it, and believes the Certificate to be lost, destroyed, or stolen.

4. In order to induce the Corporation to issue a new stock certificate to replace the Certificate, the undersigned agrees to indemnify, defend, and hold harmless the Corporation, its shareholders, directors, and officers from any and all claims, loss, or damage whatsoever arising out of or related in any manner to the Certificate or arising out of the issuance of a replacement certificate.

Date: _____, 20____

_____

STATE OF
COUNTY OF
On _____, _____, there personally appeared before me, _____, who ☐ is personally known to me ☐ produced _____ as identification, and being duly sworn on oath stated that the facts stated in the above Affidavit are true.

_____
Notary Public
My Commission Expires:

Consent to Action without Formal Meeting by the Directors of

_____

The undersigned directors of the corporation hereby adopt the following resolution:

RESOLVED, that _____ of the bylaws of the corporation is amended to read in its entirety as follows:

"The annual meeting of the shareholders shall be held on any day of the month of _____ of each year as may be determined by the board of directors."

This resolution shall be effective at _____. m. on the _____ of _____, 20_____.

_____

_____, Director

_____

_____, Director

_____

_____, Director

Consent to Action without Formal Meeting by the Directors of

_____

The undersigned directors of the corporation hereby adopt the following resolution:

RESOLVED, that, pursuant to _____, of the bylaws of the corporation, the annual meeting of shareholders shall take place at _____. m. on the _____ day of _____, 20___ at _____ _____, and further

RESOLVED, that officers of the corporation are authorized and directed to give such notice of the meeting to shareholders of record on _____, 20___ as may be required by law and the bylaws of the corporation.

This resolution shall be effective at _____. m. on the _____ of _____, 20_____.

_____

_____, Director

_____

_____, Director

_____

_____, Director

Consent to Action without Formal Meeting by the Directors of

_____

The undersigned directors of the corporation hereby adopt the following resolution:

RESOLVED, that, pursuant to _____, of the bylaws of the corporation, the substitute annual meeting of shareholders shall take place at _____. m. on the _____ day of _____ at _____, and further

RESOLVED, that officers of the corporation are authorized and directed to give such notice of the meeting to shareholders of record on _____, 20___ as may be required by law and the bylaws of the corporation.

This resolution shall be effective at _____. m. on the _____ day of _____, 20 ____.

_____

_____, Director

_____

_____, Director

_____

_____, Director

Consent to Action without Formal Meeting by the Directors of

_____

The undersigned directors of the corporation hereby adopt the following resolution:

RESOLVED, that, pursuant to _____ of the bylaws of the corporation, a special meeting of shareholders shall take place at _____. m. on the _____ day of _____ at _____, and further

RESOLVED, that the meeting is called for the following purpose(s):

and further

RESOLVED, that the appropriate officers of the corporation are authorized and directed to give such notice of the meeting to shareholders of record on _____, 20___ as may be required by law and bylaws of the corporation.

This resolution shall be effective at _____. m. on the _____ day of _____, 20 ____.

_____

_____, Director

_____

_____, Director

_____

_____, Director

President's Call for Special Meeting of the Shareholders

To the Secretary of _____

Pursuant to Article _____, Section _____ of the bylaws of the Corporation, there is hereby called a special meeting of the shareholders of the Corporation to be held on _____, at _____ ____.m., at _____, for the following purpose(s):

You are hereby authorized and directed to give such notice of the meeting to shareholders of record on _____ as may be required by law and the bylaws of the Corporation.

Date: _____, 20_____

_____
President

Shareholders' Call for Special Meeting of the Shareholders

To the Secretary of _____

Pursuant to Article _____, Section _____ of the bylaws of the Corporation, the undersigned shareholders of _____,
representing not less than one-tenth of the shares entitled to vote on the issues described below, hereby request that the President call a special meeting of the shareholders of the Corporation to be held on_____ , at _____ ____.m., at _____
_____, for the following purpose(s):

You are hereby authorized and directed to give such notice of the meeting to shareholders of record on _____ as may be required by law and the bylaws of the Corporation.

Date: _____, 20____

_____
[Name of shareholder and no. of shares owned]

_____
[Name of shareholder and no. of shares owned]

_____
[Name of shareholder and no. of shares owned]

_____
[Name of shareholder and no. of shares owned]

Notice of Annual Meeting of the Shareholders of

_____

Date:

TO: All Shareholders

The annual meeting of the shareholders of the Corporation will be held on
_____, 20___, at _____ ____.m., at _____
_____.

The purposes of the meeting are:

1. To elect directors.

2. To transact such business as may properly come before the meeting and any adjournment or adjournments thereof.

By order of the board of directors:

_____
Corporate Secretary

Notice of Special Meeting of the Shareholders of

_____

Date:

TO: All Shareholders

A special meeting of the shareholders of the Corporation will be held on
_____, 20____, at _____ ____.m., at _____
_____.

The purposes of the meeting are:

By order of the board of directors:

_____
Corporate Secretary

Affidavit of Mailing

The undersigned, being duly sworn, hereby affirms the following:

1. I am the Corporate Secretary of _____
_____ (the "Corporation").

2. On _____ I caused notice of the _____
meeting of the shareholders of the Corporation to be deposited in the United States
Post Office at _____, in sealed envelopes,
postage prepaid, addressed to each shareholder of the Corporation of record on
_____ at his or her last known address as it appeared on
the books of the Corporation.

3. A copy of such notice is attached to and incorporated by reference into this affidavit.
Date: _____, 20____

_____
Secretary

STATE OF
COUNTY OF
On _____, _____, there personally appeared before
me, _____, who, being duly sworn, deposed
and said that he/she is the Secretary of _____,
and that the facts stated in the above Affidavit are true.

_____
Notary Public
My Commission Expires:

Shareholders' Waiver of Notice

The undersigned Shareholder(s) of _____
hereby waive any and all notice required by law or by the articles of incorporation or
bylaws of the Corporation and consent to the holding of   ☐ the annual   ☐ a special
meeting of the shareholders of the corporation on _____ at
_____ _____.m., at _____
_____ for the following purposes:

_____   Date:_____
Shareholder

_____   Date:_____
Shareholder

_____   Date:_____
Shareholder

_____   Date:_____
Shareholder

_____   Date:_____
Shareholder

_____   Date:_____
Shareholder

Agenda of Meeting of the Shareholders of

_____

Date of Meeting: _____

Appointment of Proxy

The undersigned Shareholder (the "Shareholder") of _____
_____ (the "Corporation") hereby appoints
_____ as proxy, with full power of substitution,
for and in the name of the Shareholder to attend all shareholders meetings of the
Corporation and to act, vote, and execute consents with respect to any or all shares of
the Corporation belonging to the Shareholder as fully and to the same extent and effect
as the Shareholder. This appointment may be revoked by the Shareholder at any time;
but, if not revoked, shall continue in effect until _____.

The date of this proxy is _____.

_____

Shareholder

Appointment of Proxy

The undersigned Shareholder (the "Shareholder") of _____
_____ (the "Corporation") hereby appoints
_____ as proxy, with full power of substitution,
for and in the name of the Shareholder to attend the ☐ annual   ☐ special
shareholders' meeting of the Corporation to be held on _____,
at _____ ____.m., at _____,
and to act and vote at such meeting and any adjournment thereof with respect to any or
all shares of the Corporation belonging to the Shareholder as fully and to the same
extent and effect as the Shareholder. Any appointment of proxy previously made by the
Shareholder for such meeting is hereby revoked.

The date of this proxy is _____.

_____

Shareholder

Appointment of Proxy

The undersigned Shareholder (the "Shareholder") of _____
_____ (the "Corporation") hereby appoints
_____ as proxy, with full power of substitution,
for and in the name of the Shareholder to attend the ☐ annual ☐ special shareholders'
meeting of the Corporation to be held on _____,
at _____ ____.m., at _____,
and to act and vote at such meeting and any adjournment thereof with respect to any or
all shares of the Corporation belonging to the Shareholder as directed below and in his
or her discretion as to any other business that may properly come before the meeting or
any adjournment:

Any appointment of proxy previously made by the Shareholder for such meeting is
hereby revoked.

The date of this proxy is _____.

_____
Shareholder

Shareholder Ballot

Annual Shareholders' Meeting of

_____

Held on: _____

The undersigned shareholder and/or proxy holder votes the shares described below as follows:

FOR ELECTION OF DIRECTORS:

	Name of director	Shares voted for	Shares voted against
1.	_____	_____	_____
2.	_____	_____	_____
3.	_____	_____	_____
4.	_____	_____	_____
5.	_____	_____	_____
6.	_____	_____	_____

Number of shares voted by the undersigned in person: _____

Number of shares voted by the undersigned as proxy: _____

Total shares voted by this ballot: _____

A copy of the proxy form(s) authorizing the undersigned to vote by proxy as above is attached to this ballot.

_____

[signature]

_____

[name printed]

Consent to Action without Formal Meeting by the Directors of

_____

The undersigned directors of the corporation hereby adopt the following resolution:

RESOLVED, that to the extent permitted by law, it is the intent of the board of directors that the corporation shall henceforth pay regular quarterly dividends on the common shares of the corporation in the amount of $_____ per share of common stock issued and outstanding, and further

RESOLVED, that the declaration and payment of such regular dividends shall in every case be subject to the board's reasonable judgment as to their advisability at the time of such declaration.

This resolution shall be effective at _____. m. on the _____ of _____, 20_____.

_____

_____, Director

_____

_____, Director

_____

_____, Director

Consent to Action without Formal Meeting by the Directors of

_____

The undersigned directors of the corporation hereby adopt the following resolution:

RESOLVED, that there is declared a cash dividend on the common shares of the corporation in the amount of $_____ per share issued and outstanding, payable on _____, 20___ to shareholders of record on _____, 20___, and further

RESOLVED, that officers of the corporation are authorized and directed to take such actions as may be necessary or desirable to give effect to the above resolution and to properly record the payment of the dividend in the accounts of the company.

This resolution shall be effective at _____. m. on the _____ of _____, 20_____.

_____

_____, Director

_____

_____, Director

_____

_____, Director

Consent to Action without Formal Meeting by the Directors of

_____

The undersigned directors of the corporation hereby adopt the following resolution:

RESOLVED, that there is declared a cash dividend on the preferred shares of the corporation in the amount of $_____ per share issued and outstanding, payable on _____, 20___ to shareholders of record on _____, 20___, and further

RESOLVED, that officers of the corporation are authorized and directed to take such actions as may be necessary or desirable to give effect to the above resolution and to properly record the payment of the dividend in the accounts of the company.

This resolution shall be effective at _____. m. on the _____ of _____, 20_____.

_____

_____, Director

_____

_____, Director

_____

_____, Director

Consent to Action without Formal Meeting by the Directors of

_____

The undersigned directors of the corporation hereby adopt the following resolution:

RESOLVED, that there is declared a stock dividend on the common shares of the corporation at the rate of _____ share(s) of common stock for each share issued and outstanding, payable on _____, 20___ to shareholders of record on _____, 20___, and further

RESOLVED, that officers of the corporation are authorized and directed to take such actions as may be necessary or desirable to issue new stock certificates, to otherwise give effect to the above resolution, and to properly record the payment of the dividend and issuance of stock in the accounts and records of the corporation.

This resolution shall be effective at _____. m. on the _____ of _____, 20_____.

_____

_____, Director

_____

_____, Director

_____

_____, Director

Consent to Action without Formal Meeting by the Directors of

_____

The undersigned directors of the corporation hereby adopt the following resolution:

RESOLVED, that there is declared a dividend on the common shares of the corporation payable in shares of _____ at the rate of _____ share(s) of common stock for each share of this corporation issued and outstanding, payable on _____, 20___ to shareholders of record on _____, 20___, and further

RESOLVED, that officers of the corporation are authorized and directed to take such actions as may be necessary or desirable to issue stock certificates, to otherwise give effect to the above resolution, and to properly record the payment of the dividend and issuance of stock in the accounts and records of the appropriate corporation.

This resolution shall be effective at _____. m. on the _____ of _____, 20_____.

_____

_____, Director

_____

_____, Director

_____

_____, Director

Consent to Action without Formal Meeting by the Directors of

_____

The undersigned directors of the corporation hereby adopt the following resolution:

RESOLVED, that _____ is appointed to the office of
_____ of the corporation effective _____,
20____, to hold such office until his or her death, resignation, retirement, removal,
disqualification, or the appointment of a successor.

This resolution shall be effective at _____. m. on the _____ of _____,
20_____.

_____

_____, Director

_____

_____, Director

_____

_____, Director

Consent to Action without Formal Meeting by the Directors of

_____

The undersigned directors of the corporation hereby adopt the following resolution:

RESOLVED, that the following individuals are appointed to the offices indicated opposite their names, each of them to hold such office beginning on the effective date of appointment and until his or her death, resignation, retirement, removal, disqualification, or the appointment of a successor:

Name: Office: Effective date of appointment:

This resolution shall be effective at _____. m. on the _____ of _____, 20_____.

_____

_____, Director

_____

_____, Director

_____

_____, Director

Employment Agreement

This employment agreement is made by between _____
(the "Employee") and _____ (the "Corporation").
It is agreed by the Employee and the Corporation as follows:

1. The Board of Directors of the corporation has duly appointed the Employee to the office of _____ subject to the terms and conditions of this agreement.

2. Such appointment shall be effective on _____ at which time the Employee shall begin employment and assume the duties and authorities of _____.

3. The duties of the _____ shall be as follows:

4. The Employee's salary and benefits during the term of this agreement shall be as stated in this paragraph, and may be adjusted from time to time by action of the Board of Directors of the Corporation.

5. Employment pursuant to this agreement shall be:

☐ for a period of _____ years beginning on the effective date stated above.

☐ at will and may be ended by the Employee or by action of the Board of Directors of the corporation at any time and for any reason.

This agreement was executed by the Employee and by the Corporation by authority of its Board of Directors on _____.

Corporation: Employee:

By: _____   _____

Consent to Action without Formal Meeting by the Directors of

_____

The undersigned directors of the corporation hereby adopt the following resolution:

WHEREAS, the management of the corporation has presented to the board of directors a proposed employment contract between the corporation and _____ as _____ of the corporation, which contract is incorporated into this resolution by reference (management storage file no. _____) and has recommended the approval of such contract, it is, after due consideration

RESOLVED, that the referenced employment contract between the corporation and _____ as _____ of the corporation is approved and ratified, and further

RESOLVED, that the appropriate officers of the corporation are authorized and directed to execute such contract.

This resolution shall be effective at _____. m. on the _____ of _____, 20_____.

_____

_____, Director

_____

_____, Director

_____

_____, Director

Consent to Action without Formal Meeting by the Directors of

_____

The undersigned directors of the corporation hereby adopt the following resolution:

RESOLVED, that the corporation shall pay to _____,
for services rendered as _____ of the corporation, an annual
salary of $_____ in equal monthly payments (subject to requirements for
withholding amounts for taxes, etc.), such salary to be effective on
_____, and further

RESOLVED, that as _____, _____
shall be entitled to receive _____

_____
_____ during the period of his or her employment by the corporation.

This resolution shall be effective at _____. m. on the _____ of _____,
20_____.

_____

_____, Director

_____

_____, Director

_____

_____, Director

Consent to Action without Formal Meeting by the Directors of

_____

The undersigned directors of the corporation hereby adopt the following resolution:

RESOLVED, that the resignation of _____
as _____ of the corporation, effective
_____. m., _____, 20____, is accepted.

This resolution shall be effective at _____. m. on the _____ of _____,
20_____.

_____

_____, Director

_____

_____, Director

_____

_____, Director

Consent to Action without Formal Meeting by the Directors of

_____

The undersigned directors of the corporation hereby adopt the following resolution:

RESOLVED, that _____ is removed from the office of
_____ of the corporation effective _____. m.,
_____, 20___.

This resolution shall be effective at _____. m. on the _____ of _____,
20_____.

_____

_____, Director

_____

_____, Director

_____

_____, Director

Certification of Officers by the Secretary of

_____

I hereby certify that I am the Corporate Secretary of the Corporation, that the individuals listed below have been duly elected to the offices of the Corporation appearing opposite their names, and that they continue to hold such offices on the date of this certification:

President: _____   Vice President: _____

Secretary: _____   Treasurer: _____

Other: _____   Other: _____

Signed and the seal of the corporation affixed on _____.

_____

Corporate Secretary

Consent to Action without Formal Meeting by the Directors of

_____

The undersigned directors of the corporation hereby adopt the following resolution:

RESOLVED, that effective _____ the annual salary of _____
_____ shall be increased from its present rate
to $_____ per year payable _____,
subject to customary withholding requirements.

This resolution shall be effective at _____. m. on the _____ of _____,
20_____.

_____

_____, Director

_____

_____, Director

_____

_____, Director

Consent to Action without Formal Meeting by the Directors of

_____

The undersigned directors of the corporation hereby adopt the following resolution:

RESOLVED, that on or before _____ the appropriate officer of the corporation is authorized and directed to pay to _____, on behalf of the corporation, a bonus in the amount of $_____ in addition to his or her regular salary.

This resolution shall be effective at _____. m. on the _____ of _____, 20_____.

_____

_____, Director

_____

_____, Director

_____

_____, Director

Consent to Action without Formal Meeting by the Directors of

_____

The undersigned directors of the corporation hereby adopt the following resolution:

RESOLVED, that beginning _____ the annual salaries of the individuals named below shall be the amounts stated opposite their names (subject to customary withholding requirements) payable in the manner indicated, and that such salaries shall remain in effect until changed or superseded by action of the board of directors:

Name: Annual salary: Payment period:

This resolution shall be effective at _____. m. on the _____ of _____, 20_____.

_____

_____, Director

_____

_____, Director

_____

_____, Director

Consent to Action without Formal Meeting by the Directors of

_____

The undersigned directors of the corporation hereby adopt the following resolution:

WHEREAS, management has presented to the board of directors a proposed engagement letter between _____ and the corporation pursuant to which such firm will provide auditing services to the corporation for the fiscal year ended _____ (the engagement letter is located in management storage file number _____), and

WHEREAS, after discussion, the board of directors believes it to be in the best interests of the corporation to enter into such agreement, it is therefore

RESOLVED, that the proposed engagement letter for auditing services between the corporation and _____ is hereby approved and ratified, and further

RESOLVED, that the corporation shall seek the ratification of such appointment by the shareholders of the corporation at its next annual meeting of shareholders, and further

RESOLVED, that the appropriate officers of the corporation are authorized and directed to execute the referenced agreement and to take such actions as are necessary to obtain ratification of the engagement by shareholders.

This resolution shall be effective at _____. m. on the _____ of _____, 20_____.

_____

_____, Director

_____

_____, Director

_____

_____, Director

Consent to Action without Formal Meeting by the Directors of

_____

The undersigned directors of the corporation hereby adopt the following resolution:

WHEREAS, management has presented to the board of directors a proposed engagement letter between _____
and the corporation pursuant to which the firm will provide legal services to the corporation in connection with _____
(the engagement letter is located in management storage file number
_____), and

WHEREAS, after discussion, the board of directors believes it to be in the best interests of the corporation to enter into such agreement, it is therefore

RESOLVED, that the proposed engagement letter for legal services between the corporation and _____ is approved, ratified, and confirmed.

This resolution shall be effective at _____. m. on the _____ of _____, 20_____.

_____

_____, Director

_____

_____, Director

_____

_____, Director

Consent to Action without Formal Meeting by the Shareholders of

_____

The undersigned shareholders of the corporation hereby adopt the following resolution:

RESOLVED, that the employee health care plan, a copy of which is attached to this Consent to Action (the Plan), is adopted and approved, and further

RESOLVED, that the officers of the corporation are authorized and directed to take such action as is necessary or desirable to implement the Plan.

This resolution shall be effective at _____. m. on the _____ of _____, 20_____.

_____

_____, Shareholder

_____

_____, Shareholder

_____

_____, Shareholder

_____

_____, Shareholder

_____

_____, Shareholder

Consent to Action without Formal Meeting by the Shareholders of

_____

The undersigned shareholders of the corporation hereby adopt the following resolution:

RESOLVED, that the officers of the corporation are authorized and directed to contract with an insurance provider for a group life insurance program with the following basic provisions:

1. Life insurance shall be provided to all employees with _____ or more years of service with the corporation;

2. Each employee's life insurance policy shall be _____ _____.

3. The entire cost of the group life insurance program shall be paid by the corporation.

This resolution shall be effective at _____. m. on the _____ of _____, 20_____.

_____

_____, Shareholder

_____

_____, Shareholder

_____

_____, Shareholder

_____

_____, Shareholder

_____

_____, Shareholder

Consent to Action without Formal Meeting by the Shareholders of

_____

The undersigned shareholders of the corporation hereby adopt the following resolution:

RESOLVED, that the employee retirement plan, a copy of which is attached to this Consent to Action (the Plan), is hereby adopted and approved, and further

RESOLVED, that the officers of the corporation are authorized and directed to take whatever action they deem necessary or desirable to implement the Plan, including but not limited to retaining legal counsel or other financial professionals to ensure that the Plan complies with any federal or state requirements for registration and to obtain any tax classification or benefits as may be directed in the Plan.

This resolution shall be effective at _____. m. on the _____ of _____, 20_____.

_____

_____, Shareholder

_____

_____, Shareholder

_____

_____, Shareholder

_____

_____, Shareholder

_____

_____, Shareholder

Consent to Action without Formal Meeting by the Shareholders of

_____

The undersigned shareholders of the corporation hereby adopt the following resolution:

RESOLVED, that the profit sharing plan, a copy of which is attached to this Consent to Action (the Plan), is adopted and approved, subject to the receipt of assurances regarding legal and tax treatment of the Plan as provided in this resolution below, and further

RESOLVED, that the President and Secretary of the corporation, or their designees, are authorized and directed to take any action reasonably necessary to implement the Plan, including but not limited to executing a trust agreement pursuant to the Plan, and further

RESOLVED, that the officers of the corporation are authorized and directed to retain legal counsel to provide whatever services the officers deem necessary or desirable in order to receive legal assurance that the Plan is qualified under applicable provisions of the Internal Revenue Code for the tax treatment contemplated by the Plan and to provide the board of directors with an opinion satisfactory to the board as to legal compliance of the plan with the Internal Revenue Code and other applicable law, and further

RESOLVED, that the officers of the corporation are authorized and directed to take such actions as may be necessary or desirable to put the profit sharing plan into operation.

This resolution shall be effective at _____. m. on the _____ of _____, 20_____.

_____

_____, Shareholder

_____

_____, Shareholder

_____

_____, Shareholder

_____

_____, Shareholder

_____

_____, Shareholder

Consent to Action without Formal Meeting by the Shareholders of

_____

The undersigned shareholders of the corporation hereby adopt the following resolution:

RESOLVED, that the stock option plan, a copy of which is attached to this Consent to Action (the Plan), is adopted and approved, and further

RESOLVED, that a total number _____ shares of the common stock of this corporation shall be set aside for sale pursuant to the terms of the Plan.

This resolution shall be effective at _____. m. on the _____ of
_____, 20_____.

_____

_____, Shareholder

_____

_____, Shareholder

_____

_____, Shareholder

_____

_____, Shareholder

_____

_____, Shareholder

Consent to Action without Formal Meeting by the Shareholders of

_____

The undersigned shareholders of the corporation hereby adopt the following resolution:

RESOLVED, that the comprehensive employee benefit plan, a copy of which is attached to this Consent to Action (the Plan), is adopted and approved, and further

RESOLVED, that the officers of the corporation are authorized and directed to take whatever action they deem reasonably necessary to implement the Plan, including but not limited to retaining legal counsel or other professional advisors to ensure that the Plan complies with applicable federal or state requirements and to obtain any tax classification or tax benefits as may be contemplated by the Plan.

This resolution shall be effective at _____. m. on the _____ of _____, 20_____.

_____

_____, Shareholder

_____

_____, Shareholder

_____

_____, Shareholder

_____

_____, Shareholder

_____

_____, Shareholder

Limited Power of Attorney

_____ (the "Corporation")
hereby grants to _____ (the "Agent") a
limited power of attorney. As the Corporation's attorney in fact, the Agent shall have full
power and authority to undertake and perform the following on behalf of the
Corporation:

By accepting this grant, the Agent agrees to act in a fiduciary capacity consistent with
the reasonable best interests of the corporation. This power of attorney may be revoked
by the Corporation at any time; however, any person dealing with the Agent as attorney
in fact may rely on this appointment until receipt of actual notice of termination.

IN WITNESS WHEREOF, the undersigned corporation has executed this power of
attorney under seal and by authority of its board of directors as of the date stated
above.

By: _____
President

Attest:

_____
Secretary

STATE OF
COUNTY OF

I certify that _____ personally
appeared before me on _____ and acknowledged that (s)he
is Secretary of _____
and that by authority duly given and as the act of the corporation, the foregoing
instrument was signed in its name by its President, sealed with its corporate seal and
attested by him/her as its Secretary.

_____
Notary Public
My Commission Expires:

I hereby accept the foregoing appointment as attorney in fact on _____.

_____
Attorney in Fact

General Power of Attorney

_____ (the "Corporation") hereby grants
to _____ (the "Agent") a general power of attorney. As
the Corporation's attorney in fact, the Agent shall have full power and authority to undertake any
and all acts which may be lawfully undertaken on behalf of the corporation including but not
limited to the right to buy, sell, lease, mortgage, assign, rent or otherwise dispose of any real or
personal property belonging to the Corporation; to execute, accept, undertake and perform
contracts in the name of the Corporation; to deposit, endorse, or withdraw funds to or from any
bank depository of the Corporation; to initiate, defend or settle legal actions on behalf of the
Corporation; and to retain any accountant, attorney or other advisor deemed by the Agent to be
necessary to protect the interests of the Corporation in relation to such powers.

By accepting this grant, the Agent agrees to act in a fiduciary capacity consistent with the
reasonable best interests of the Corporation. This power of attorney may be revoked by the
Corporation at any time; however, any person dealing with the Agent as attorney in fact may
rely on this appointment until receipt of actual notice of termination.

IN WITNESS WHEREOF, the undersigned corporation has executed this power of attorney
under seal and by authority of its board of directors as of the date stated above.

By: _____

President

Attest:

_____
Secretary

STATE OF
COUNTY OF

I certify that _____ personally appeared
before me on _____ and acknowledged that (s)he is Secretary of
_____ and that by authority
duly given and as the act of the corporation, the foregoing instrument was signed in its name by
its President, sealed with its corporate seal and attested by him/her as its Secretary.

_____
Notary Public
My Commission Expires:

I hereby accept the foregoing appointment as attorney in fact on _____.

_____
Attorney in Fact

Revocation of Power of Attorney

The appointment of _____
as the attorney in fact of the undersigned Corporation (the "Corporation") made on
_____ is hereby revoked and terminated by the Corporation
effective on this date.

Signed and the corporate seal affixed on _____, 20_____.

By: _____

President

Attest:

_____

Secretary

Consent to Action without Formal Meeting by the Directors of

_____

The undersigned directors of the corporation hereby adopt the following resolution:

WHEREAS, the corporation's current designated registered agent for service of process
_____, it is therefore

RESOLVED, that the person named below, located at the address below, is appointed to serve as the corporation's registered agent for service of process

and further

RESOLVED, that the officers of the corporation are authorized and directed to file such documents and notices as may be necessary or desirable to give effect to this resolution.

This resolution shall be effective at _____. m. on the _____ of _____, 20_____.

_____

_____, Director

_____

_____, Director

_____

_____, Director

Indemnification Agreement

This indemnification agreement is entered into by and between _____,
(the "Corporation") and _____, (the "Director").

In consideration of the Director's consent to serve or to continue serving as a director of the Corporation
and other valuable consideration, the parties agree for themselves, their successors and assigns, as
follows.

1. Subject to the terms and limitations provided in this agreement, the Corporation hereby agrees to
indemnify and hold the Director harmless to the fullest extent permitted by law against the expenses,
payments, and liabilities described in this agreement and incurred by the Director by reason of the fact
that the Director is or was a director, officer, employee, or agent of the Corporation or serves or served, at
the request of the Corporation, as a director, officer, partner, trustee, employee, or agent of any other
enterprise or as a trustee or administrator under an employee benefit plan.

> 1.1. The expenses, payments, and liabilities referred to above are:
>
> > 1.1.1. Reasonable expenses, including attorneys' fees, incurred by the Director in
> > connection with any threatened, pending, or completed inquiry, proceeding, action,
> > suit, investigation, or arbitration, whether civil, criminal, or administrative, and any
> > appeal there from, whether or not brought by or on behalf of the Corporation.
> >
> > 1.1.2. Any payment made by the Director in satisfaction of any judgment, money decree,
> > fine, excise tax, penalty, or reasonable settlement for which the Director became
> > liable in any matter described in subparagraph 1.1.1 above.
> >
> > 1.1.3. Reasonable expenses, including legal fees, incurred by the Director in enforcing
> > his or her rights under this paragraph.
>
> 1.2. To the fullest extent allowed by law, the Corporation shall pay the expenses and payments
> described in paragraph 1.1 above in advance of the final disposition of any matter.

2. The rights of the Director hereunder shall inure to the benefit of the Director and his or her heirs, legal
representative, and assigns.

3. The Director shall have the rights provided for in this agreement whether or not he or she is an officer,
director, employee, or agent at the time such liabilities or expenses are imposed or incurred, and whether
or not the claim asserted against the Director is based on matters that predate the execution of this
agreement.

4. The rights of the Director under this agreement are in addition to and not exclusive of any other rights
to which he or she may be entitled under any statute, agreement, insurance policy, or otherwise.

5. The Corporation agrees to use its best reasonable efforts to obtain and pay for a policy of insurance to
protect and insure the Director's rights under this agreement.

IN WITNESS WHEREOF, the parties have executed this agreement under seal and by authority of its
board of directors on the _____ day of _____, 20_____.

Corporation: Director:

By: _____   _____
              President

Attest : _____, Secretary

Consent to Action without Formal Meeting by the Directors of

_____

The undersigned directors of the corporation hereby adopt the following resolution:

WHEREAS, the management of the corporation has presented to the board of directors a proposed policy of insurance providing errors and omissions coverage for the officers and directors of the corporation and insuring the company's obligations to pay indemnification to its officers and directors pursuant to the articles of incorporation and/or bylaws of the company and various contractual arrangements, and

WHEREAS, management has recommended the approval to the purchase of the policy, it is, after due consideration

RESOLVED, that the policy of insurance negotiated with _____ and titled _____ presented to the board of directors (the Policy), which Policy is incorporated by reference into this Consent to Action by reference (management storage file no _____), is approved and ratified, and further

RESOLVED, that the appropriate officers are authorized and directed to take such actions and execute such documents as are necessary or desirable to place such policy in effect and to make premium payments from corporate funds so as to keep such policy in force until further action by the board of directors.

This resolution shall be effective at _____. m. on the _____ of _____, 20_____.

_____

_____, Director

_____

_____, Director

_____

_____, Director

Consent to Action without Formal Meeting by the Directors of

_____

The undersigned directors of the corporation hereby adopt the following resolution:

RESOLVED, that pursuant to _____ of the bylaws
of the corporation, _____ of such
bylaws is amended to read in its entirety as follows:

This resolution shall be effective at _____. m. on the _____ of _____,
20_____.

_____

_____, Director

_____

_____, Director

_____

_____, Director

Consent to Action without Formal Meeting by the Directors of

_____

The undersigned directors of the corporation hereby adopt the following resolution:

RESOLVED, that, pursuant to _____ of the bylaws of the corporation, the bylaws are amended by the addition of a new provision at _____ to read in its entirety as follows:

This resolution shall be effective at _____. m. on the _____ of _____, 20_____.

_____

_____, Director

_____

_____, Director

_____

_____, Director

Consent to Action without Formal Meeting by the Directors of

_____

The undersigned directors of the corporation hereby adopt the following resolution:

RESOLVED, that pursuant to the laws of the state of _____ and the articles and bylaws of the corporation, the board of directors recommends to the shareholders of the corporation that its articles of incorporation be amended by changing _____ to read in its entirety as follows:

and further

RESOLVED, that the directors recommend to the shareholders that they vote in favor of the proposed amendment, and further

RESOLVED, that the submission of the proposed amendment to the shareholders for approval shall be on the condition that the directors, by majority vote, may withdraw and cancel the amendment at any time prior to its effective date, and further

RESOLVED, that the appropriate officers of the corporation are authorized and directed to call a special meeting of the shareholders, giving appropriate notice, on _____, 20___, for the purpose of approving or disapproving such proposed amendment, or to obtain shareholder approval of the amendment by Consent to Action without Formal Meeting of the Shareholders; and, upon approval by the shareholders, to execute and file articles of amendment and to take such other actions as may be necessary or desirable to give effect to the proposed amendment and the foregoing resolution.

This resolution shall be effective at _____. m. on the _____ of _____, 20_____.

_____

_____, Director

_____

_____, Director

_____

_____, Director

Consent to Action without Formal Meeting by the Shareholders of

_____

The undersigned shareholders of the corporation hereby adopt the following resolution:

WHEREAS, the directors of the corporation have proposed that its articles of incorporation be amended in the manner set out below and have recommended to the shareholders that such amendment be adopted by its shareholders, it is therefore

RESOLVED, that the proposal and recommendation by the directors is ratified and approved and that the articles of incorporation is of the corporation are amended by changing _____ to read in its entirety as follows:

This resolution shall be effective at _____. m. on the _____ of _____, 20_____.

_____

_____, Shareholder

_____

_____, Shareholder

_____

_____, Shareholder

_____

_____, Shareholder

_____

_____, Shareholder

Consent to Action without Formal Meeting by the Directors of

_____

The undersigned directors of the corporation hereby adopt the following resolution:

RESOLVED, that the corporation shall assume and henceforth conduct its
_____ business under the name
_____,
and further

RESOLVED, that the appropriate officers of the corporation are authorized and directed to execute and file such certificates and declarations as may be required by law and to take such other acts as may be necessary or desirable to give effect to the foregoing resolution.

This resolution shall be effective at _____. m. on the _____ of _____, 20_____.

_____

_____, Director

_____

_____, Director

_____

_____, Director

Consent to Action without Formal Meeting by the Directors of

_____

The undersigned directors of the corporation hereby adopt the following resolution:

RESOLVED, that pursuant to the laws of the state of _____ and the articles and bylaws of the corporation, the board of directors recommends to the shareholders of the corporation that its articles of incorporation be amended to change the name of the corporation from its current name to _____, and further

RESOLVED, that such change be accomplished by amending _____ to read in its entirety as follows:

Article _____. The name of the corporation is _____,

and further

RESOLVED, that the directors recommend to the shareholders that they vote in favor of the proposed amendment, and further

RESOLVED, that the submission of the proposed amendment to the shareholders for approval shall be on the condition that the directors, by majority vote, may withdraw and cancel the amendment at any time prior to its effective date, and further

RESOLVED, that the appropriate officers of the corporation are authorized and directed to call a special meeting of the shareholders, giving appropriate notice, on _____ for the purpose of approving or disapproving such proposed amendment or to obtain shareholder approval of the proposed amendment by Consent to Action without Formal Meeting of the Shareholders; and, upon approval by the shareholders, to execute and file articles of amendment and to take such other actions as may be necessary or desirable to give effect to the proposed amendment and the foregoing resolution.

This resolution shall be effective at _____. m. on the _____ of _____, 20_____.

_____

_____, Director

_____

_____, Director

_____

_____, Director

Consent to Action without Formal Meeting by the Shareholders of

_____

The undersigned shareholders of the corporation hereby adopt the following resolution:

WHEREAS, the directors of the corporation have proposed that its articles of incorporation be amended to change the name of the corporation, and have recommended to the shareholders that such amendment be adopted by its shareholders, it is therefore

RESOLVED, that the proposal and recommendation by the directors is ratified and approved and that the articles of incorporation is of the corporation are amended by changing _____ to read in its entirety as follows:

Article ___. The name of the corporation is _____.

This resolution shall be effective at _____. m. on the _____ of _____, 20_____.

_____

_____, Shareholder

_____

_____, Shareholder

_____

_____, Shareholder

_____

_____, Shareholder

_____

_____, Shareholder

Consent to Action without Formal Meeting by the Directors of

_____

The undersigned directors of the corporation hereby adopt the following resolution:

WHEREAS, management of the corporation has recommended to the board of directors that the corporation undertake business activities in the state of _____ and have advised the board that, in order to do so, it is necessary to obtain a certificate of authority to engage in business in that state, it is therefore

RESOLVED, that the officers of the corporation are authorized and directed to apply for and obtain a certificate of authority to carry on business in the state of _____, and further

RESOLVED, that _____ at _____
_____
is appointed to serve as the corporation's registered agent for service of process in the state of _____, and further

RESOLVED, that the officers of the corporation are authorized to file such applications and other documents and to take such further actions as may be necessary or desirable to give effect to this resolution.

This resolution shall be effective at _____. m. on the _____ of _____, 20_____.

_____

_____, Director

_____

_____, Director

_____

_____, Director

Consent to Action without Formal Meeting by the Directors of

_____

The undersigned directors of the corporation hereby adopt the following resolution:

WHEREAS the directors of the corporation have determined that it is in the best interests of the corporation that it merge with its wholly owned subsidiary (the Merging Corporation), it is therefore

RESOLVED, that the following plan of merger between this corporation and its wholly owned subsidiary, _____, is hereby approved and adopted:

Plan of Merger

A. The name of the parent corporation into which the subsidiary shall merge is _____, which shall be the Surviving Corporation, and the name of the subsidiary corporation which shall merge into the parent is _____, which shall be the Merging Corporation.

B. On the effective date of the merger, the Merging Corporation shall merge into the Surviving Corporation and the corporate existence of the Merging Corporation shall cease. The shares of the Merging Corporation shall not be converted into shares, obligations or other securities of the Surviving Corporation or any other corporation or into cash or other property in whole or in part. The outstanding shares of the Surviving Corporation will not be converted, exchanged or altered in any manner, but shall remain outstanding shares of the Surviving Corporation.

C. The directors of the Surviving Corporation may, in their discretion, abandon this merger at any time before its effective date.

D. The effective date of this merger shall be the close of business on the date articles of merger relating to this merger are filed as required by law.

Further RESOLVED, that the corporation, as shareholder of the Merging Corporation, waives all notice of the proposed merger, and further

RESOLVED, that the appropriate officers of the corporation are authorized and directed to execute and file articles of merger and to take such other actions as may be necessary or desirable to give effect to the above resolution.

This resolution shall be effective at _____. m. on the _____ of _____, 20_____.

_____

_____, Director

_____

_____, Director

_____

_____, Director

Articles of Merger of

_____

into

_____

These Articles of Merger are submitted by _____
_____, organized under the laws of _____
(the "Surviving Corporation") for the purpose of merging its subsidiary corporation
_____, organized under the laws of
_____ (the "Merging Corporation") into the
Surviving Corporation.

1. The following Plan of Merger has been duly approved by the board of directors of the surviving corporation:

Plan of Merger

A. The name of the parent corporation into which the subsidiary shall merge is
_____, which shall be the Surviving
Corporation, and the name of the subsidiary corporation which shall merge into the
parent is _____, which shall be the
Merging Corporation.

B. On the effective date of the merger, the Merging Corporation shall merge into the Surviving Corporation and the corporate existence of the Merging Corporation shall cease. The shares of the Merging Corporation shall not be converted into shares, obligations, or other securities of the Surviving Corporation or any other corporation or into cash or other property in whole or in part. The outstanding shares of the Surviving Corporation will not be converted, exchanged, or altered in any manner, but shall remain outstanding shares of the Surviving Corporation.

C. The directors of the Surviving Corporation may, in their discretion, abandon this merger at any time before its effective date.

D. The effective date of this merger shall be the close of business on the date articles of merger relating to this merger are filed as required by law.

2. Shareholder approval of the merger was not required because the Surviving Corporation was the owner of 100% of the outstanding shares of the Merging Corporation, and the Plan of Merger does not provide for any amendment to the articles of incorporation of the Surviving Corporation.

These articles of merger were signed by the corporation on _____,
20____.

By: _____

Consent to Action without Formal Meeting by the Directors of

_____

The undersigned directors of the corporation hereby adopt the following resolution:

WHEREAS, the directors of the corporation, after due consideration, have determined that it is in the best interests of the corporation that it enter into a merger with _____ under the terms of a plan of merger set out below, it is therefore

RESOLVED, that pursuant to the laws of the state of _____ and the articles and bylaws of the corporation, the board of directors recommends to the shareholders of the corporation that the following Plan of Merger be adopted by the shareholders:

Plan of Merger

A. _____, which shall be the Merging Corporation, shall merge into _____, which shall be the Surviving Corporation.

B. On the effective date of the merger, the Merging Corporation shall merge into the Surviving Corporation, and the corporate existence of the Merging Corporation shall cease. On the effective date of the merger, each outstanding share of the Merging Corporation shall be converted into _____ share(s) of the Surviving Corporation. The outstanding shares of the Surviving Corporation will not be converted, exchanged, or altered in any manner, but shall remain outstanding shares of the Surviving Corporation.

C. Each shareholder of the Merging Corporation holding a certificate representing share(s) of such corporation shall surrender the certificate and shall be entitled to receive certificate(s) representing the shares of the Surviving Corporation to which the Shareholder is entitled under this Plan of Merger. After the effective date of the merger and before such surrender, each certificate representing shares of the Merging Corporation shall be deemed for all purposes to evidence ownership of the shares of the Surviving Corporation to which the Shareholder is entitled under this Plan of Merger.

D. The directors of the Surviving Corporation or the Merging Corporation may, in their discretion, abandon this merger at any time before its effective date.

E. The effective date of this merger shall be the close of business on the date articles of merger relating to this Plan of Merger are filed as required by law.

Further RESOLVED, that the submission of the Plan of Merger to the shareholders for approval shall be on the condition that the directors, by majority vote, may withdraw and cancel such proposed merger at any time before its effective date, and further

RESOLVED, that the appropriate officers of the corporation are hereby authorized and directed to call a special meeting of the shareholders, giving appropriate notice, on _____, 20___, for the purpose of approving or disapproving the Plan of Merger, or to obtain shareholder approval of the Plan of Merger by Consent to Action without Formal Meeting; and, upon approval by the shareholders of the corporations participating in the proposed merger to execute and file articles of merger and to take such other actions as may be necessary or desirable to give effect to the Plan of Merger and this resolution.

This resolution shall be effective at _____. m. on the _____ of _____, 20_____.

_____

_____, Director

_____

_____, Director

_____

_____, Director

Consent to Action without Formal Meeting by the Shareholders of

_____

The undersigned shareholders of the corporation hereby adopt the following resolution:

WHEREAS, the directors of the corporation have proposed the adoption of a Plan of Merger accomplishing the merger of _____ into _____, and have recommended to the shareholders that the Plan of Merger be adopted, it is therefore

RESOLVED, that such proposal and recommendation by the directors is ratified and approved and that the following Plan of Merger is adopted:

Plan of Merger

A. _____, which shall be the Merging Corporation, shall merge into _____, which shall be the Surviving Corporation.

B. On the effective date of the merger, the Merging Corporation shall merge into the Surviving Corporation, and the corporate existence of the Merging Corporation shall cease. On the effective date of the merger, each outstanding share of the Merging Corporation shall be converted into _____ share(s) of the Surviving Corporation. The outstanding shares of the Surviving Corporation will not be converted, exchanged or altered in any manner, but shall remain outstanding shares of the Surviving Corporation.

C. Each shareholder of the Merging Corporation holding a certificate representing share(s) of such corporation shall surrender the certificate and shall be entitled to receive certificate(s) representing the shares of the Surviving Corporation to which the Shareholder is entitled under this Plan of Merger. After the effective date of the merger and before such surrender, each certificate representing shares of the Merging Corporation shall be deemed for all purposes to evidence ownership of the shares of the Surviving Corporation to which the Shareholder is entitled under this Plan of Merger.

D. The directors of the Surviving Corporation or the Merging Corporation may, in their discretion abandon this merger at any time before its effective date.

E. The effective date of this merger shall be the close of business on the date articles of merger relating to this Plan of Merger are filed as required by law.

This resolution shall be effective at _____. m. on the _____ of _____, 20_____.

_____

_____, Shareholder

_____

_____, Shareholder

_____

_____, Shareholder

_____

_____, Shareholder

_____

_____, Shareholder

Articles of Merger of

_____

into

_____

These Articles of Merger are submitted by _____,
organized under the laws of _____ (the
"Surviving Corporation") for the purpose of merging _____
_____, organized under the laws of _____
_____ (the "Merging Corporation") into the Surviving
Corporation.

1. The following Plan of Merger has been duly approved by the boards of directors of
the Surviving Corporation and the Merging Corporation:

2. The designation and number of outstanding shares, and the number of votes entitled
to be cast by each voting group entitled to vote separately on such Plan as to the
Merging Corporation were:

Designation: _____ Shares outstanding: _____ Votes entitled to be cast: _____

The number of votes cast for such Plan by shareholders of the Merging Corporation
was _____ which was sufficient for approval of the Plan by the
shareholders of the Merging Corporation.

3. The designation and number of outstanding shares, and the number of votes entitled
to be cast by each voting group entitled to vote separately on such Plan as to the
Surviving Corporation were:

Designation: _____ Shares outstanding: _____ Votes entitled to be cast: _____

The number of votes cast for such Plan by shareholders of the Surviving Corporation was _____ which was sufficient for approval of the Plan by the shareholders of the Surviving Corporation.

These articles of merger were signed by the corporation on _____.

By: _____

Title: _____

Consent to Action without Formal Meeting by the Directors of

_____

The undersigned directors of the corporation hereby adopt the following resolution:

WHEREAS, management of the corporation has entered into negotiations with _____ for the sale and purchase of the outstanding shares of _____ by this company, and after due consideration the directors have determined that such transaction under the terms and conditions expressed in the _____ presented to the directors (the Agreement) (a copy of the Agreement is located in management Storage file No. _____) is in the best interests of the Corporation, it is therefore

RESOLVED, that the purchase of the outstanding shares of _____ _____ by this corporation under the terms and conditions of the Agreement executed by management dated _____, 20___, is approved, ratified and confirmed, and further

RESOLVED, that the appropriate officers of the corporation are authorized and directed to take such actions as may be necessary or desirable to give effect the above resolution and the Agreement.

This resolution shall be effective at _____. m. on the _____ of _____, 20_____.

_____

_____, Director

_____

_____, Director

_____

_____, Director

Consent to Action without Formal Meeting by the Directors of

_____

The undersigned directors of the corporation hereby adopt the following resolution:

WHEREAS, management of the corporation has entered into negotiations with _____ for the sale and purchase of substantially all of the assets of _____ by this company, and after due consideration the directors have determined that such transaction under the terms and conditions expressed in the _____ presented to the directors (the Agreement) (a copy of the Agreement is located in management Storage file No. _____) is in the best interests of the Corporation, it is therefore

RESOLVED, that the purchase of the assets of _____ by this corporation under the terms and conditions of the Agreement executed by management dated _____, 20___, is approved, ratified, and confirmed, and further

RESOLVED, that the appropriate officers of the corporation are authorized and directed to take such actions as may be necessary or desirable to give effect the above resolution and the Agreement.

This resolution shall be effective at _____. m. on the _____ of _____, 20_____.

_____

_____, Director

_____

_____, Director

_____

_____, Director

Stock Ledger

Certificates Issued

Transfer Shares

Cert. No.	No. of Shares	Date Acquired	Shareholder Name and Address	From Whom Transferred	Amount Paid	Date of Transfer	To Whom Transferred	Cert. No Surrendered	No. of Shares Transferred	Cert. No.

Form 2553
(Rev. March 2005)

Department of the Treasury
Internal Revenue Service

Election by a Small Business Corporation
(Under section 1362 of the Internal Revenue Code)
▶ See Parts II and III on back and the separate instructions.
▶ The corporation may either send or fax this form to the IRS. See page 2 of the instructions.

OMB No. 1545-0146

Notes:
1. **Do not** file **Form 1120S,** U.S. Income Tax Return for an S Corporation, for any tax year before the year the election takes effect.
2. This election to be an S corporation can be accepted only if all the tests are met under **Who May Elect** on page 1 of the instructions; all shareholders have signed the consent statement; an officer has signed this form; and the exact name and address of the corporation and other required form information are provided.

Part I   Election Information

Please Type or Print

Name (see instructions)	**A** Employer identification number
Number, street, and room or suite no. (If a P.O. box, see instructions.)	**B** Date incorporated
City or town, state, and ZIP code	**C** State of incorporation

D Check the applicable box(es) if the corporation, after applying for the EIN shown in **A** above, changed its name ☐ or address ☐

E Election is to be effective for tax year beginning (month, day, year) . . . . ▶   /   /

F Name and title of officer or legal representative who the IRS may call for more information

G Telephone number of officer or legal representative
(   )

H If this election takes effect for the first tax year the corporation exists, enter month, day, and year of the **earliest** of the following: (1) date the corporation first had shareholders, (2) date the corporation first had assets, or (3) date the corporation began doing business . . . . ▶   /   /

I Selected tax year: Annual return will be filed for tax year ending (month and day) ▶ ----------------------------

If the tax year ends on any date other than December 31, except for a 52-53-week tax year ending with reference to the month of December, complete Part II on the back. If the date you enter is the ending date of a 52-53-week tax year, write "52-53-week year" to the right of the date.

J Name and address of each shareholder or former shareholder required to consent to the election. (See the instructions for column K)	**K** Shareholders' Consent Statement. Under penalties of perjury, we declare that we consent to the election of the above-named corporation to be an S corporation under section 1362(a) and that we have examined this consent statement, including accompanying schedules and statements, and to the best of our knowledge and belief, it is true, correct, and complete. We understand our consent is binding and may not be withdrawn after the corporation has made a valid election. (Sign and date below.)		**L** Stock owned or percentage of ownership (see instructions)		**M** Social security number or employer identification number (see instructions)	**N** Shareholder's tax year ends (month and day)
	Signature	Date	Number of shares or percentage of ownership	Date(s) acquired		

Under penalties of perjury, I declare that I have examined this election, including accompanying schedules and statements, and to the best of my knowledge and belief, it is true, correct, and complete.

Signature of officer ▶   Title ▶   Date ▶

For Paperwork Reduction Act Notice, see page 4 of the instructions.   Cat. No. 18629R   Form **2553** (Rev. 3-2005)

Form 2553 (Rev. 3-2005)   Page **2**

Part II Selection of Fiscal Tax Year (All corporations using this part must complete item O and item P, Q, or R.)

O   Check the applicable box to indicate whether the corporation is:

   1. ☐ A new corporation **adopting** the tax year entered in item I, Part I.

   2. ☐ An existing corporation **retaining** the tax year entered in item I, Part I.

   3. ☐ An existing corporation **changing** to the tax year entered in item I, Part I.

P   Complete item P if the corporation is using the automatic approval provisions of Rev. Proc. 2002-38, 2002-22 I.R.B. 1037, to request **(1)** a natural business year (as defined in section 5.05 of Rev. Proc. 2002-38) or **(2)** a year that satisfies the ownership tax year test (as defined in section 5.06 of Rev. Proc. 2002-38). Check the applicable box below to indicate the representation statement the corporation is making.

   1. Natural Business Year ▶ ☐ I represent that the corporation is adopting, retaining, or changing to a tax year that qualifies as its natural business year as defined in section 5.05 of Rev. Proc. 2002-38 and has attached a statement verifying that it satisfies the 25% gross receipts test (see instructions for content of statement). I also represent that the corporation is not precluded by section 4.02 of Rev. Proc. 2002-38 from obtaining automatic approval of such adoption, retention, or change in tax year.

   2. Ownership Tax Year ▶ ☐ I represent that shareholders (as described in section 5.06 of Rev. Proc. 2002-38) holding more than half of the shares of the stock (as of the first day of the tax year to which the request relates) of the corporation have the same tax year or are concurrently changing to the tax year that the corporation adopts, retains, or changes to per item I, Part I, and that such tax year satisfies the requirement of section 4.01(3) of Rev. Proc. 2002-38. I also represent that the corporation is not precluded by section 4.02 of Rev. Proc. 2002-38 from obtaining automatic approval of such adoption, retention, or change in tax year.

Note: *If you do not use item P and the corporation wants a fiscal tax year, complete either item Q or R below. Item Q is used to request a fiscal tax year based on a business purpose and to make a back-up section 444 election. Item R is used to make a regular section 444 election.*

Q   Business Purpose—To request a fiscal tax year based on a business purpose, check box Q1. See instructions for details including payment of a user fee. You may also check box Q2 and/or box Q3.

   1. Check here ▶ ☐ if the fiscal year entered in item I, Part I, is requested under the prior approval provisions of Rev. Proc. 2002-39, 2002-22 I.R.B. 1046. Attach to Form 2553 a statement describing the relevant facts and circumstances and, if applicable, the gross receipts from sales and services necessary to establish a business purpose. See the instructions for details regarding the gross receipts from sales and services. If the IRS proposes to disapprove the requested fiscal year, do you want a conference with the IRS National Office?
   ☐ Yes   ☐ No

   2. Check here ▶ ☐ to show that the corporation intends to make a back-up section 444 election in the event the corporation's business purpose request is not approved by the IRS. (See instructions for more information.)

   3. Check here ▶ ☐ to show that the corporation agrees to adopt or change to a tax year ending December 31 if necessary for the IRS to accept this election for S corporation status in the event (1) the corporation's business purpose request is not approved and the corporation makes a back-up section 444 election, but is ultimately not qualified to make a section 444 election, or (2) the corporation's business purpose request is not approved and the corporation did not make a back-up section 444 election.

R   Section 444 Election—To make a section 444 election, check box R1. You may also check box R2.

   1. Check here ▶ ☐ to show the corporation will make, if qualified, a section 444 election to have the fiscal tax year shown in item I, Part I. To make the election, you must complete **Form 8716,** Election To Have a Tax Year Other Than a Required Tax Year, and either attach it to Form 2553 or file it separately.

   2. Check here ▶ ☐ to show that the corporation agrees to adopt or change to a tax year ending December 31 if necessary for the IRS to accept this election for S corporation status in the event the corporation is ultimately not qualified to make a section 444 election.

Part III Qualified Subchapter S Trust (QSST) Election Under Section 1361(d)(2)*

Income beneficiary's name and address	Social security number
Trust's name and address	Employer identification number

Date on which stock of the corporation was transferred to the trust (month, day, year) . . . . ▶   /   /

In order for the trust named above to be a QSST and thus a qualifying shareholder of the S corporation for which this Form 2553 is filed, I hereby make the election under section 1361(d)(2). Under penalties of perjury, I certify that the trust meets the definitional requirements of section 1361(d)(3) and that all other information provided in Part III is true, correct, and complete.

_____   _____
Signature of income beneficiary or signature and title of legal representative or other qualified person making the election   Date

*Use Part III to make the QSST election only if stock of the corporation has been transferred to the trust on or before the date on which the corporation makes its election to be an S corporation. The QSST election must be made and filed separately if stock of the corporation is transferred to the trust **after** the date on which the corporation makes the S election.

Form **2553** (Rev. 3-2005)

Instructions for Form 2553

Department of the Treasury
Internal Revenue Service

(Rev. March 2005)

Election by a Small Business Corporation

Section references are to the Internal Revenue Code unless otherwise noted.

General Instructions

Purpose

A corporation or other entity eligible to elect to be treated as a corporation must use Form 2553 to make an election under section 1362(a) to be an S corporation. An entity eligible to elect to be treated as a corporation that meets certain tests discussed below will be treated as a corporation as of the effective date of the S corporation election and does not need to file Form 8832, Entity Classification Election.

The income of an S corporation generally is taxed to the shareholders of the corporation rather than to the corporation itself. However, an S corporation may still owe tax on certain income. For details, see *Tax and Payments* in the Instructions for Form 1120S, U.S. Income Tax Return for an S Corporation.

Who May Elect

A corporation or other entity eligible to elect to be treated as a corporation may elect to be an S corporation only if it meets all the following tests.

1. It is (a) a domestic corporation, or (b) a domestic entity eligible to elect to be treated as a corporation that timely files Form 2553 and meets all the other tests listed below. If Form 2553 is not timely filed, see Rev. Proc. 2004-48, 2004-32 I.R.B. 172.

2. It has no more than 100 shareholders. A husband and wife (and their estates) are treated as one shareholder for this test. A member of a family can elect under section 1361(c)(1) to treat all members of the family as one shareholder for this test. All other persons are treated as separate shareholders.

3. Its only shareholders are individuals, estates, exempt organizations described in section 401(a) or 501(c)(3), or certain trusts described in section 1361(c)(2)(A).

For information about the section 1361(d)(2) election to be a qualified subchapter S trust (QSST), see the instructions for Part III. For information about the section 1361(e)(3) election to be an electing small business trust (ESBT), see Regulations section 1.1361-1(m). For guidance on how to convert a QSST to an ESBT, see Regulations section 1.1361-1(j)(12). If these elections were not timely made, see Rev. Proc. 2003-43, 2003-23 I.R.B. 998.

4. It has no nonresident alien shareholders.

5. It has only one class of stock (disregarding differences in voting rights). Generally, a corporation is treated as having only one class of stock if all outstanding shares of the corporation's stock confer identical rights to distribution and liquidation proceeds. See Regulations section 1.1361-1(l) for details.

6. It is not one of the following ineligible corporations.

a. A bank or thrift institution that uses the reserve method of accounting for bad debts under section 585.

b. An insurance company subject to tax under subchapter L of the Code.

c. A corporation that has elected to be treated as a possessions corporation under section 936.

d. A domestic international sales corporation (DISC) or former DISC.

7. It has or will adopt or change to one of the following tax years.

a. A tax year ending December 31.

b. A natural business year.

c. An ownership tax year.

d. A tax year elected under section 444.

e. A 52-53-week tax year ending with reference to a year listed above.

f. Any other tax year (including a 52-53-week tax year) for which the corporation establishes a business purpose.

For details on making a section 444 election or requesting a natural business, ownership, or other business purpose tax year, see Part II of Form 2553.

8. Each shareholder consents as explained in the instructions for column K.

See sections 1361, 1362, and 1378, and their related regulations for additional information on the above tests.

A parent S corporation can elect to treat an eligible wholly-owned subsidiary as a qualified subchapter S subsidiary. If the election is made, the subsidiary's assets, liabilities, and items of income, deduction, and credit are treated as those of the parent. For details, see Form 8869, Qualified Subchapter S Subsidiary Election.

When To Make the Election

Complete and file Form 2553 (a) at any time before the 16th day of the 3rd month of the tax year the election is to take effect, or (b) at any time during the tax year preceding the tax year it is to take effect. An election made no later than 2 months and 15 days after the beginning of a tax year that is less than 2½ months long is treated as timely made for that tax year.

An election made after the 15th day of the 3rd month but before the end of the tax year generally is effective for the next tax year. However, an election made after the 15th day of the 3rd month will be accepted as timely filed if the corporation can show that the failure to file on time was due to reasonable cause.

To request relief for a late election, the corporation generally must request a private letter ruling and pay a user fee in accordance with Rev. Proc. 2005-1, 2005-1 I.R.B. 1 (or its successor). However, the ruling and user fee requirements may not apply if the following revenue procedures apply.

• If an entity eligible to elect to be treated as a corporation (a) failed to timely file Form 2553, and (b) has

not elected to be treated as a corporation, see Rev. Proc. 2004-48, 2004-32 I.R.B. 172.
• If a corporation failed to timely file Form 2553, see Rev. Proc. 2003-43, 2003-23 I.R.B. 998.
• If Form 1120S was filed without an S corporation election and neither the corporation nor any shareholder was notified by the IRS of any problem with the S corporation status within 6 months after the return was timely filed, see Rev. Proc. 97-48, 1997-43 I.R.B. 19.

Where To File

Send the original election (no photocopies) or fax it to the Internal Revenue Service Center listed below. If the corporation files this election by fax, keep the original Form 2553 with the corporation's permanent records.

If the corporation's principal business, office, or agency is located in:	Use the following Internal Revenue Service Center address or fax number:
Connecticut, Delaware, District of Columbia, Illinois, Indiana, Kentucky, Maine, Maryland, Massachusetts, Michigan, New Hampshire, New Jersey, New York, North Carolina, Ohio, Pennsylvania, Rhode Island, South Carolina, Vermont, Virginia, West Virginia, Wisconsin	Cincinnati, OH 45999 Fax: (859) 669-5748
Alabama, Alaska, Arizona, Arkansas, California, Colorado, Florida, Georgia, Hawaii, Idaho, Iowa, Kansas, Louisiana, Minnesota, Mississippi, Missouri, Montana, Nebraska, Nevada, New Mexico, North Dakota, Oklahoma, Oregon, South Dakota, Tennessee, Texas, Utah, Washington, Wyoming	Ogden, UT 84201 Fax: (801) 620-7116

Acceptance or Nonacceptance of Election

The service center will notify the corporation if its election is accepted and when it will take effect. The corporation will also be notified if its election is not accepted. The corporation should generally receive a determination on its election within 60 days after it has filed Form 2553. If box Q1 in Part II is checked, the corporation will receive a ruling letter from the IRS in Washington, DC, that either approves or denies the selected tax year. When box Q1 is checked, it will generally take an additional 90 days for the Form 2553 to be accepted.

Care should be exercised to ensure that the IRS receives the election. If the corporation is not notified of acceptance or nonacceptance of its election within 2 months of the date of filing (date faxed or mailed), or within 5 months if box Q1 is checked, take follow-up action by calling 1-800-829-4933.

If the IRS questions whether Form 2553 was filed, an acceptable proof of filing is (a) a certified or registered mail receipt (timely postmarked) from the U.S. Postal Service, or its equivalent from a designated private delivery service (see Notice 2004-83, 2004-52 I.R.B.

1030 (or its successor)); (b) Form 2553 with an accepted stamp; (c) Form 2553 with a stamped IRS received date; or (d) an IRS letter stating that Form 2553 has been accepted.

 Do not file Form 1120S for any tax year before the year the election takes effect. If the corporation is now required to file Form 1120, U.S. Corporation Income Tax Return, or any other applicable tax return, continue filing it until the election takes effect.

End of Election

Once the election is made, it stays in effect until it is terminated. IRS consent generally is required for another election by the corporation (or a successor corporation) on Form 2553 for any tax year before the 5th tax year after the first tax year in which the termination took effect. See Regulations section 1.1362-5 for details.

Specific Instructions

Part I

Name and Address

Enter the corporation's true name as stated in the corporate charter or other legal document creating it. If the corporation's mailing address is the same as someone else's, such as a shareholder's, enter "c/o" and this person's name following the name of the corporation. Include the suite, room, or other unit number after the street address. If the Post Office does not deliver to the street address and the corporation has a P.O. box, show the box number instead of the street address. If the corporation changed its name or address after applying for its employer identification number, be sure to check the box in item D of Part I.

Item A. Employer Identification Number (EIN)

Enter the corporation's EIN. If the corporation does not have an EIN, it must apply for one. An EIN can be applied for:
• Online—Click on the EIN link at *www.irs.gov/businesses/small*. The EIN is issued immediately once the application information is validated.
• By telephone at 1-800-829-4933 from 7:00 a.m. to 10:00 p.m. in the corporation's local time zone.
• By mailing or faxing Form SS-4, Application for Employer Identification Number.

If the corporation has not received its EIN by the time the return is due, enter "Applied for" in the space for the EIN. For more details, see Pub. 583.

Item E. Effective Date of Election

 Form 2553 generally must be filed no later than 2 months and 15 days after the date entered for item E. For details and exceptions, see When To Make the Election on page 1.

A corporation (or entity eligible to elect to be treated as a corporation) making the election effective for its first tax year in existence should enter the earliest of the following dates: (a) the date the corporation (entity) first had shareholders (owners), (b) the date the corporation (entity) first had assets, or (c) the date the corporation (entity) began doing business. This same date will be entered for item H.

A corporation (entity) not making the election for its first tax year in existence that is keeping its current tax year should enter the beginning date of the first tax year for which it wants the election to be effective.

A corporation (entity) not making the election for its first tax year in existence that is changing its tax year and wants to be an S corporation for the short tax year needed to switch tax years should enter the beginning date of the short tax year. If the corporation (entity) does not want to be an S corporation for this short tax year, it should enter the beginning date of the tax year following this short tax year and file Form 1128, Application To Adopt, Change, or Retain a Tax Year. If this change qualifies as an automatic approval request (Form 1128, Part II), file Form 1128 as an attachment to Form 2553. If this change qualifies as a ruling request (Form 1128, Part III), file Form 1128 separately. If filing Form 1128, enter "Form 1128" on the dotted line to the left of the entry space for item E.

Column K. Shareholders' Consent Statement

For an election filed before the effective date entered for item E, only shareholders who own stock on the day the election is made need to consent to the election.

For an election filed on or after the effective date entered for item E, all shareholders or former shareholders who owned stock at any time during the period beginning on the effective date entered for item E and ending on the day the election is made must consent to the election.

If the corporation filed a timely election, but one or more shareholders did not file a timely consent, see Regulations section 1.1362-6(b)(3)(iii). If the shareholder was a community property spouse who was a shareholder solely because of a state community property law, see Rev. Proc. 2004-35, 2004-23 I.R.B. 1029.

Each shareholder consents by signing and dating either in column K or on a separate consent statement. The following special rules apply in determining who must sign.
● If a husband and wife have a community interest in the stock or in the income from it, both must consent.
● Each tenant in common, joint tenant, and tenant by the entirety must consent.
● A minor's consent is made by the minor, legal representative of the minor, or a natural or adoptive parent of the minor if no legal representative has been appointed.
● The consent of an estate is made by the executor or administrator.
● The consent of an electing small business trust (ESBT) is made by the trustee and, if a grantor trust, the deemed owner. See Regulations section 1.1362-6(b)(2)(iv) for details.
● If the stock is owned by a qualified subchapter S trust (QSST), the deemed owner of the trust must consent.
● If the stock is owned by a trust (other than an ESBT or QSST), the person treated as the shareholder by section 1361(c)(2)(B) must consent.

Continuation sheet or separate consent statement. If you need a continuation sheet or use a separate consent statement, attach it to Form 2553. It must contain the name, address, and EIN of the corporation and the information requested in columns J through N of Part I.

Column L

Enter the number of shares of stock each shareholder owns on the date the election is filed and the date(s) the stock was acquired. Enter -0- for any former shareholders listed in column J. An entity without stock, such as a limited liability company (LLC), should enter the percentage of ownership and date(s) acquired.

Column M

Enter the social security number of each individual listed in column J. Enter the EIN of each estate, qualified trust, or exempt organization.

Column N

Enter the month and day that each shareholder's tax year ends. If a shareholder is changing his or her tax year, enter the tax year the shareholder is changing to, and attach an explanation indicating the present tax year and the basis for the change (for example, an automatic revenue procedure or a letter ruling request).

Signature

Form 2553 must be signed and dated by the president, vice president, treasurer, assistant treasurer, chief accounting officer, or any other corporate officer (such as tax officer) authorized to sign.

If Form 2553 is not signed, it will not be considered timely filed.

Part II

Complete Part II if you selected a tax year ending on any date other than December 31 (other than a 52-53-week tax year ending with reference to the month of December).

Note. Generally, the corporation cannot obtain automatic approval of a fiscal year under the natural business year (Box P1) or ownership tax year (Box P2) provisions if it is under examination, before an area office, or before a federal court with respect to any income tax issue and the annual accounting period is under consideration. For details, see section 4.02 of Rev. Proc. 2002-38, 2002-22 I.R.B. 1037.

Box P1

Attach a statement showing separately for each month the amount of gross receipts for the most recent 47 months. A corporation that does not have a 47-month period of gross receipts cannot automatically establish a natural business year.

Box Q1

For examples of an acceptable business purpose for requesting a fiscal tax year, see section 5.02 of Rev. Proc. 2002-39, 2002-22 I.R.B. 1046, and Rev. Rul. 87-57, 1987-2 C.B. 117.

Attach a statement showing the relevant facts and circumstances to establish a business purpose for the requested fiscal year. For details on what is sufficient to establish a business purpose, see section 5.02 of Rev. Proc. 2002-39.

If your business purpose is based on one of the natural business year tests provided in section 5.03 of

Rev. Proc. 2002-39, identify if you are using the 25% gross receipts, annual business cycle, or seasonal business test. For the 25% gross receipts test, provide a schedule showing the amount of gross receipts for each month for the most recent 47 months. For either the annual business cycle or seasonal business test, provide the gross receipts from sales and services (and inventory costs, if applicable) for each month of the short period, if any, and the three immediately preceding tax years. If the corporation has been in existence for less than three tax years, submit figures for the period of existence.

If you check box Q1, you will be charged a user fee of $1,500 ($625 if your gross income is less than $1 million) (subject to change — see Rev. Proc. 2005-1 or its successor). Do not pay the fee when filing Form 2553. The service center will send Form 2553 to the IRS in Washington, DC, who, in turn, will notify the corporation that the fee is due.

Box Q2

If the corporation makes a back-up section 444 election for which it is qualified, then the section 444 election will take effect in the event the business purpose request is not approved. In some cases, the tax year requested under the back-up section 444 election may be different than the tax year requested under business purpose. See Form 8716, Election To Have a Tax Year Other Than a Required Tax Year, for details on making a back-up section 444 election.

Boxes Q3 and R2

If the corporation is not qualified to make the section 444 election after making the item Q2 back-up section 444 election or indicating its intention to make the election in item R1, and therefore it later files a calendar year return, it should write "Section 444 Election Not Made" in the top left corner of the first calendar year Form 1120S it files.

Part III

In Part III, certain qualified subchapter S trusts (QSSTs) may make the QSST election required by section 1361(d)(2). Part III may be used to make the QSST election only if corporate stock has been transferred to the trust on or before the date on which the corporation makes its election to be an S corporation. However, a statement can be used instead of Part III to make the election. If there was an inadvertent failure to timely file a QSST election, see the relief provisions under Rev. Proc. 2003-43.

Note. Use Part III only if you make the election in Part I (that is, Form 2553 cannot be filed with only Part III completed).

The deemed owner of the QSST must also consent to the S corporation election in column K of Form 2553.

Paperwork Reduction Act Notice. We ask for the information on this form to carry out the Internal Revenue laws of the United States. You are required to give us the information. We need it to ensure that you are complying with these laws and to allow us to figure and collect the right amount of tax.

You are not required to provide the information requested on a form that is subject to the Paperwork Reduction Act unless the form displays a valid OMB control number. Books or records relating to a form or its instructions must be retained as long as their contents may become material in the administration of any Internal Revenue law. Generally, tax returns and return information are confidential, as required by section 6103.

The time needed to complete and file this form will depend on individual circumstances. The estimated average time is:

Recordkeeping . . . . 9 hr., 19 min.

Learning about the law or the form . . . . 3 hr., 9 min.

Preparing, copying, assembling, and sending the form to the IRS . . . . 4 hr., 38 min.

If you have comments concerning the accuracy of these time estimates or suggestions for making this form simpler, we would be happy to hear from you. You can write to Internal Revenue Service, Tax Products Coordinating Committee, SE:W:CAR:MP:T:T:SP, 1111 Constitution Ave. NW, IR-6406, Washington, DC 20224. Do not send the form to this address. Instead, see *Where To File* on page 2.

Noncompetition and Nondisclosure Agreement

This agreement is made between _____ (the "Employee") and _____ (the "Corporation"). The Employee agrees to the terms of this agreement in consideration of the Employee's continued employment by the Corporation and additional consideration consisting of _____
_____, which the Employee acknowledges is consideration paid by the Corporation over and above the consideration due to the Employee pursuant to his or her usual terms of employment. The Employee also acknowledges the receipt and sufficiency of such consideration to support his or her promises made in this agreement.

1. The Employee agrees that upon termination of employment for any reason, he or she will not enter into competition with the Corporation, its successors or assigns, in the area and for the period of time stated below.

2. For purposes of this agreement, the term "competition" shall mean any activity of the Employee consisting of or related to (a) soliciting orders for any product or service competitive with the Corporation, (b) contracting, for the purpose of soliciting business, any customer, client or account of the Corporation in existence during the term of his or her employment by the Corporation, (c) disclosing confidential information of the Corporation, including but not limited to trade secrets, customer lists, supplier lists and prices, and pricing schedules, or without in any way limiting the foregoing, (d):

Any such activity shall be considered "competition" whether undertaken directly or indirectly, as an owner, officer, director, employee, consultant, stockholder, partner, or in any other relationship with a competing business.

3. The period of time referred to in paragraph 1 above shall be _____ months following the termination of the Employee's employment by the Corporation, and the area referred to in paragraph 1 above shall be limited to the following:

4. Violation of this agreement by the Employee will entitle the Corporation to an injunction to prevent such competition or disclosure, with posting of any bond by the Corporation; and will entitle the Corporation to other legal remedies, including attorneys' fees and costs.

5. This agreement may not be modified except in writing signed by both parties.

This agreement was executed by the Employee and by the Corporation by authority of its Board of Directors on _____, _____.

Dated: _____   Dated: _____

Employee: Corporation:

_____   By: _____

Consent to Action without Formal Meeting by the Directors of

_____

The undersigned directors of the corporation hereby adopt the following resolution:

RESOLVED, that the corporation shall borrow from _____
the sum of $_____ at the rate of interest and payable
according to the terms of a promissory note presented to the directors for their approval
(the Note) (located in management Storage File No. _____), and further

RESOLVED, that the president or vice president, and secretary or assistant secretary of
the corporation are authorized and directed to execute the Note under the seal of the
corporation, to receive the proceeds of the loan, to deposit the loan proceeds into the
depository accounts of the corporation, and to take such other actions as may be
necessary or desirable to give effect to this resolution.

This resolution shall be effective at _____. m. on the _____ of _____,
20_____.

_____

_____, Director

_____

_____, Director

_____

_____, Director

Consent to Action without Formal Meeting by the Directors of

_____

The undersigned directors of the corporation hereby adopt the following resolution:

RESOLVED, that the corporation shall lend to _____
the sum of $_____ and further

RESOLVED, that the _____ of the
corporation is authorized to issue a check to _____
for the sum of $_____ upon receipt of a promissory note signed by the
borrower providing for the repayment of the principle of the loan and payment of interest
at the rate of _____ per cent per annum, and subject to the following additional
terms:

This resolution shall be effective at _____. m. on the _____ of _____,
20_____.

_____

_____, Director

_____

_____, Director

_____

_____, Director

Consent to Action without Formal Meeting by the Directors of

_____

The undersigned directors of the corporation hereby adopt the following resolution:

WHEREAS, management of the corporation, under authority previously given by this board of directors, have entered into negotiations for the purchase of real property located at _____ _____ (the Property) and have recommended to the directors that the corporation agree to the purchase of the Property for the sum of $_____ under the terms of a "Contract for the Sale and Purchase of Real Property" dated _____, 20___, (a copy of the contract is located in management storage file no _____), and

WHEREAS, management has recommended that the corporation purchase the Property using the proceeds of a loan negotiated by management from _____ under the terms of a "loan Agreement" dated _____, 20___, (management storage file no. _____), and

WHEREAS, after due consideration, the board of directors believes such transactions to be in the best interests of the corporation, it is therefore,

RESOLVED, that the "Contract for the Sale and Purchase of Real Property" dated _____ between _____ and the corporation and the "Loan Agreement" dated _____ between _____ _____ and the corporation presented to this board for its consideration are approved, ratified, and confirmed, and further

RESOLVED, that the appropriate officers of the corporation are authorized and directed, with the advice of corporate legal counsel, to execute other documents, including without limitation notes, mortgages and deeds of trust, in order to complete the described borrowing of money and purchase of real property according to the terms of such agreements, and to take such further actions as may be necessary or desirable to give effect to this resolution.

This resolution shall be effective at _____. m. on the _____ of _____, 20_____.

_____

_____, Director

_____

_____, Director

_____

_____, Director

Consent to Action without Formal Meeting by the Directors of

_____

The undersigned directors of the corporation hereby adopt the following resolution:

WHEREAS, management of the corporation, under authority previously given by this board of directors, have entered into negotiations for the sale of real property belonging to the corporation located at _____
and have recommended to the directors that the corporation agree to the sale of such property for the amount of $_____ under the terms and conditions contained in a "Contract for the Sale and Purchase of Real Property" dated _____, 20___, (a copy of such contract is located in management storage file no. _____), and

WHEREAS, after due consideration, the board of directors believes the transaction to be in the best interests of the corporation, it is therefore,

RESOLVED, that the "Contract for the Sale and Purchase of Real Property" dated _____, 20___, between the corporation and _____ _____ presented to this board for its consideration is approved, ratified, and confirmed, and further,

RESOLVED, that the appropriate officers of the corporation are authorized and directed, with the advice of corporate legal counsel, to execute other documents, including without limitation a deed for the transfer of such property, in order to complete the sale of the property according to the terms of the approved agreement, and to take such further actions as may be necessary or desirable to give effect to this resolution.

This resolution shall be effective at _____. m. on the _____ of _____, 20_____.

_____

_____, Director

_____

_____, Director

_____

_____, Director

Consent to Action without Formal Meeting by the Directors of

_____

The undersigned directors of the corporation hereby adopt the following resolution:

WHEREAS, management of the corporation, under authority previously given by this board of directors, have entered into negotiations for the long term lease of real property located at _____ and have recommended to the directors that the corporation agree to the lease of such property under the terms and conditions contained in a "Contract for the Lease of Real Property" dated _____, 20___, (a copy of such contract is located in management storage file no. _____), and

WHEREAS, after due consideration, the board of directors believes such transaction to be in the best interests of the corporation, it is therefore,

RESOLVED, that the "Contract for the Lease of Real Property" dated _____ , 20___, between _____ and the corporation presented to this board for its consideration is approved, ratified, and confirmed, and further,

RESOLVED, that the appropriate officers of the corporation are authorized and directed, to take such further actions as may be necessary or desirable to give effect to this resolution

This resolution shall be effective at _____. m. on the _____ of _____, 20_____.

_____

_____, Director

_____

_____, Director

_____

_____, Director

Consent to Action without Formal Meeting by the Directors of

_____

The undersigned directors of the corporation hereby adopt the following resolution:

WHEREAS, management of the corporation have recommended to the directors that the corporation agree to the _____ of _____ for the sum of $_____ under the terms of a contract dated _____, 20___, (a copy of such contract is located in management storage file no. _____), and

WHEREAS, after due consideration, the board of directors believes such transaction to be in the best interests of the corporation, it is therefore,

RESOLVED, that the contract dated _____, 20___, between _____ and the corporation presented to this board for its consideration are approved, ratified. and confirmed, and further,

RESOLVED, that the appropriate officers of the corporation are authorized and directed to take such further actions as may be necessary or desirable to give effect to this resolution.

This resolution shall be effective at _____. m. on the _____ of _____, 20_____.

_____

_____, Director

_____

_____, Director

_____

_____, Director

Consent to Action without Formal Meeting by the Directors of

_____

The undersigned directors of the corporation hereby adopt the following resolution:

WHEREAS, management of the corporation have recommended to the directors that the corporation agree to the rental of _____ under the terms of a lease agreement dated _____, 20___, (a copy of such contract is located in management storage file no. _____), and

WHEREAS, after due consideration, the board of directors believes such transaction to be in the best interests of the corporation, it is therefore,

RESOLVED, that the contract dated _____, 20___, between _____ and the corporation presented to this board for its consideration are approved, ratified, and confirmed, and further,

RESOLVED, that the appropriate officers of the corporation are authorized and directed to take such further actions as may be necessary or desirable to give effect to this resolution.

This resolution shall be effective at _____. m. on the _____ of _____, 20_____.

_____

_____, Director

_____

_____, Director

_____

_____, Director

Assignment of Assets

This agreement is made this _____ day of _____, _____, by and between _____ ("Shareholder") and _____, a _____ corporation ("Corporation"), who agree as follows:

1. The Shareholder hereby transfers and assigns the assets listed on the attached Exhibit "A" to the Corporation.

2. In consideration for said transfer and assignment of assets, the Corporation shall issue to the Shareholder _____ shares of _____ stock in the Corporation, with a par value of $_____ per share.

Shareholder: Corporation:

_____   By: _____

Articles of Amendment of

_____

The Articles of Incorporation of _____
are hereby amended as follows:

The date of these Articles of Amendment is _____.

By: _____

Certification of Secretary of

_____

I HEREBY CERTIFY that I am the Corporate Secretary of _____ _____; that I am the custodian of the official corporate records of all stock ownership; and that, as of this date, there is a total of _____ shares of capital stock of the corporation issued and outstanding.

Signed and the seal of the Corporation affixed, _____, 20____.

_____
Secretary

Certification of Secretary of

_____

I HEREBY CERTIFY that I am the Corporate Secretary of _____
_____; and that the attached (describe documents):

are true and accurate copies of the records and documents of the corporation.

Signed and the seal of the Corporation affixed, _____, 20____.

_____
Secretary

STATE OF
COUNTY OF
On _____, 20_____, there personally appeared before
me, _____, who, being duly sworn, deposed
and said that he/she is the Secretary of _____,
and that the facts stated in the above Affidavit are true.

_____
Notary Public
My Commission Expires:

The State of _____

Articles of Incorporation
of

_____

The undersigned hereby executes these Articles of Incorporation for the purpose of incorporating under the Business Corporation Law of the State of _____.

1. The name of the corporation is _____.

2. The number of shares the corporation shall have authority to issue is _____.

3. The street address (and mailing address, if different)(including county) of the initial registered office of the corporation and the name of the registered agent of the corporation located at that address is

4. (Optional) The names and addresses of the individuals who will serve as initial directors of the corporation are

5. (Optional) Additional provisions not inconsistent with law for managing the corporation, regulating the internal affairs of the corporation, and establishing the powers of the corporation and its directors and shareholders:

6. The name and address of each incorporator of the corporation is

In witness whereof, these Articles of Incorporation have been subscribed by the incorporator(s) this ____ day of _____, 20____.

_____

Consent to Action without Formal Meeting of Directors of

_____

Organizational Activity

The undersigned, being all of the Directors of the Corporation, hereby adopt the following resolutions:

RESOLVED, that the Articles of Incorporation as filed with the Secretary of State of the State of _____, and presented to the directors by the secretary of the Corporation (the "secretary"), are hereby accepted and approved, and that the secretary is authorized and directed to place the duplicate original of the Articles, together with the original filing receipt of the Secretary of State, in the minute book of the Corporation.

RESOLVED, that the Bylaws presented to the directors by the secretary are hereby adopted as the Bylaws of the Corporation, and that the secretary is authorized and directed to insert a copy of such Bylaws, certified as such by the secretary, in the minute book of the Corporation immediately following the Articles of Incorporation.

RESOLVED, that the corporate seal presented to the directors by the secretary is hereby adopted as the seal of the Corporation, and that an impression of such seal be made in the margin of these minutes.

> [Imprint Seal]

RESOLVED, that the form of share certificate presented to the directors by the secretary is hereby adopted as the form of share certificate for the Corporation, and that the secretary is authorized and directed to attach a sample of such certificate to these resolutions.

RESOLVED, that stock subscription agreements for shares of the Corporation, dated _____, and described below

Name	_Number of shares_	_Consideration_

are hereby accepted on behalf of the corporation, and that the president and secretary, upon receipt of the consideration stated, are authorized and directed to issue certificates for such shares to the respective shareholders.

RESOLVED, that the president of the Corporation is authorized and directed to pay charges and expenses related to the organization of the Corporation and to reimburse any person who has made such payments on behalf of the Corporation.

RESOLVED, that the persons listed below are hereby appointed to the offices indicated opposite their names, and that a determination of compensation of such officers shall be delayed for consideration at a later date.

Name   _Office_

RESOLVED, that funds of the Corporation shall be deposited in _____ and that standard printed resolutions supplied by such Bank and presented by the secretary to the directors shall be adopted by the directors and incorporated and attached to these resolutions.

RESOLVED, that the registered office and registered agent of the corporation as stated in the Articles of Incorporation shall be and remain the registered office and agent of the Corporation until the same is changed by resolution of the directors in accordance with the applicable law.

RESOLVED, that the following Plan for the issuance of common stock of the Corporation and qualification of such stock as "small business corporation" stock under Section 1244 of the Internal Revenue Code of 1986, as amended, is hereby adopted:

1. The corporation shall offer and issue under this Plan, a maximum of _____ shares of its common stock at a maximum price of $_____ per share and a minimum price equal to the par value of the shares, if any.

2. This plan shall be terminated by (a) the complete issuance of all shares offered hereunder, (b) appropriate action terminating the Plan by the board of directors and the shareholders of the Corporation, or (c) the adoption of a new Plan by the shareholders for the issuance of additional stock under IRC Section 1244.

3. No increase in the basis of outstanding stock shall result from a contribution to capital under this Plan.

4. No stock offered under this Plan shall be issued on the exercise of a stock right, stock warrant, or stock option, unless such right, warrant, or option is applicable solely to unissued stock offered under this Plan and is exercised during the period of the Plan.

5. Shares of the Corporation subscribed for prior to the adoption of this Plan, including shares subscribed for prior to the date the corporation comes into existence, may be issued hereunder, provided, however, that the said stock is not in fact issued prior to the adoption of this Plan.

6. No shares of stock shall be issued under this plan for a payment which, including prior payments, exceeds the maximum amount that may be receive under the Plan.

7. Any offering or portion of an offer outstanding that is unissued at the time of the adoption of this plan is hereby withdrawn.

8. Any matters related to the issue of shares under this Plan shall be resolved so as to comply with applicable law and regulations so as to qualify such issue under Section 1244 of the Internal Revenue Code. Any shares issued under this Plan which are finally determined not to be so qualified, and only such shares, shall be determined not to be in the Plan, and any other Shares not so disqualified shall not be affected by such disqualification.

9. Any matters related to the issue of shares under this Plan shall be resolved so as to comply with applicable law and regulations so as to qualify such issue under Section 1244 of the Internal Revenue Code. Any shares issued under this Plan which are finally determined not to be so qualified, and only such shares, shall be determined not to be in the Plan, and any other Shares not so disqualified shall not be affected by such disqualification.

10. The aggregate amount offered hereunder plus the equity capital of the Corporation shall not exceed $1,000,000.

RESOLVED, that these resolutions shall be effective on _____, 20_____.

_____

_____, Director

_____

_____, Director

_____

_____, Director

Bylaws of

_____

Article 1. Offices of the corporation.

Section 1. Principal office. The principal office of the corporation and other offices of the corporation shall be at the locations, within or without the corporation's state of incorporation (the "State"), as the directors may specify from time to time.

Section 2. Registered office. The registered office of the corporation required by law to be maintained in the State may be, but need not be, the same as its principal office.

Article 2. Shareholders' meetings.

Section 1. Annual meeting. The annual meeting of shareholders shall be held in the fifth month following the end of each fiscal year of the corporation on any day of that month as determined by the board of directors.

Section 2. Special meetings. Special meetings of the shareholders for any purpose or purposes permitted by law may be called by the president of the corporation or by the board of directors. Such meetings shall also be called by the president at the request of the holders of not less than one tenth of the outstanding shares of the corporation entitled to vote at the meeting.

Section 3. Location. Meetings of the shareholders may be held at any location, within or without the State, designated by the board of directors or, in the absence of a designation by the board of directors, by the person or persons who call such meeting. If no designation is made, the meeting shall be held at the principal office of the corporation.

Section 4. Notice. Notice of annual and special meetings of the shareholders shall be given at the time and to the shareholders required by applicable law. Additional or expanded notice may be given at the discretion of the directors or officers of the corporation. Any shareholder may waive notice of any meeting before or after the meeting. Such waiver must be in writing signed by the shareholder and delivered to the secretary of the corporation for inclusion in the minutes of the meeting.

Section 5. Quorum and voting. Except as otherwise required by applicable law, a majority of the outstanding shares of the corporation entitled to vote, represented in person or by proxy, shall constitute a quorum at a meeting of the shareholders. Each outstanding share entitled to vote shall be entitled to one vote upon each matter voted on at a meeting of shareholders. Except as otherwise required by applicable law, the vote of a majority of the shareholders present in person or by proxy at a meeting at which a quorum is present shall be the act of the shareholders.

Section 6. Proxies. At meetings of the shareholders, a shareholder may vote in person or by proxy executed in writing in compliance with applicable law and filed with the secretary of the corporation at or before the time of the meeting.

Section 7. Informal action by shareholders. Any action required or permitted by law to be taken by the shareholders at a meeting may be taken without a meeting if one or more consents in writing, setting forth the action so taken, shall be signed by all of the shareholders entitled to vote at a meeting.

Article 3. Directors' meetings.

Section 1. General powers. The business and affairs of the corporation shall be managed by the board of directors.

Section 2. Number. The number of directors constituting the board of directors shall be not less than three nor more than nine. Within such limits, the number may be fixed or changed from time to time by the vote of a majority of the shareholders or by vote of a majority of the directors.

Section 3. Regular meetings. A regular meeting of the board of directors shall be held immediately after, and at the same place as, the annual meeting of shareholders. The board of directors may, by resolution, provide for additional regular meetings of the board.

Section 4. Special meetings. Special meetings of the directors for any purpose or purposes permitted by law may be called by the president of the corporation or by any two directors. The person or persons who call such meeting may fix any time or place for the holding of such meeting.

Section 5. Notice. Notice of regular and special meetings of the board of directors shall be given in the manner and at the time required by applicable law. Additional or expanded notice may be given at the discretion of the directors or officers of the corporation. Any director may waive notice of any meeting before or after the meeting. Such waiver must be in writing signed by the director and delivered to the secretary of the corporation for inclusion in the minutes of the meeting.

Section 6. Quorum and voting. Except as otherwise required by applicable law, a majority of the directors, shall constitute a quorum at a meeting of the directors. Each director shall be entitled to one vote upon each matter voted on at a meeting of the directors. Except as otherwise required by applicable law, the vote of a majority of the directors present at a meeting at which a quorum is present shall be the act of the board of directors.

Section 7. Informal action by directors. Any action required or permitted by law to be taken by the directors at a meeting may be taken without a meeting if one or more consents in writing, setting forth the action so taken, shall be signed by all of the directors entitled to vote at a meeting.

Section 8. Vacancies and removal. Directors may be removed from office and vacancies on the board of directors may be filled in any manner allowed by applicable law.

Article 4. Officers.

Section 1. Number. The officers of the corporation shall be a president, one or more vice presidents, and a secretary appointed by the board of directors. The board of directors may appoint such other additional officers as it may see fit from time to time. Subject to contractual agreements approved by the board of directors, officers of the corporation shall serve at the pleasure of the board of directors, and shall have the authority and duties specified from time to time by the board of directors, and shall receive salary and benefits as may be approved by the board of directors.

Article 5. Books and Records.

Section 1. Books and records. The corporation shall create and maintain such books and records, including minutes of meetings, stock ledgers, and financial records, as may be required by law and any such additional records as may be specified by the directors and officers from time to time.

Section 2. Inspection by shareholders. To the extent required by applicable law, and to the additional extent permitted from time to time by the directors, shareholders shall have the right to inspect the books and records of the corporation.

Article 6. Miscellaneous.

Section 1. Share certificates. Shareholders of the corporation shall be entitled to one or more certificates representing shares owned by such shareholders. Share certificates shall be in the form specified from time to time by the board of directors.

Section 2. Dividends and distributions. The board of directors may from time to time declare, and the corporation may pay, dividends on outstanding shares of the corporation, subject to limitations provided by law and the articles of incorporation of the corporation.

Section 3. Seal. The board of directors may adopt, and from time to time modify, a corporate seal.

Section 4. Fiscal year. The fiscal year of the corporation shall be the period designated by the board of directors.

Section 5. Amendment. These bylaws may be amended from time to time by the directors or the shareholders in the manner permitted by applicable law.

Certification

The foregoing bylaws are certified to be the bylaws of the corporation as adopted by the board of directors on the _____ day of _____, 20 ____.

_____
Secretary

Statement of Change of Registered Office and/or Registered Agent

Pursuant to the laws of the state of _____, the undersigned corporation submits the following for the purpose of changing its registered office and/or registered agent in the State of _____.

The name of the corporation is: _____.

The mailing address, street address and county of the corporation's registered office currently on file is:

The name of the current registered agent is: _____.

1. The mailing address, street address and county of the new registered office of the corporation is: [to be completed only if the registered office is being changed]

2. The name of the new registered agent and the new agent's consent to appointment appears below: [to be completed only if the registered agent is being changed]

_____   _____
Typed name   Signature

3. The address of the corporation's registered office and the address of the business office of its registered agent, as changed, will be identical.

4. This statement will be effective upon filing, unless a date and/or time is specified:
_____

This is the _____ day of _____, 20 _____.

Name of corporation: _____

Signature: _____

Typed name and title: _____

Application for Certificate of Authority

Pursuant to the laws of the state of _____, the undersigned corporation hereby applies for a Certificate of Authority to transact business in the State of _____, and for that purpose submits the following:

1. The name of the corporation is _____, and if the corporate name is unavailable for use in the State of _____, the name the corporation wishes to use is _____.

2. The state or country under whose laws the corporation was organized is:
_____.

3. The date of incorporation was _____; its period of duration is: _____.

4. The street address of the principal office of the corporation is:

5. The mailing address if different from the street address of the principal office of the corporation is:

6. The street address and county of the registered office in this State is:

7. The mailing address if different from the street address of the registered office in this State is:

8. The name of the registered agent in this State is: _____.

9. The names, titles, and usual business addresses of the current officers of the corporation are:

Name   *Title*   *Business address*

10. Attached is a certificate of existence (or document of similar import), duly authenticated by the secretary of state or other official having custody of corporate records in the state or country of incorporation.

11. If the corporation is required to use a fictitious name in order to transact business in this state, a copy of the resolution of its board of directors, certified by its secretary, adopting the fictitious name is attached.

12. This application will be effective upon filing, unless a delayed date and/or time is specified: _____.

This is the _____ day of _____, 20 ____.

Name of corporation: _____

Signature: _____

Typed name and title: _____

Consent to Action without Formal Meeting by the Directors of

_____

The undersigned directors of the corporation hereby adopt the following resolution:

RESOLVED, that pursuant to the laws of the state of _____ the corporation shall be dissolved and that any officer or director of the corporation is hereby authorized and directed to complete, execute and file with the Secretary of State of _____ Articles of Dissolution accomplishing such dissolution, and further

RESOLVED, that such dissolution shall be effective on the effective date of such Articles of Dissolution.

This resolution shall be effective at _____. m. on the _____ of _____, 20_____.

_____

_____, Director

_____

_____, Director

_____

_____, Director

Consent to Action without Formal Meeting by the Directors of

_____

The undersigned directors of the corporation hereby adopt the following resolution:

RESOLVED, that pursuant to the laws of the state of _____,
the board of directors recommends to the shareholders of the corporation that the
corporation be dissolved, and that the shareholders approve the recommendation, and
further

RESOLVED, that the appropriate officers of the corporation are authorized and directed
to call a special meeting of the shareholders, giving appropriate notice, or to arrange for
approval of the recommendation by consent to action without formal meeting of the
shareholders, and further

RESOLVED, that upon approval by the shareholders and at such time as he/she deems
in the best interests of the corporation, the President or his/her designee shall have
authority to execute and file articles of dissolution and to take such other actions as may
be necessary or desirable to give effect to the proposed dissolution and this resolution.

This resolution shall be effective at _____. m. on the _____ of _____,
20_____.

_____

_____, Director

_____

_____, Director

_____

_____, Director

Consent to Action without Formal Meeting by the Shareholders of

_____

The undersigned shareholders of the corporation hereby adopt the following resolution:

WHEREAS, the directors of the corporation have proposed that the corporation be dissolved and have recommended to the shareholders that they approve such dissolution, it is therefore

RESOLVED, that the proposal of the directors that the corporation be dissolved is ratified, and approved, and that the corporation shall be dissolved.

This resolution shall be effective at _____. m. on the _____ of _____, 20_____.

_____

_____, Shareholder

_____

_____, Shareholder

_____

_____, Shareholder

_____

_____, Shareholder

_____

_____, Shareholder

The State of _____

Articles of Dissolution of a Business Corporation

Pursuant to the laws of this, the undersigned corporation hereby submits the following Articles of Dissolution for the purpose of dissolving the corporation.

1. The name of the corporation is: _____.

2. The names, titles, and addresses of the officers of the corporation are:

3. The names and addresses of the directors of the corporation are:

4. The dissolution of the corporation was authorized on the _____ day of _____ , 20___.

5. Shareholder approval for the dissolution was obtained as required by law.

6. These articles will be effective upon filing, unless a delayed date and/or time is specified: _____.

This the _____ day of _____, 20___.

Name of corporation: _____

Signature: _____

Typed name and title: _____

Index